THE HOUSE HANDBOOK

MWPS-16

The House
HANDBOOK

Guidelines for Building or Remodeling Your Home

MWPS
MidWest Plan Service
A Foundation of Knowledge

Copyright® 2006, MidWest Plan Service
All rights reserved.

Designed by Kathy J. Walker

MidWest Plan Service
122 Davidson Hall
Iowa State University
Ames, Iowa 50011-3080

For additional copies of this publication and a free catalog of other agricultural publications,
call 1-800-562-3618
or
visit our website at: www.mwps.org

Library of Congress
Cataloging-in-Publication Data

The house handbook: guidelines for building or remodeling your home.
    p. cm.
  Rev. ed. of: House plannig handbook. 1988.
  "MWPS-16"
  ISBN 0-89373-101-3
  1. Architecture, Domestic—United States—Designs and plans. I. MidWest Plan Service.
II. Title: House planning handbook.

NA7205.H685 2006   2006045031
728'.37—dc22

The last number is the print number:
9 8 7 6 5 4 3 2

MWPS would like to thank the following people for providing support to this project:

Diane Huntrods, Editor, Ames, Iowa

John Moore, Editor, Ames, Iowa

Letitia Wetterauer, Illustrator, Alpine, Texas

Steve Theis, Rottlund Homes of Iowa, Inc.
West Des Moines, Iowa 50266

Brian Stauffer, Photographer
University of Illinois, College of ACES
Urbana, IL 61801

MWPS would like to recognize the following external reviewers for providing support to this project:

Kathleen Parrott, PhD, CKE
Professor, Housing, Virginia Tech

Victoria Brinn Feinberg, PhD, IIDA, CID
Professor, Family & Consumer Sciences
California State University - Northridge

MWPS would like to acknowlege the following for financial support for graphic development and review of this book:

USDA Cooperative State Research, Education and Extension Service, (CSREES)
(http://www.csrees.usda.gov) through the Healthy Homes program.

CONTENTS

ABOUT THE AUTHORS

Mary Yearns

Mary H. Yearns is a Professor and Extension Housing Specialist at Iowa State University. She led the revision efforts for this project. Her subject matter interests focus on the housing needs of an aging population and persons with disabilities. She has been a pioneer in creating interactive exhibits to demonstrate the benefits of universal design and home accessibility that have been used at home shows, fairs, and conferences in Iowa and across the nation.

Marilyn Bode

Marilyn Bode, Ph.D., is a state specialist with Iowa State University Extension. She was previously the housing specialist with the Extension Service at Kansas State University and wrote the chapter on bedrooms while she was working there. She has her B.S., M.S., and Ph.D. degrees from Iowa State University. She has also been an Extension Housing Specialist at the University of Minnesota.

Marilyn Bruin

Marilyn J. Bruin, Ph.D., is an Associate Professor/Extension Housing Specialist in Design, Housing, and Apparel at the University of Minnesota. Marilyn has an integrated program of outreach, research, and service. Her teaching and research interests center on families at risk for maintaining independent, adequate, and affordable housing. She teaches courses on children's environments, housing for the elderly and special populations, and supportive housing and well as developing and managing *RentWise*, a comprehensive tenant education program.

Marilou Cheple

Marilou Cheple is an Extension Educator for the Department of Bio-based Products at the University of Minnesota. She teaches and conducts research and outreach programs on cold climate housing concerns including moisture issues, energy conservation, and alternative building systems. She has been involved in the development of building codes and sustainable building practices. Her bachelor's degree is from Iowa State University and her master's from the University of Minnesota.

Ted Funk, P.E.

Ted Funk is an Extension Agricultural Engineer in the Department of Agricultural and Biological Engineering, University of Illinois at Urbana-Champaign. During his career he has led state Extension programs in residential indoor air quality and energy conservation, and he has helped teach an undergraduate course in residential housing.

Tom Greiner, P.E.

Tom Greiner, Ph.D., is a retired Extension Agricultural Engineer from Iowa State University, where he worked for more than 25 years. He has written extensively on housing issues such as drainage, indoor air quality, and heating. He is known as a national expert on radon and carbon monoxide poisoning and has been a technical consultant for or featured on ABC's 20/20, Bob Vila's programs, and This Old House.

Kenneth Hellevang, P.E.

Ken Hellevang has a Ph.D. degree in engineering, is a registered professional engineer, and is a Professor at North Dakota State University. As an Extension Engineer, he provides education and technical assistance in structures and indoor environmental engineering, primarily related to home moisture and molds, and in crop post-harvest engineering. He has authored or co-authored more than 150 publications and numerous magazine and news articles.

David Kammel, P.E.

David W. Kammel is an Agricultural Engineer and Professor in the Biological Systems Engineering Department at the University of Wisconsin-Madison working in Extension. He received his Ph.D. in 1985. He provides Extension educational programs related to construction and livestock housing. His hobby is remodeling his own home.

Frederick Wm. (Bill) Koenig, P.E.

Bill Koenig has been the engineer at MWPS for 15 years. During that time, he has served as project engineer, development coordinator, and technical editor for more than 30 major educational publications, including various construction, wiring, and concrete handbooks. Bill has been an active member of ASABE (American Society of Agricultural and Biological Engineers) and was a 2005 inductee of the Rural Builder's Hall of Fame.

Sarah Kirby

Sarah Kirby, Ph.D., is an Associate Professor and Housing Specialist with the North Carolina Cooperative Extension Service. Prior to moving to North Carolina in 1995, she was the Housing Specialist for the Oklahoma Cooperative Extension Service for almost ten years. She received her Ph.D. from Oklahoma State University in 1989. Her areas of educational programming include accessible and adaptable housing, residential energy efficiency, affordable housing, maintenance and repair, moisture control, and housing for the lifespan.

John Merrill

John Merrill is a recently retired professor from the School of Human Ecology at the University of Wisconsin-Madison where he served for more than 20 years as Wisconsin's Extension Housing Specialist. During his tenure in Madison he was a regular guest on the state's public radio network answering questions about housing technology. He also wrote a monthly news column on housing technology circulated to newspapers throughout Wisconsin. He authored many extension publications on housing issues including one titled Remodeling: Where to Begin. He holds a Doctorate of Architecture from the University of Michigan.

Morgan Powell, P.E.

Morgan Powell has been at Kansas State University for 29 years where he is Professor and Extension Engineer. As Extension Engineer, he provides education and technical assistance in many aspects of soil and water issues. He has authored or co-authored more than 140 bulletins, 12 handbooks, and numerous other educational materials. He earned a Ph.D. degree in engineering from Utah State University, an M.S. from the University of Missouri-Columbia, and a B.S. from Kansas State University. Prior to joining Kansas State University, he worked for CH2M Hill as a consulting engineer. He has been a registered professional engineer since 1976.

Wanda Olson

Wanda Olson is a Professor and Extension Specialist Emeritus for the Department of Design, Housing, and Apparel at the University of Minnesota. Her outreach and research program was focused on technology and its impact in residential environments. Research with Becky Yust culminated in revision of kitchen planning guidelines for designers to effectively incorporate new technology. She also was instrumental in dual-language publications for new immigrant communities to educate them about environmental hazards such as carbon monoxide, lead, and excessive moisture in homes. Her bachelor's degree is from Augsburg College and her master's from the University of Minnesota.

Linda Reece-Adler

Linda Adler is an Extension Home Furnishing Specialist, University of Kentucky Cooperative Extension Service, Lexington, KY. She holds degrees in interior design from Iowa State University and has written extensively on interior design, home care, and housing issues.

Rich Seifert

Rich Seifert is a Professor at the University of Alaska-Fairbanks. He has been the Cooperative Extension Service "Energy guy" at UAF for 24 years. He has a bachelor's degree in physics from West Chester State University in Pennsylvania, and a master's degree in engineering physics from the University of Alaska. He has authored numerous technical and public information papers and pamphlets on housing issues, indoor air quality, radon, renewable energy, and building design, and he maintains a keen interest in sustainable design and construction.

Janis Stone

Janis Finley Stone, Ph.D., Iowa State University Professor Emeritus, was an Extension Specialist in Textiles and Clothing, retiring in 2003. She was a member of the USDA NC-170 Regional Research group for 20 years and of the AHAM Major Appliance Consumer Action Panel for seven years. Her work focuses on farm and sun safety issues, clothing care, and protective clothing.

Kenneth R. Tremblay, Jr.

Kenneth R. Tremblay, Jr., Ph.D., is a Cooperative Extension Housing Specialist and Professor of Housing and Design, Department of Design and Merchandising, Colorado State University. Author of *Social Aspects of Housing* and *Small House Designs*, he has published more than 100 articles on housing and design issues.

Michael P. Vogel

Michael P. Vogel, Ph.D., has been Professor and Housing and Environmental Health Specialist with Montana State University Extension Service since 1982. His primary responsibility at MSU is developing housing education programs and resources for Montana consumers and tribes. While at MSU, he has contributed to 6 books, produced 96 technical training manuals, 49 research/technical reports, and 163 consumer-oriented publications dealing with housing and environmental health. He serves as the Executive Director of the Housing Education and Research Association, Director of the U.S. EPA Region VIII Peaks to Prairies Pollution Prevention Information Center, and Director of the Central Department of Energy Weatherization Training Center at Montana State University.

Joseph L. Wysocki

Joseph L. Wysocki, Ph.D., is National Program Leader, Housing and Indoor Environments, Cooperative State Research, Education and Extension Service, USDA. He had program responsibilities related to affordable housing, indoor environments including air and water quality, healthy homes, and energy. He held positions at the University of Illinois, Penn State University, and Virginia Tech. His Ph.D. in housing is from Cornell University and his B.S. in interior design is from Drexel University. He is a former President of the Housing Education and Research Association.

Becky Yust

Becky Yust, Ph.D., is Professor and Head of the Department of Design, Housing, and Apparel at the University of Minnesota. Her research and teaching are in the area of housing studies and the interaction between households and housing. In addition to kitchen planning research with Wanda Olson, other research has included energy conservation and environmental issues; the role of housing in the vitality of rural communities; and issues of housing affordability and adequacy. Her Ph.D. is from The Ohio State University; her bachelor's and master's from Colorado State University.

THE HOUSE HANDBOOK

CHAPTER 1

Creating a Resident-friendly Home

A DECISION TO BUILD OR REMODEL A HOUSE, to buy your first house, or even to change houses opens the door to a challenging, perhaps frustrating, but exciting experience. This handbook presents guidelines to help you sort through many factors, organize your thinking, and make decisions. It focuses on planning, because time spent in forethought saves time, money, and frustration later; delays caused by changing your mind are often costly in materials and labor. Select carefully from the large number of alternatives at each stage, and then change a decision only with good reason.

Whether you build a new house or remodel your current one, certain municipal, state, and federal building codes and regulations will apply. Your builder, or contractor, will work with a permit inspector to meet municipal requirements. The United States has recently developed one national residential code, the International Residential Code (IRC). The IRC has been adopted by many states, jurisdictions, and localities and is the basis for many of the recommendations in this book.

Use this book as a guide to help you build or find a home that best suits your needs. That home might not be your dream home or the most expensive home in your income bracket, but it will be the home that best balances cost with individual and family needs, evolving lifestyles, space, convenience, and protection. What follows are the basic and most important elements that will guide you in building or buying a better home.

The Resident-friendly Home

People choose homes for many different reasons, but at the top of everyone's list should be a resident-friendly home. A resident-friendly home will serve the needs of your own family for a lifetime and be usable by other individuals and families in the future. A resident-friendly home easily adapts to the various ages and stages of family life, whether you are a single person, a young couple just starting out, a family with teenagers, or a retiree.

The family life cycle

Begin the process of developing a resident-friendly home by analyzing where you fit in the family life cycle. Are you single? Do you have young children? Is retirement approaching? Then consider how you live. Do you entertain frequently or seldom, work at home or in another location? How your family lives should help determine the type, layout, shape, and style of housing that

One of the central themes of this book is to encourage those who are building or remodeling a home to incorporate the concept of universal design in the building process. Throughout the book, you will see references to this design concept and to certain building criteria and dimensions necessary to meet universal needs. You may be wondering what universal design means and why incorporating it into a building project is a good idea. Simply put, universal design means building a home that provides comfort and ease of use for anyone living in or visiting a home, regardless of age or ability. While kitchens and baths often receive the most emphasis in discussions about universal design, the concept is important in all parts of the home. Some basic elements of a home that incorporates universal design are the following:

- A first floor with a bathroom and a bedroom.
- Accessible rooms with hallways at least 42 inches wide and doors at least 32 inches wide.
- A walk-in or roll-in shower.
- Grab bars installed in shower and tub areas.

Continued

- Accessible storage, with at least half of the storage no higher than 54 inches.
- Lighting features that include outlets and switches located 18 to 46 inches from the floor.
- Easy-grip controls such as lever handles on doors and faucets.
- Easily accessible work surfaces and appliances.
- Safe flooring features, including low or no thresholds and no-step entries.
- Smoke detectors, carbon monoxide detectors, and night lights.

will meet your needs and wants adequately, comfortably, and functionally. First assess the living patterns of your household as a group and then the patterns of each member.

Living patterns

To determine living patterns, consider the time your family devotes to various activities at home. Considering the following types of activities may help:

- Social (outside the household).
- Family.
- Individual (study, hobbies, work).
- Private (dressing, bathing, personal time).
- Work (meals, laundry, cleaning, gardening, school, or employment interests).
- Leisure (television, computer use, games, music).

If there are or will be elderly or physically challenged persons in your household, consider their needs now. It will be difficult and expensive to change kitchens, baths, halls, doorways, and bedrooms to accommodate their needs later. Consider the needs of pets in getting indoors and out as well as your needs in caring for them. Try to picture the future and anticipate activity patterns and needs in 5, 10, and 20 years. If the empty nest stage is near, adding space for teenagers to entertain may be justified by alternative uses for the new space later.

All households differ; houses take on different characteristics once a family settles in. With careful planning, multiple use rooms, and some compromises, it is usually possible to meet a family's needs and match its lifestyle.

Basic features

One goal of this publication is to encourage people to develop a home that incorporates an adaptable and universally useful floor plan, integrates indoor and outdoor living spaces, employs an innovative use of materials and technology (including building green), and features a design that creates storage spaces without detracting from the home's overall living areas.

Expect to make many compromises. No plan is perfect, but the best plan is one that meets basic criteria that make a home usable for a lifetime:

- **Affordable.** An affordable home makes the best use of a family's financial and labor resources. An affordable home conserves energy, and the savings in purchased energy can be used elsewhere. When you budget the life cycle cost of your home, include a maintenance budget of about 5 percent for upkeep of the home's exterior and major interior systems, thus maintaining your home's value.
- **Attractive.** An attractive home has a functional form, a style harmonious with its environment, and aesthetic elements such as shape and color that enhance its livability.
- **Convenient.** A convenient home has comfortable spaces that can accommodate the needs of a family at many stages. Convenient homes are designed to be usable by a wide range of humans including children, older people, and those of different sizes and abilities.
- **Efficient.** An efficient home is a functional home that uses natural resources wisely.

• **Healthy.** A healthy home provides a protected environment for its occupants. This protected environment offers physical safety, including fire protection, electrical safety, and indoor air quality, and can be maintained over the structure's lifetime.

Throughout the handbook, these criteria will be highlighted with the following icons:

 Affordable

 Attractive

 Convenient

 Efficient

 Healthy

These icons will point you to concepts or practices that will help you meet the goal of developing an integrated house and landscape plan that fits a variety of life stages, lifestyles, pocketbooks, and locations.

Book Organization

This book contains 17 chapters. Following this introductory chapter, three chapters provide the crucial information that you need to jumpstart the process of building a new home or remodeling an existing one. Chapter 2 details how to select and collaborate with such home-building professionals as designers, lenders, real estate agents, and builders; Chapter 3 explains how to develop or choose an appropriate floor plan for your situation; and Chapter 4 describes how to locate and select a suitable building site.

With the groundwork in place, the handbook narrows its focus, highlighting specific areas within the house. In Chapters 5 through 11, the book surveys social areas, kitchens, bathrooms, bedrooms, home offices, laundry areas, and garages.

Chapters 12 through 16 deal with those necessary but often unnoticed housing components that pervade every room in the house. These chapters discuss the entries, halls, stairs, and doors that provide access to and throughout the house; storage areas; foundations; utilities; and the variety of materials that go into making a house more attractive, affordable, convenient, efficient, and healthy.

Recognizing that remodeling presents some special challenges, Chapter 17, which ends with a simple case study, is designed to help you decide if remodeling is right for you and your home. It also provides suggestions to make a remodeling project more successful.

No one publication can provide all the information or design ideas you are likely to want or need, but the material in the following chapters will provide the information needed to build a resident-friendly home—an affordable, attractive, convenient, efficient, healthy, and up-to-code house—for you and those living with you as you progress through the typical family life cycle.

Resources

Chapters 2 through 17 each contain a list of resources pertinent to the topic covered in that chapter; use these resources to begin gathering information about all components of the house. A wide range of information on house planning also is available from a variety of other sources including:

- Home improvement centers.
- Magazines and publications.
- Home shows and tours.
- House plans available on the Internet.
- Builders and designers.

Lumber yards generally carry a variety of house planning books in their literature section. Magazines and other publications can help define the style and general design that you want your house to embody. Home shows and tours can also be helpful to see the latest technology and design features. You can even access Internet websites that sell house plans, taking a virtual tour of their homes. However, you will most likely develop your own house plan by interacting with local design and house-building companies, because they will be familiar with the typical housing in your area and the types of materials that are best suited for your location.

It may be easier to start with a basic plan from a builder you know and like, and then adapt the plan to your specific criteria. Local home builders often have a set of basic plans they use as a building template, making minor adaptations for each owner who contracts with them.

CHAPTER 2

Working with Professionals

ONE OF THE FIRST DECISIONS that you will make as you plan and build a new house or remodel your current house is determining which professionals you want on your construction team. At the very least, you will be interacting with contractors. If, like most people, you do not have an existing relationship with a contractor, you will need to interview and select one. What questions do you ask and how do you establish a good working relationship with the contractor? This chapter will offer suggestions about how to interact with professionals and how to deal with issues that may arise during construction and with those that might arise as the process nears completion.

Types of Professionals

A typical house construction project involves several different individuals and companies. During the planning and construction process, you may interact with many professionals, including lenders, real estate agents, designers, contractors, and local government officials. However, some of these people, such as surveyors, subcontractors, and permit inspectors, may interact with your builder more than with you. In any case, communication among these different groups is critical to the successful completion of the project.

Construction and design professionals

Architects. You may commission an architect at an architectural and engineering firm or design firm to prepare a custom house design based on your needs and desires. Because an architect will develop the detailed plans and specifications and other contract documents for your construction project, an architect is generally the first individual that you will put under contract.

An architect is trained to lead you through the planning process. Although that process can be very complex, it should not be confusing if done correctly. The architect will work with you in a series of phases including (1) schematic design, (2) design development, (3) preparing construction documents, (4) bidding or negotiating, and (5) construction. When the plans and specifications are complete, you may begin negotiations with pre-selected contractors or solicit competitive bids for all or various portions of the work.

Contractors and subcontractors. Individuals or companies involved in the business of house construction are known as contractors because they operate under a contract arrangement directly with you or with another contractor. Contractors who enter into a contract with you are called prime contractors.

Because an architect will develop the detailed plans and specifications for your house, an architect is generally the first individual that you will put under contract.

- **Seek to hire competent professional contractors** who respect you, assist you in making tough choices, and offer you knowledgeable suggestions and alternatives that can reduce your cost and get you into the house you have always dreamed of owning.

- **Request written contracts** with all of the professionals involved in your home construction.

- **If you hire a contractor** to build your house, keep in daily contact with him or her and plan to spend as much time as possible at the site.

- **Whenever you need to communicate** with the contractor about your project, discuss the issue verbally and then put it in writing.

- **When you purchase a new home,** participate in a home inspection to visually evaluate the mechanical and structural condition of the house.

Those contractors who contract to do work for another contractor are called subcontractors.

Contractors are also categorized as either general or specialty contractors. General contractors perform a wide range of construction activity and often oversee the subcontractors' work. Specialty contractors limit their activities to one or more construction specialties such as electrical, plumbing, or excavation. Keep in mind that the terms general or specialty have nothing to do with contractual relationships. A general contractor may be employed as either a prime contractor or a subcontractor. The same goes for any specialty contractor.

To make sure the construction process meets a reasonable timeline with minimal mistakes, open lines of communication are essential among the contractors involved in the project.

Interior designers. You may choose to hire an interior designer to advise you about the interior furnishings of the home, including furniture, fixtures, and lighting. An interior designer can help make a small room appear larger by arranging furniture and wall hangings or through the use of color or lighting. Likewise, an interior designer can divide up a large room into smaller more comfortable areas. It may be desirable to hire an interior designer at the same time you hire an architect to take advantage of the designer's knowledge of space planning for location of furniture, fixtures, and lighting to work out the best possibilities for room arrangement. In some states, the licensed or certified interior designer may only *observe* the work of the subcontrac-

tors and report it to the owner or contractor.

Kitchen and bath designers. Kitchen and bath designers work primarily on remodeling and new construction projects. Kitchens and baths are areas of the house that have many technical requirements and can be complex to design, build, or remodel. These designers have specialized training beyond the background of an interior designer.

Kitchen and bath designers will work with a contractor or subcontractor through all construction stages. Be sure to check a designer's qualifications before hiring. A person with a certified kitchen designer (CKD) or certified bath designer (CBD) designation is a professional who has met the training and educational requirements of the National Kitchen and Bath Association.

Landscape architects. You may also wish to hire a landscape architect to help you locate the best site for your house and to design and develop the land surrounding your house. A landscape architect can help you manage the environmental features of your site, including wind and sunlight orientation and site drainage.

Surveyors. You may need surveyors to document the land you purchase, especially if the land is not located in a development or is located outside of an urban area. Developers usually have the surveying done before their lots are sold and then communicate the information through a real estate agent. In the case of an extensive external remodeling project, you may need a surveyor to determine if the proposed modifications fit on your property and meet local zoning and setback requirements.

Financial and legal professionals

Lenders. As one of your primary contacts, lenders determine budget and loan conditions for the construction loan. They will set up payment schedules for the loan and escrows to handle the financial requirements of the construction process. If you are building a new house, they will most likely hold the mortgage that you will be paying to achieve eventual ownership of the property.

Real estate agents. Real estate agents may be working for you or the individual whose property you are buying. They have the contacts to find the house or land that you are seeking. In the case of new construction, the real estate agent may represent a developer of the land where you will be building or the owners of the land you want to purchase.

Attorneys. Like real estate agents, attorneys may be working for you or the individual whose property you are buying. You will need an attorney to help draw up a purchase contract and to examine the title to the property you are purchasing. You will also want an attorney to review the contracts that you develop with construction and design professionals.

Permit inspectors. Local governing authorities generally require permits for construction. Typical inspections might include electrical, plumbing, foundation, framing, and safety. The contractor usually communicates with permit inspectors. The inspection process generally involves completing a certain stage of work and then having it inspected before the next stage of work begins. Having each stage of construction inspected before proceeding facilitates the construction process because mistakes can be corrected before they are covered up or become too costly to repair.

Selecting a Contractor

When investing in your home, you need to ensure that your contractors are qualified to undertake your building or remodeling project. You want professional contractors who respect you, assist you in making tough choices, and offer you knowledgeable suggestions and alternatives that can reduce your cost and get you into the house you have always dreamed of owning. To help narrow your selection, ask a prospective contractor the following questions:

- How long have you been in business?
- What education and training do you have?
- Do you have training in residential design?
- Do you have any professional certifications?
- Have you successfully worked on similar projects?
- How many projects of this type have you completed?
- Can you provide a list of names and addresses of previous customers?
- Are you insured?
- Will you provide a performance bond?
- Do you provide a written warranty and/or performance standards?
- Are you a member of a builders' association or other professional group?
- Are you registered or licensed with the state?

 If a home inspection report indicates substantial problems with a house but you are still interested in buying it, you may be able to either negotiate a lower price with the seller or have the seller fix the problems.

After receiving a list of references, call them to confirm that they would do business with the contractor again. Questions you can ask include:

- Does the contractor have a good reputation with local banks and suppliers?
- Were you pleased with the contractor's finished work?
- Were you able to communicate easily and openly with the contractor? (Most problems arise from poor communication.)
- Was the project completed within a reasonable time?

Other than building inspectors, you should request written contracts with all of the professionals involved in your construction project. The contracts protect you and the other party from miscommunications and can save you money. While your main contract will likely be with the contractor, you will also likely have contracts with the land developer or real estate agent for the land and with some subcontractors such as the landscaper and designer. In turn, the contractor will have contracts with subcontractors. Make sure you read the contracts and ask the lawyer representing you to read them as well. Money and contracts keep the process honest and beneficial to all parties involved.

Your Relationships with Construction Professionals

It is definitely to your advantage to understand the relationship among the various groups involved in a construction project. The most common arrangements are:

- Working with both a design firm and one or more construction contractors.
- Working with a design/build firm.
- Assuming the role of your own general contractor.

A homeowner can work with a design firm and contractors. In this case, a general contractor is the prime contractor. One or more subcontractors are hired, typically by the general contractor. The design firm is also under contract to inspect work as the contractors perform it.

A design-build firm is a company that has a contract with an owner to both design and build a house meeting certain specified requirements. New construction involving design/build firms is commonly referred to as turnkey construction. A single design/build firm commonly designs and constructs the basic house, that is, is under contract to do all of the work. Since the same organization is both designing and building the house, coordination problems are minimized, and construction can begin before completion of the final design. Although they may not be advertised as design/build firms, many specialty contractors have design capabilities that are used extensively on small projects. For example, the same firm both designs and installs the electrical wiring system in most homes.

You can assume the role of general contractor, that is, coordinate the day-to-day work of all directly employed labor working on the construction project, and of all companies under contract. When serving in this dual role, you are known as an owner/general contractor. Figure 2-1 depicts this arrangement, which requires that you be knowledgeable about the details of the project and have good relationships with the contractors. Since most homeowners do not have existing relationships with contractors, this arrangement can be challenging at best. In addition, being a general contractor can be time consuming.

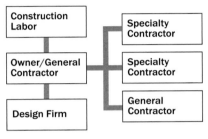

FIGURE 2-1.
Owner functions as general contractor.

Considerations During Construction

During a building project, you should expect to spend significant time at the building site. You should also expect to make many decisions, and some will involve construction changes. This section offers advice about both situations.

Oversight of construction

The construction process can be long and involved. As the owner, you need to make the time to monitor the process and make the decisions necessary to keep it moving. If you hire a contractor, you should be in daily contact with him or her and plan to spend as much time as possible at the site. Visit the site at

least weekly during the early stages of construction and more frequently as the project nears completion. If you are there, you will be able to answer questions on the spot, which will eliminate future problems. You can also hire someone to monitor the construction for you, but for most people, part of the excitement of a building project is to be actively involved in its progress.

Changes during construction

Always note any construction changes on paper. Once you start building, it becomes very expensive (not to mention time consuming) to make changes. Whenever you need to communicate with the contractor about your project, discuss the issue verbally and then put it in writing. If you order a change to the project, write the builder a memo describing the change, and keep a copy for yourself. Hundreds, if not thousands, of decisions are made in the course of a building project; it would be impossible for anyone to keep all of the details straight. By putting change requests on paper, you will have a chance to think through what you are trying to say, and the contractor will have a document that he or she can refer to. If a problem occurs, the written change order will provide a means of determining exactly what was said and when.

Punch lists

A punch list is a list specifying items that are not finished, are not working properly, or do not look right as the project nears completion. The contractor usually agrees to the punch list before the job is finished, and it becomes part of the closing documents. Make sure you include every item you want the contractor to fix. Once the punch list has been finalized, the contractor may not return and fix other items (other than warranty items) without charge. If you are building from scratch, you will want to delay paying the contractor in full until the work is completed.

Resources

American Society of Home Inspectors: http://www.ashi.org, 800-743-2744

Home Builders Association of Iowa: http://www.hbaiowa.org

National Kitchen and Bath Association: http://www.nkba.org

National Association of Home Builders: http://www.nahb.org

Toolbase Services: http://www.toolbase.org

CHAPTER 3

Designing a Home

PLANNING A NEW HOUSE or even major remodeling of your current house can cause information overload; there are many details to process and incorporate into a plan. Start by collecting ideas; then assess your present house to determine which ideas work and which do not. You may find a stock plan in a home plan publication or plan magazine that suits your needs or could work with minor modifications. Armed with that knowledge, you can confidently evaluate floor plans and decide which one will best meet your household's needs. Begin the process by determining what your family's interests are and what activities are important to your family.

Identifying Activities and Interests

Each household is unique, and housing needs vary according to the number, ages, and interests of household members. A good floor plan will provide spaces for the activities that are most important to that household.

To determine your household's activities and interests, analyze how you use space in your current home. First, write the name of each room in your home in a separate box. Then, list all of the activities that occur in the room. Make sure you list all of the activities that really do take place there. For example, in addition to being a food preparation and storage area, a kitchen often fulfills other functions such as serving as an office, homework area, or gathering spot. See Table 3-1. Ask all household members to add to the list of activities for each room.

Now take a look at the list. Ask yourself the following questions:

- Do some rooms seem to be mislabeled for the kinds of activities going on within them? For example, is that room you are calling a dining room being used instead as an office or as a computer game room?
- Are certain rooms jam-packed with activities while others are seldom used? For example, if you are short of space, do you really need to maintain a separate guest room that visitors occupy only occasionally?
- Do you have conflicting uses of space at the same time? For example, is one person trying to read while another practices the saxophone?
- Are there some activities that you would enjoy doing but lack the space for right now? Crafts, sewing, or woodworking require plenty of space to spread out. Build in custom storage to accommodate oversize items your household uses frequently such as art paper, fabric bolts, or sports equipment.

Considering a Floor Plan

Whether you are building a new home or thinking about remodeling your present one, ask yourself six basic questions to help you decide if the floor plan you are considering will be convenient and comfortable for your household:

1. Does it accommodate your activities and interests?
2. Does it meet your need for both public and private spaces?
3. Does it create efficient traffic patterns and room relationships?
4. Will it provide adequate space for your household furnishings and possessions?
5. Does it incorporate the concept of universal design?
6. Is it an adaptable design?

Table 3-1. Example list of room activities.

Room: *Kitchen*

Activities that take place in this room:
— *prepare food*
— *put away groceries*
— *talk on phone*
— *watch TV*
— *pay bills*
— *do and supervise homework*
— *do crafts*

Avoid the temptation to solve space problems simply by adding separate rooms for each activity. If rooms are used only a few times a year, they are an extremely expensive investment. Consider whether you would get more enjoyment and versatility by eliminating seldom-used rooms, possibly a formal living room or dining room, and adding extra space to areas that will be used more frequently. If you cannot afford a larger house now, buy a smaller home or select a building lot and a plan that would allow you to expand the house when the need arises.

- As your household's lifestyle changes, do you anticipate changes to activities and interests? For example, you may not use formal spaces much now, but in a few years when the children are grown, you may use these spaces to entertain guests more often.

If you have answered yes to any of these questions, you may need to rethink how you will use space in a new or remodeled home.

Need for Public and Private Spaces

Every house needs both public and private spaces. When household members want to be with others, they will look for the public spaces that incorporate living, dining, and kitchen functions.

When they want to be alone, they will look for private spaces that are visually or acoustically separated from the public areas.

With today's fast-paced lifestyles, many households feel more comfortable with an informal, open plan that places the kitchen as the hub of activity. Food entices family and friends to congregate and socialize. The formal living and dining room and a separate family room are eliminated in this arrangement, but quiet spaces are still needed for renewal and retreat.

An open-space plan offers many advantages. For example, it:
- Makes a smaller home seem larger because spaces are visually connected.
- Accommodates larger groups in a smaller home.
- Allows more flexible room arrangements (Figure 3-1).

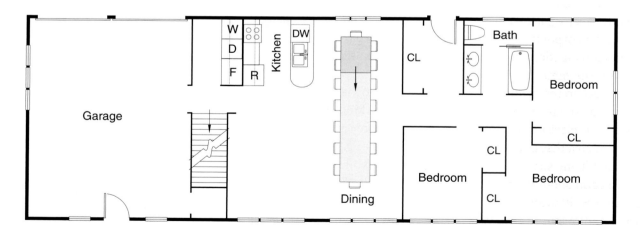

Note: The dining table in the figure illustrates the space available for table expansion. Most tables will not expand to the length shown, but more likely, a second, more portable table will be brought in to extend the seating area. In addition, the extended table arrangement is only temporary; otherwise, it would interfere with traffic flow from the kitchen to the bedroom areas.

FIGURE 3-1.
In an open-space arrangement, a dining table can be expanded for special meals.

Check your floor plan to see if the rooms will accommodate your furniture and still leave enough space to move about. (Draw furniture pieces to size on graph paper, cut out, and lay over the plan to see if everything fits. A computer software program can also be used to check furniture size and placement.)

- Adapts to changing family lifestyles.
- Can be easily changed to accommodate different events.
- Reduces housing costs (one large room takes less square footage, has fewer walls, and is thus less expensive to build than several smaller rooms). Reducing the amount of space may provide some budget flexibility to add custom features such as built-in storage and to upgrade the quality of materials and finishes.

Careful planning is needed to create privacy and reduce noise conflicts in an open-space plan. You can make an open-space plan more appealing by incorporating some or all of the following ideas:

- **Expand the main bedroom.** Add extra space to the main bedroom to serve as an area for quiet reading or television viewing or as an office area that is separate from the main living space. For more information about bedrooms, see **Chapter 8, Bedrooms.**
- **Add "nooks and crannies."** Use alcoves and bump-outs to create cozy reading and conversation areas within a larger room.
- **Widen stair landings.** Make a stair landing slightly larger to

Developing a Floor Plan

A good floor plan will reflect your household's activities and interests, accommodate both public and private activities, have efficient traffic patterns and room relationships, incorporate universal design features, and be flexible and adaptable in response to changing needs. Check your floor plan to see if the rooms will accommodate your furniture and still leave enough space to move about.

Using a computer software program or using paper cut outs that are scaled to fit a floor plan are good ways to visualize a room and house. Some common floor plan symbols are shown here. Look at various room arrangements and make sure that space is allowed for people to move around and to have easy access to all parts of the room. When you use a computer software program, be sure to use actual sizes of the furniture that you will be using in your rooms and not standard-sized furniture that may be used in the program.

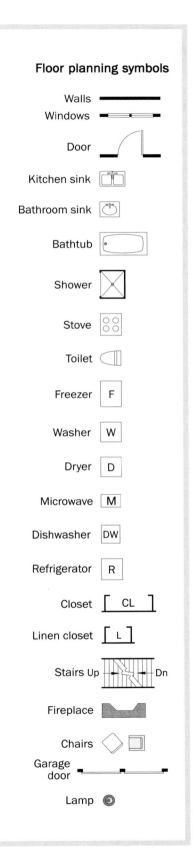

Floor planning symbols

Walls
Windows
Door
Kitchen sink
Bathroom sink
Bathtub
Shower
Stove
Toilet
Freezer   F
Washer   W
Dryer   D
Microwave   M
Dishwasher   DW
Refrigerator   R
Closet   [CL]
Linen closet   [L]
Stairs Up   Dn
Fireplace
Chairs
Garage door
Lamp

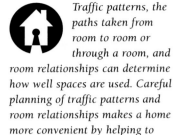

Traffic patterns, the paths taken from room to room or through a room, and room relationships can determine how well spaces are used. Careful planning of traffic patterns and room relationships makes a home more convenient by helping to minimize unnecessary steps, avoid congestion in busy work areas, and protect privacy.

serve as a reading area or as an area for a computer workstation.

• **Plan for multipurpose spaces.** Plan a guest bedroom to serve double duty as an office. When guests arrive, the desk and office clutter can be hidden behind the bi-fold doors of a closet.

Traffic Patterns and Room Relationships

When you first step into a house or look at a floor plan, visualize how people will be moving through the house. They should be able to quickly walk from the main entrance to other areas of the house without going through other rooms; the best traffic patterns allow access to all activity areas from the entrances without using any room as a corridor (Figures 3-2 and 3-3). If the traffic pattern is poor (Figure 3-4), look for another plan rather than wasting time evaluating individual rooms. A good traffic pattern will:

• Be direct, convenient, and logical.
• Provide easy flow of traffic between different levels of the home.
• Help separate private areas from public activity areas.
• Use hallways to control movement (Figure 3-2).
• Provide direct path from garage to kitchen for convenience in carrying groceries into the house and taking out trash.

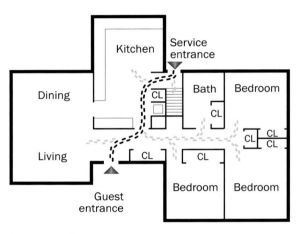

Traffic from either entrance uses the central hall for access to all rooms.

FIGURE 3-2.
Good traffic pattern—entry to central hall.

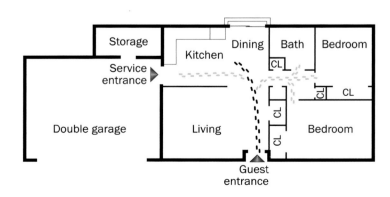

The guest entry to the living room does not interfere with furniture arrangement or activities. There is a direct path from garage to kitchen.

FIGURE 3-3.
Good traffic pattern in a small house.

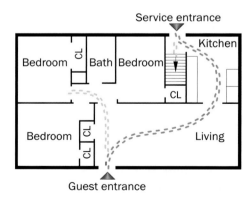

Traffic through the kitchen work area creates conflicts with meal preparation; the diagonal path across the living room wears the floor covering unevenly.

FIGURE 3-4.
Poor traffic pattern.

- Go through edges or corners of rooms, rather than cutting through the middle, to avoid interrupting activities in a room.
- Not interfere with or limit furniture arrangement (Figure 3-3).

Remodeling requires meticulous consideration of the most advantageous traffic patterns. Avoid reducing the usefulness of current space by making it a traffic lane to a new addition. Traffic lanes cannot be used as living space. When you take away the traffic lanes and storage areas and the space required to operate doors, the floor space remaining is the usable "living area" of your home. To reduce building costs, minimize halls and pathways so your plan has a high proportion of usable living space.

In a multilevel house, consider traffic patterns between levels. When locating stairs, emphasize convenience. For example, if recreation and entertainment areas occupy the basement, the stairs should start in the central hall (Figure 3-5). But if the basement is used as a workroom or mudroom, the stairs should be placed close to the service entrance (Figure 3-6). When locating stairs, also consider space use at each level. Put the stairs to the second floor above the basement stairs for efficient space use (Figure 3-7). For more information about stairs, see **Chapter 12, Entries, Doors, Halls, and Stairs**.

Room relationships affect the efficiency of the traffic patterns. Some strategies to consider are these:

- Place greater emphasis on the location of the informal eating area in relation to the kitchen than on the convenience of the

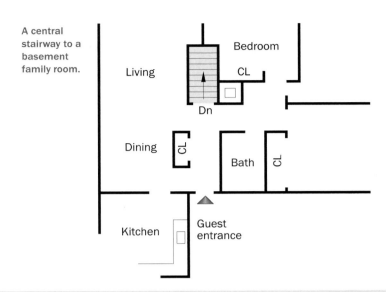

FIGURE 3-5.
A stairway from a central hall.

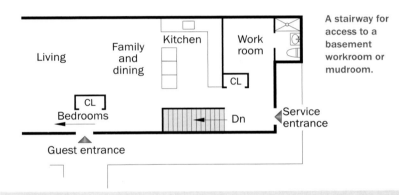

FIGURE 3-6.
A stairway near a service entrance.

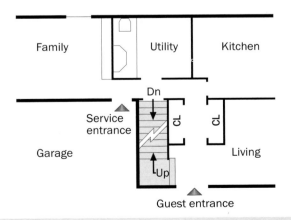

FIGURE 3-7.
Stairs on a main floor.

kitchen to the formal dining room that is used only occasionally.

• Provide convenient access from the kitchen to the food-serving area on the deck or patio. Avoid carrying food through the garage.

• Locate bathrooms to protect privacy. They should not be visible from public spaces or from the main entrance to the home. Figure 3-8 shows a poor location for the laundry and half bath. Instead of being a private space, the room is used as a hallway and opens off the dining room as well.

• Place a premium on privacy. If there is only one bathroom, it should be accessible without going through another room. For greater flexibility, compartmentalize the space by placing the tub/shower and toilet in a separate area from the lavatory (Figure 3-9).

• Design the outdoor living area to be an extension of indoor living spaces (Figure 3-10).

• Locate a children's play area where it can be seen from inside the house. Provide a half bath near the outdoor play area.

Universal Design

Because people come in a variety of ages, sizes, and abilities, your house should be designed to be convenient and comfortable both now—and when your needs change in the future. Universal design involves designing homes that are more convenient for everyone. Such homes are accessible to friends and

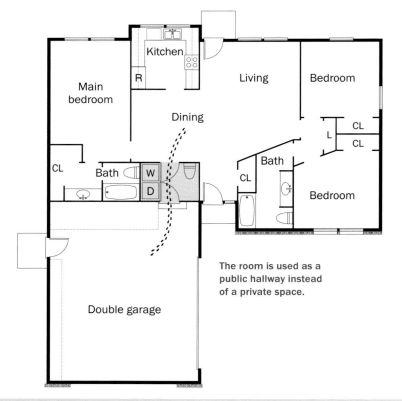

The room is used as a public hallway instead of a private space.

FIGURE 3-8.
Poor location for a laundry and half bath.

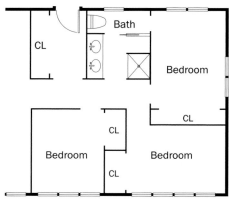

A pocket door separates the two parts of the bathroom so two people can use the room at the same time. Note convenient access from main bedroom to toilet area.

FIGURE 3-9.
A compartmentalized bathroom.

family with special needs: a parent pushing a baby stroller, a teenager hobbling on a sprained ankle, or a grandmother using a wheelchair or walker. Universal design features add very little to the initial cost of building or remodeling but can be difficult or expensive to add later. The following features are basic to the concept of universal design:

- **No-step entrance.** To create an attractive entrance, carefully grade and landscape the area instead of building a ramp. See **Chapter 12. Entries, Doors, Halls, and Stairs** for more information on no-step entrances.

- **Essential activity areas on main level.** Although not every part of a house needs to be accessible, be sure to have a place for eating, bathing, and sleeping on the no-step level of the home. A two-story house or a home with a basement is acceptable if the main level is accessible. Laundry equipment should also be located on the main level.

- **Wide doorways.** Doorways to the essential activity areas on the no-step level need to have at least a 32-inch wide clear

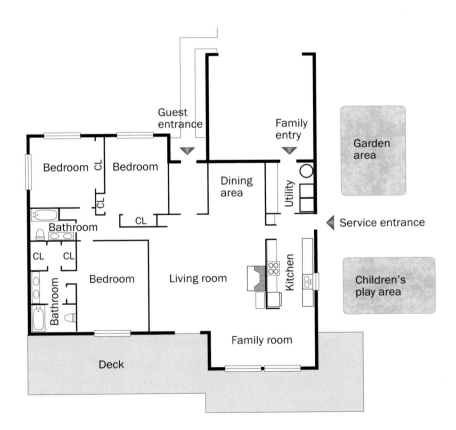

The living room and family room areas will be the rooms with the most windows. These rooms have the best view of the most attractive parts of your lawn and yard, and face south so they can take advantage of the sun's warmth in cold climates.

FIGURE 3-10.
Consider how interior and exterior spaces relate.

opening. If you are remodeling, you may be able to make the usable doorway space wider by installing pocket doors or swing-away hinges or by removing part of the doorframe (Figure 3-11).

- **Wide halls and pathways.** Make halls on the no-step level at least 42 inches wide.
- **Maneuvering space.** Make sure the entrance and at least one bathroom on the main level have a 60-inch "turning circle" of open floor space for guests or household members who use wheelchairs (Figure 3-12).

Adaptable Design

An adaptable floor plan will allow you to make future changes with minimum effort and expense. For example, a family room for a young family could eventually be turned into a bedroom for a retired couple if a bathroom and storage closets are located nearby. The following adaptable features simplify future changes:

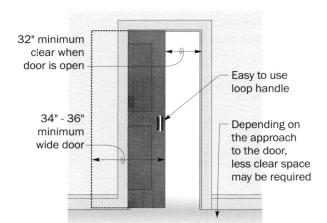

32" minimum clear when door is open

34" - 36" minimum wide door

Easy to use loop handle

Depending on the approach to the door, less clear space may be required

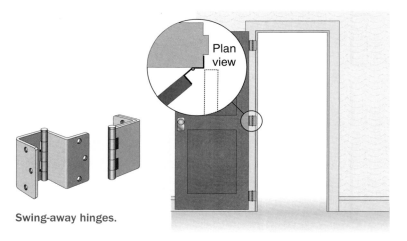

Swing-away hinges.

Plan view

Swing-away hinges allow the door to swing out of the door opening and increase the clear space by 1" to 1-1/2".

FIGURE 3-11.
Existing doorways can be made wider by using pocket doors or doors with swing-away hinges.

FIGURE 3-12.
A 5-foot turning circle in bathroom.

5'

- **Convertible space on main level.** Provide a room with doors for privacy that can be used in many ways. A room that starts out as an office or quiet reading area on the main level could be converted to a bedroom for the later years. It could also be used as a separate space for practicing musical instruments or as a temporary bedroom for a sick child. Locate this convertible space near a bathroom, and include flexible storage.

- **Flexible storage.** Build in as much storage as you can afford, near the location where items will be used most often. As a rule of thumb, allow a minimum of 10 percent of the living area of your home for storage. Built-in storage can change the shape of a room or create awkward traffic lanes, so plan where it should be placed even if it is too costly to install during construction. Include adjustable brackets in closets and cabinets to make it easy to raise or lower rods and shelves to adapt to items of various size and shape. For additional storage ideas, see **Chapter 13, Household Storage**.

- **Wall reinforcement in bathrooms.** Under the drywall, reinforce the walls around the tub and toilet with plywood sheeting, enabling grab bars to be added later, if needed. This feature is essential for at least the one bathroom that will be located on the no-step level of your home. For safety sake, be sure towel bars and grab bars are firmly anchored into the wall studs with long screws.

- **Adjustable cabinets and counters.** Consider installing base cabinets that could be removed or counters that could be lowered to create a seated work area in the kitchen (Figure 3-13). Cabinets and counters that can be raised or lowered will accommodate tall and short people as well as seated users. Appliances such as dishwashers and ovens can be raised or lowered to make it easier to reach the controls. Some companies even make pneumatic lifts for cabinets and counters. For more information, see **Chapter 6, Kitchens**.

Universal design features add very little to the initial cost of building or remodeling but are difficult or expensive to add later. Build in flexibility to adapt spaces as needs change. Include these adaptable features to allow future changes with minimum effort and expense.

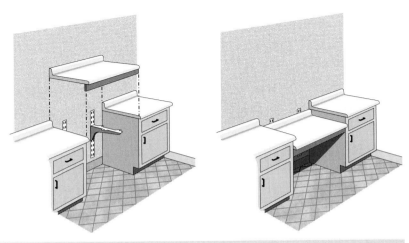

FIGURE 3-13.
Adjustable cabinets and counters.

Resources

Barrier Free Environments Incorporated. 1991. *The Accessible Housing Design File.* New York, NY: Van Nostrand Reinhold.

Building Research Council. *Council Notes.* School of Architecture, University of Illinois at Urbana-Champaign. http://brc.arch.uiuc.edu/Pubcatalog.htm#council%20notes%20set

Housing Education and Research Association (HERA). *Introduction to Housing.* New York, NY: Prentice Hall. 2005.

Housing: www.extension.iastate.edu/housing.

Kicklighter, Clois E. and Joan C. Kicklighter. 1998. *Residential Housing and Interiors.* Tinley Park, IL: The Goodheart-Willcox Company, Inc.

Lewis, Evelyn L. and Carolyn S. Turner. 2000. *Housing Decisions.* Tinley Park, IL: The Goodheart-Willcox Company, Inc.

Mace, R.M. 1998. Universal design in housing. *Assistive Technology* 10:21-28.

Sherwood, Ruth F. 1997. *Homes: Today and Tomorrow, Fifth Edition.* New York, NY: Glencoe, McGraw-Hill.

Susanka, Sarah and Kira Obolensky. 1998. *The Not So Big House: A Blueprint for the Way We Really Live.* Newton, CT: Taunton Press, Inc.

Universal Design and Home Accessibility: www.extension.iastate.edu/universaldesign

Universal Design in Housing: www.design.ncsu.edu/cud/pdf_files/UDinHousing.pdf

Wentling, James W. 1990. *Housing by Lifestyle: The Component Method of Residential Design.* New York, NY: McGraw-Hill Publishing Company.

Selecting a Location
or a Building Site

CAREFUL CHOICE OF THE LOCATION AND SITE of your new home is essential. Too often, those considering where to buy or build choose unwisely and lose the value of their investment. It is unwise to buy or build in a location if you are not familiar with the nearby area and its resources. In addition to general considerations for choosing a location or building site, this chapter addresses the special considerations required when buying or building a house in a rural location.

General Considerations for Site Selection

Real estate agents are known for their frequent mantra "location, location, location." This book uses this mantra with a slightly different focus, stressing the concept of "context, context, context." Learning about the site on which a home is located or will be located is very helpful in the planning and decision-making process. The natural, social, and physiographic contexts include such factors as weather exposure, soil conditions, topography, drainage, neighborhood conditions, transportation options, school locations, tax prospects, the value of a site, and ultimately the value of a home. For example, in the Twenty-first century the cost of fossil fuel probably will increase, and these location elements will be important aspects in determining a home's desirability and sustainability. As you go through the site evaluation process, be diligent in your efforts; after all, the site you select is the place where you will live!

Neighbors and the neighborhood

Try to learn if the neighbors are compatible with your lifestyle. Find out if at least some neighbors will be in your age and interest group with children in the same age group as yours. Consider knocking on the doors of the nearest neighbors to determine this type of information.

Neighborhood character is important. Is the neighborhood attractive and well maintained? In general, buy or build in a well-maintained or improving neighborhood, not a deteriorating one. The average value of houses in the neighborhood greatly affects the value of a house.

Zoning ordinances and legal limitations

Check the title and deed to your property. Then review zoning ordinances, local regulations that restrict property use and type of construction as well as set the minimum lot size, number of family units in each building, maximum

Before you look for a specific site, begin by thinking about such general considerations as neighbors and the neighborhood as well as transportation facilities and traffic patterns. Determine which community resources, such as schools, health care facilities, and recreational facilities, are most important to your family. Determine if suitable resources such as these are available in the surrounding area. Learn as much as possible about a building site's physical attributes such as lot orientation and soil characteristics.

If your future house will be modest in size but situated among large houses, its value may be enhanced. If you have the one large house in a neighborhood, the reverse may be true. In any case, a well-maintained house in a good quality neighborhood increases resale value and increases the chances of a good return on investment.

height of a building, minimum setbacks (how close a house can be located to property lines and adjacent streets), and side yard requirements. Utility companies may have easements on a property so they can repair or replace lines. Is your lot and the area around you zoned to suit your needs? Is the area zoned for single or multiple family use? Are fences permitted? Do zoning ordinances allow for a home business if you have one? Are you restricted to the number of cars or clients that you may have visit at any one time? Are there business taxes levied by the city or state? Are zoning ordinances changing, or have they been stable for some time? Remember that zoning changes can help or hurt you.

Some areas have restrictions such as covenants that might be in a deed, subdivision regulations, or regulations imposed by a homeowner's association. A homeowner's association may have mandatory membership fees. Fees collected by an association may be used to finance upkeep of the neighborhood.

An architect can be a good resource to make sure that any construction or remodeling you are planning fits into the architecture and zoning requirements of a neighborhood.

Growth patterns

If possible, check with local planning officials for clues to future growth and its potential effects on your property. Property values in the path of a city's expansion may rise. If, however, the city is growing away from the property, the neighborhood may deteriorate, causing the houses

to lose value. Growth may also influence placement of future highways and rights of way. Avoid surprises. Check into what easements and rights of way may be used by public utilities or that may be subject to seizure by eminent domain in the future.

Odor, noise, dust, and other nuisances

Sometimes, distance is the best guarantee that your quality of living will not be affected by external factors. If, for example, a building site is located near a municipal or county disposal facility or landfill, distance from the facility is the only guarantee that a site will be unaffected. Even with the best management, such facilities come with odor, mosquitoes, and rodents.

If you are thinking about a rural location, be aware that some manufacturing plants and livestock operations can generate unpleasant odors. To minimize odors carried by prevailing summer winds, keep houses at least one-quarter mile from manufacturing plants or livestock operations that may generate unpleasant odors.

In the same way that you evaluate nuisance odors, determine the noises you want to avoid and their prevalence in a prospective neighborhood. Locate the source of the noise. Evaluate seasonal prevailing wind directions. Do not buy property downwind from a source unless there is enough distance to dilute its effects. For example, racetracks can be noisy and dusty and can create heavy traffic. Likewise, sites near airports typically have high noise levels and heavy traffic.

Transportation and traffic

Being able to get to and from work easily and quickly saves time and reduces stress. Is public transportation in the form of buses or a subway system available, well established, and likely to continue? Is road maintenance, including snow removal, reliable?

Living near a major street or intersection is convenient, but you may want to avoid noise and exhaust fumes. Consider the possibility that traffic patterns will change; as undeveloped areas grow, traffic patterns can change, and roads can become congested. Traffic that is currently near the house can be too great a hazard, and later, the road may be widened or relocated.

Barriers can be erected near major roads to minimize noise, but these types of barriers are not always effective. In addition, they can limit views, create shade, and affect wind patterns.

Community Resources

In addition to the general factors discussed in the previous section, you need to consider how accessible a site is to community resources such as schools, shopping, health care facilities, police and fire protection, recreational facilities, and places of worship. Evaluate the resources important to you. If the area lacks them, you may want to look elsewhere.

To quickly obtain information about a particular area, use the research capabilities of an Internet search engine (for example, Yahoo or Google), and enter the area's zip code and the words "zip code." This should give you a list of links that will provide more information about the location you are interested in.

Use census data to learn about your neighbors and neighborhood. Contact the city planning department, or its equivalent, in your community to find out about the area. Visit the neighborhood on several occasions to find out about typical patterns of activity. Examine your needs as they relate to what features the neighborhood provides.

Schools

If you have or plan to have school-aged children, you will want to know which school district they will be attending. What programs and services does the district offer? Will your children attend a neighborhood school located within walking distance of your home? If you are comfortable having your children ride a bus to school, a site located some distance from a school may be suitable.

To learn more about a school district, call the superintendent's office, or ask your real estate agent for references. The answers you receive may influence your site selection. Keep in mind, however, that children grow up, and needs change.

General services

For convenience, you may want to live near a full-service grocery store. Where is the post office located? How far is the nearest service station and bank? If you shop often for products or services, having easy access to a major shopping area may be a high priority for you.

Health care facilities

Families need access to health care. How close is the nearest physician's office? Are dentist offices, pharmacies, clinics, and hospitals located nearby? Long distances and inconvenient travel can add risks, costs, and anxieties for those using health care services.

Police and fire protection

How available are police and fire protection? Incorporated towns and cities provide personal and property protection with a municipal police department. Rural homeowners receive similar protection from county sheriffs who patrol much larger areas and thus cannot respond as quickly as urban or suburban police officers. Likewise, firefighters and fire hydrants are commonplace in populated areas. In rural areas, on the other hand, trained volunteers often serve as firefighters, and fire hydrants may not be available. The location of fire departments and hydrants can affect insurance rates.

Recreational facilities

Is having recreational facilities nearby of interest to you? Do the facilities available add to or detract from the neighborhood? Consider how various facilities appeal to your family and how they will affect property values. A city park within walking distance allows you to take advantage of facilities you help support. However, a busy playground next door or across the street could contribute to parking issues during the day and support undesirable activities at night. Nearby creeks and rivers may be an attraction, but they can also flood or be a hazard to young children. Golf courses are quiet and beautiful, and they usually have limited traffic, but they can be busy during certain times of the year or during special events at the course. Scenic lakes can be beautiful but may become polluted, add to insect populations, and be overrun with waterfowl all year.

Places of worship

Is a place of worship for the religious faith of your choice located nearby? If you are actively involved in religious activities, you may wish to live near your place of worship. Having access to public transportation, such as city buses or subways, however, may enable you to live wherever you wish and still practice your religion.

Physical Considerations for Site Selection

As you deliberate about purchasing a specific site, consider the lot's physical attributes such as:
- Orientation.
- Size and shape.
- Soil characteristics.
- Drainage.
- Trees.

Then consider other pertinent issues such as utilities, garbage collection and disposal, pavement and curbs, driveways and parking, and sidewalks, steps, and porches. Figure 4-1 shows some basic considerations that are described in this section.

Lot orientation

If you are buying a house that you will remodel, you may have little choice about how the house is oriented, but you may still be able to reconstruct the house to take advantage of certain physical features. If you are building a new house, will your lot allow you to develop a house plan with the sun and wind orientation that you desire? If a choice is available, orient the house with respect to winter and summer sun and to prevailing winds. For example, if the long axis of the house runs east/west, you can place more windows on the south side, thus taking advantage of winter sun. To shield the house from winter winds, plant evergreen trees on the appropriate side of the house; in cold climates, this side would likely be the northwest. You may also wish to orient your house to maximize outdoor living or frame a panoramic view.

Relationship to the sun

The value of natural heating and cooling is often overlooked, but orienting a house to take advantage of natural heating and cooling opportunities makes good sense and pays for itself many times over. Having continuous sun access can be valuable, especially in colder regions. In cold weather regions, a house with a large south or southwest orientation intercepts the greatest amount of solar heat in the winter. To shade the house in these regions in the summer, place awnings or a roof overhang on south windows (Figure 4-2), and plant deciduous trees nearby (Figure 4-3). Since these trees shed their leaves in the fall, they allow more sun to reach the house and windows in the winter. On the other hand, because evergreens block the winter sun, avoid planting evergreen trees on the south side of the house in colder areas.

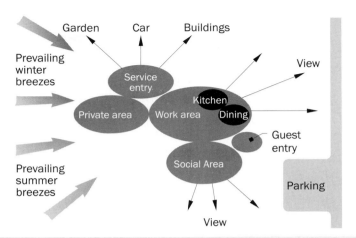

FIGURE 4-1.
House zones relative to exterior factors.

Wind

The location of trees can provide considerable protection from winter winds. In your design, consider the direction of the predominant winter wind. Plant evergreen trees and shrubs on the side of the house exposed to winter winds, providing a windbreak.

Try to orient doors, windows, and outdoor living areas to capture cooling summer breezes. Design

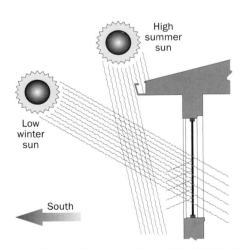

FIGURE 4-2.
Roof overhang related to winter and summer sun angle.

For most localities, planning solar shading in the summer can be accomplished easily with landscaping and good overhang design. In regions where summer cooling is more important than winter heating, plant evergreens to shade a house, especially windows. Evergreens will not lose their needles and will provide shade year round. In addition to reducing the costs of heating and cooling, overhangs also can be elegant architectural features. If practical, incorporate them into your building plan.

house entries wisely to decrease the impact of cold wind and snow. In colder climates, it is especially important to recognize predominant winter wind direction for planning doors and garage entrances so that drifting snow does not block doors regularly, thereby preventing emergency egress.

Lot size and shape

Do not crowd a large house into a small lot. Leave room to accentuate the building with plantings. Keep possible irrigation patterns in mind. A large yard means more maintenance, but the activities that it promotes—sports, entertaining, and gardening—may make the additional effort worthwhile. Smaller houses can be elegant and efficient and are often much easier to heat, cool, and maintain.

Narrow lots create challenges: the house may not fit with the best orientation of public and private areas, and an attached garage may not be possible. Although a lot at least 60 feet wide may be more expensive, it is often worth the increased cost. Wedge-shaped lots require careful house design to avoid an awkward arrangement, and they often raise the issue of having enough space for a future addition.

Soil characteristics

While evaluating a site, check with current residents and local housing inspection officials to determine if the lot has any unusual soil characteristics. Find out if the soil on a site has good surface and subsurface drainage. Does the land surrounding the site drain through or away from the site? Is the soil appropriate for a septic tank system, if one is needed? Will

the soil support a garden and vigorous lawn growth? Is the soil in a chemical waste hazard area? Is it prone to radon problems? Beware of a lot containing fill soil; it may settle. To help answer these kinds of questions, you may want to have the soil tested by a reputable soil-testing lab.

Drainage

The presence of surface water during heavy rainfall or snowmelt could indicate a problem. The design of your lot should intercept and divert surface water far enough from the house to create an adequate, well-drained yard. Avoid a site where underground flow or a high water table can interfere with basements, footings, and foundations. Ask those neighbors who use their basements for living space if wet basements are a problem. Inquire if their storm and septic sewers have ever backed up and if their homes contain sump pumps. Contact local and state health authorities about groundwater pollution.

Determine what you can about the flood history of the site, especially if it is near a permanent waterway. If the site has ever been flooded, this has significant implications for financing, flood insurance, and Federal Emergency Management Agency (FEMA) regulations regarding flood-prone sites. FEMA administers a national flood insurance program and should be consulted about flood risks and history.

Trees

If you have a choice of locations, favor one with trees, thus getting a head start on landscaping and shade. Learn about native species of trees,

especially about those on the property because they can help shade and
cool your home in the summer as
well as provide wind protection in the
winter (Figure 4-3). Consider which
trees you want to save, but recognize
that removing trees can be costly.
However, if their variety is undesirable or their location interferes with
house orientation or sun access, select
another site.

Utilities

If you are looking at a lot as a
potential building site, the lot should
have access to water, gas, electricity,
sewers, streetlights, and phone
service. Can a water line be run from
a public supply to the building site,
or will a private water supply need to
be developed? If the water will come
from a private well, will the water
have to be treated to make it acceptable for drinking and other uses? If
utility access is unavailable, what will
installing utilities cost? Who will be
responsible for paying those costs?
Check the location and depth of
sanitary and storm sewers. If they are
less than 6 feet deep, you may
encounter problems with basement
drainage. If a private sewage system
is needed, will zoning, space, and soil
type permit the use of a basic sewer
system, or will a more expensive
system be required? The time to
analyze these issues is before you
buy the lot.

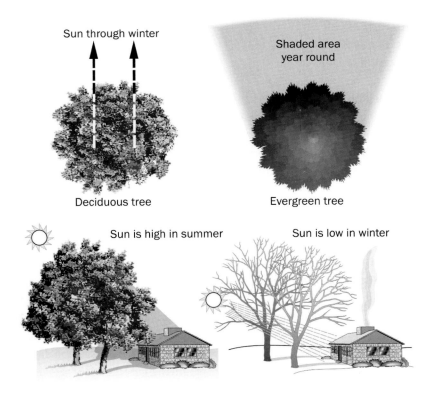

Sun through winter

Shaded area
year round

Deciduous tree

Evergreen tree

Sun is high in summer

Sun is low in winter

FIGURE 4-3.
Deciduous trees shade the house in the summer.

Garbage collection and disposal

Is curbside garbage collection available and affordable? If not, how can you dispose of household garbage? Is outdoor burning allowed? Is a municipal disposal facility or landfill located within driving distance? Can you compost without restriction?

Pavements and curbs

If you are building in a new subdivision, determine if the streets are paved and if curbs are present and paid for? If not, do owners pay for paving in front of their lot, or does the city, county, or state pay for improvements and maintenance? Ask the real estate agent for more information.

Driveways and parking

In selecting a home or a building site, carefully consider how the lot accommodates driveways and parking facilities. Does an all-weather road presently lead to the home site? If not, whose responsibility is it to build and maintain a road? If so, is access to and from the road easy? How will winter affect entry? A drive that slopes down to a garage from a higher road can be treacherous when it is slippery, snow covered, or icy. For these cases, the slope of the driveway can be decreased by having the driveway gradually descend back and forth across the hillside.

A lot should be able to accommodate the dimensions in Figures 4-4 and 4-5, which provide space to walk past a parked car without stepping off the driveway into wet grass or snow. For a double drive, increase the 12-foot width of a single drive to

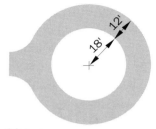

Circle driveway.

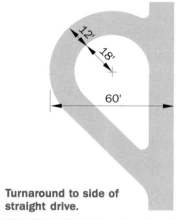

Turnaround to side of straight drive.

FIGURE 4-4.
Driveway turns for cars and pickups.

18 feet. The 30-foot outside radius (12-foot drive + 18-foot radius) can be 28 feet if the front of the car can extend beyond the drive.

Vehicles are often parked directly outside the garage door. In addition, vehicles should be able to be backed out and turned around on a nearly level surface. The area before entering the garage should be sloped slightly (1 percent, or 1/4-inch per foot minimum) away from the garage so water does not drain into the garage.

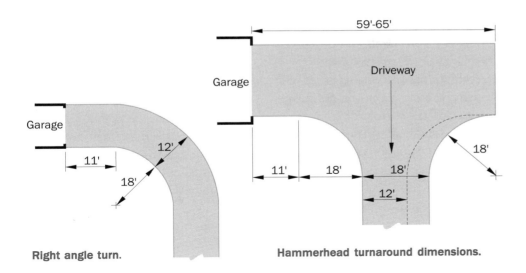

Right angle turn.

Hammerhead turnaround dimensions.

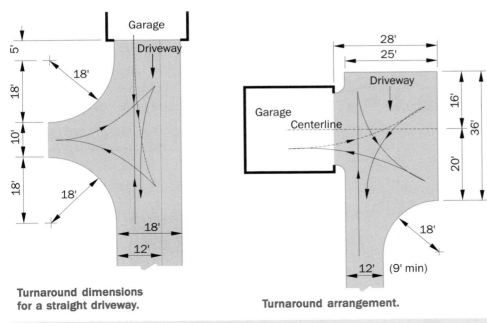

Turnaround dimensions
for a straight driveway.

Turnaround arrangement.

FIGURE 4-5.
Turns, driveways, and turnarounds.

Special Considerations for Rural Sites

For the most part, choosing a rural site is similar to selecting an urban site, but the process might be more complex and have more problems.

On one hand, a rural site may offer more freedom of location (for example, house placement, orientation, and plan selection), but it may also require consideration of the type of water and sewer system required and may involve determining the cost of gaining access to roads and utilities. These considerations can greatly affect the initial and ongoing cost of a property. Inquire about the business activities on the surrounding properties. Some rural enterprises make good neighbors, and some do not. Flies and rodents accompanying animal production can be annoying; odors from manure spread on nearby fields can be unpleasant.

Siting a farmhouse on a working farm is unique. Because it is part of a whole farm business, it must be considered in relation to the farming enterprise and farmstead facilities. If you have already located the farmstead, the issue may be fitting the house into a rather limited area. Consider locating away from the farmstead. Figure 4-6 shows many of

the external factors that affect a well-planned farmstead.

Understanding the following factors will help you select a suitable rural site:

- Approach to the house.
- Distance from the main road.
- Prevailing winds (to avoid animal odors).
- Drainage.
- View.
- Windbreaks.

Approach to the house

The site should afford a spacious area between the public road and the house. It should buffer the house from the road and should have space to provide room for farm activities as well as having adequate parking space. The lot should be situated so that the house is the first major

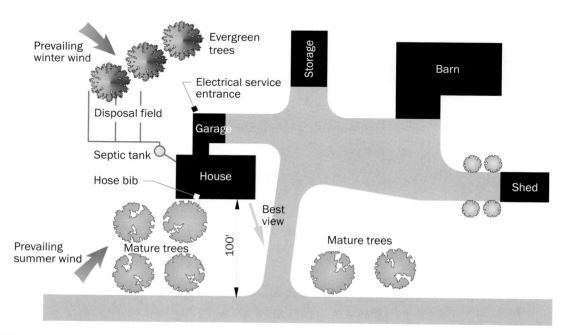

FIGURE 4-6.
Typical external factors that affect a well-planned farmstead.

building reached when entering a farmstead from public roads. Space should be available to provide guest parking for three to six cars (Figure 4-7) and turn-around space. When possible, avoid the need to back onto a public road. Design walks and landscaping to lead visitors to the guest entry but also to facilitate snow piling and removal, if winter weather conditions require that. Avoid having a driveway with shrubs and trees that make clearing snow from the driveway difficult. If possible, the house should at least 100 feet from the road, allowing for road widening and buffering noise and dust. Too much distance adds to driveway maintenance.

View

Pick a site that allows you to take advantage of pleasant countryside views from the living/social areas of the house. In general, provide a view from the kitchen or service area toward the farm courtyard and service buildings, and, if practical, the drive and public road. These views help detect accidents, fire, loose animals, or anyone coming or going from the farmstead.

Windbreaks

Be careful about selecting sites that have tree windbreaks. If healthy and properly located, they are usually desirable. They can improve comfort, but they may block a desirable view or the sun, and they can create large (75- to 100-foot wide) snowdrifts along the windbreak. Contact your county cooperative extension agent for detailed planning resources.

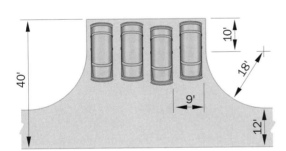

Space required for head-in parking.

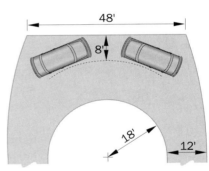

Parallel parking on circle drive.

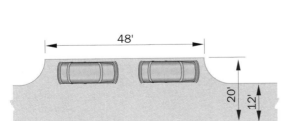

Space required for parallel parking.

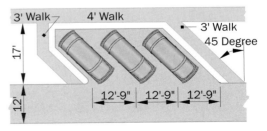

Space required for diagonal parking.

FIGURE 4-7.
Space for parking.

Snow removal

In colder climates, removing snow from roadways and parking areas may be a necessity. Select a site that provides an area on which to pile snow. The size of the area to pile snow depends on expected snowfall and melting. A site that receives a 6-inch snowfall on a 16-foot wide road that is 350 feet long and has a 50- by 50-foot parking area will have a snow volume in these areas of about 4,000 cubic feet. If all this snow is piled in one location, an area about 32-feet in diameter will be needed. The height of this pile will be about 16 feet tall!

There are few ideal areas in which to locate a snow pile. Following are some guidelines for identifying an area for a snow pile. Keep them in mind while evaluating a rural home site.

- Place the pile away from low areas and drainage ways. Snow piles can block water draining due to melting snow. This blockage can result in water accumulating around the pile and slowing down the melting of the snow pile. Accumulated water can also result in ice.
- Keep the pile away from wellheads, drinking water sources, and septic systems. Snow can contain salts and manure. Snow melt can drain towards and into drinking water locations, which can result in a contaminated water supply. Locating piles near or on wellheads and septic systems can make servicing these areas difficult. Also, the equipment used to move snow can damage wellheads and septic systems.
- Put the pile in a sunny area. Thermal and solar radiation energy from the sun can facilitate snowmelt. Snow piles located in shady areas can only benefit from thermal energy to melt snow.
- Locate the pile downwind from the site. Snow from the pile can blow onto the just clean surfaces if the pile is not properly located. Locate the pile based on winter prevailing patterns.
- Place the pile in a large, open area. Locate piles in a large open area that can allow snow to be piled from multiple snowfalls or a single heavy snowfall. It is not uncommon for people to realize that the large area they thought they had was not nearly large enough to contain the snow.
- Keep the pile near the areas being cleaned. Moving snow to a remote location can be expensive and time consuming. Locate piles at the ends of roadways or parking lots, if possible.

Resources

Entrances and Site Design. 1991. Raleigh, North Carolina: The Center for Universal Design, North Carolina State University. Publication number TP #2.00.

FEMA: www.fema.gov

Institute for Business and Home Safety: www.ibhs.org

Vehicular Transportation and Parking. 1991. Raleigh, North Carolina: The Center for Universal Design, North Carolina State University. Publication number TP #8.00.

Social Areas

SOCIAL AREAS ARE SPACES for the family to entertain guests, relax, watch television, read, listen to music, play games, enjoy the outdoors, and eat. These areas of the home are some of the most intensely used and fall under various names: living area, family area, great area, recreation area, media area, dining area, den, music area, patio, and outdoor living areas. In these areas, family members interact with each other and entertain friends and relatives. Some people use social areas to host work-related events, while others use them to enjoy hobbies and more private home-related activities.

Design Concepts

In addition to endorsing the concepts of universal and adaptable design, this chapter is based on the concept of open house design and on the ideas popularized by Sarah Susanka in her *The Not So Big House* series of books. Both concepts emphasize making the best use of available space.

Open house design

An open house design can make a small house feel like a larger house. This design concept can be incorporated in new or remodel designs. An open house design uses fewer walls and rooms. This type of house is laid out so that a space can be used for multiple functions.

A new house using the open house concept is designed with all the living or activity areas located on one floor. This arrangement allows for more flexibility in shared space use. For example, an eating area can be located adjacent to a kitchen and social room area. This space can be used for informal family dining or formal entertainment. Taking the eating area out of the kitchen allows the kitchen to become smaller and more efficient while seeming larger. This arrangement also eliminates the need for a dining room.

A house also can be remodeled to facilitate an open house design. In a house that has many small rooms, walls can be removed or relocated to open space. Before removing any walls, inspect the walls to determine if they support any loads or weight located above them. Support walls can be removed or relocated if a properly designed and installed beam and column system is used. Also, determine if any electrical wiring or water or sewer lines are located in the walls. Electrical lines can be easy to relocate, but water and sewer lines can present more of a challenge. Contact a house building professional if there are any questions or concerns in removing a wall.

Even though the types of activities in social areas vary from one household to another, all households have many similar needs. A variety of activities requires a variety of spaces in separate or multipurpose rooms. These rooms demand a large share of the space in a home. Family size, the size of groups entertained, special hobbies, and your budget determine how much space to allocate.

Take time to analyze carefully the space your family needs as you are planning your home. Remember that space is not only expensive to create, but it also must be insured, heated, cooled, furnished, and cleaned.

Even though an open design will make a house feel larger, people still need to have their own personal privacy spaces. These areas provide a warm and cozy area for people to relax, read, write, think, work on a craft, or do whatever a person wants to do in privacy. Each person living in the house should have his or her own personal privacy space. This space could be in a separate space such as a bedroom in which he or she can close the door, or the space could be something like a window seat or a corner in a room or hallway that is blocked off from other activities.

Furniture can be used to provide an open feel to small space. Use small-scale furniture with simple lines to help eliminate the feeling of overcrowding. Decorating the entire house as a unit instead of each room individually can create the feeling of spaciousness and continuity. Making a guest room double as a hobby, sewing, or television room can help increase the efficient use of a space.

The not so big house

The *Not So Big House* series of books details the ideas of a school of design that emphasizes the philosophy that people are building homes too large while neglecting the possibility of improving their homes by building smaller, more intimate, and more personal houses. This theory puts forth the idea that if people would construct smaller houses, say by one-third, and use the money saved to incorporate more personal touches then people would have a more pleasing and more livable home.

Much of the basis for the not-so-big-house design is similar to the open house design concept. The biggest difference between the two is that the not-so-big-house concept emphasizes building smaller homes and using some specific architectural design features such as the following:

- **Shelter around activity.**
  People tend to gravitate towards a corner of a room or alcove to sit. The walls provide a feeling of protection while the location allows a view out into a larger space.
- **Variety of ceiling heights.**
  Changes in ceiling height can make a room and house feel more comfortable. Instead of having the same ceiling height throughout a level in the house, vary the ceiling heights based on a room's dimensions.
- **Interior views.** Many houses are designed to include multiple windows that provide a nice view of the outside. The views within the house are just as important and should be designed to be aesthetically pleasing.
- **Diagonal views.** The size of a room can be made to feel larger if a room can focus people's attention from one corner of a room to the opposite corner. For example, a 10- by 14-foot room can seem like a 17-foot long room if the design can focus people's attention from one corner of a room to the opposite corner.

A house can be made to feel cozy through such design details as lighting, decorating themes and variations, and the framing of openings. A word of caution, reducing the size of a house by one-third does not mean the cost of the house will be reduced by one-third or 33 percent. Because the biggest cost associated with the house is with the structure and operating systems, some people have estimated that the cost savings of building not-so-big to be more like 10 to 15 percent. Also, the ideas behind the not-so-big-house concept may seem straightforward, but fully integrating them into a house successfully may be a challenge. Working with experienced professionals, including an architect, an interior decorator, a kitchen or bath designer, and a landscape designer can help integrate these concepts into a house.

General Planning Considerations

Think through the types of activities that social spaces need to accommodate in your home. A typical list of activity areas to plan for includes:

- Conversation areas.
- Television viewing areas.
- Dining spaces.
- Entertainment areas.
- Outside living areas.
- Action spaces.
- Special spaces (hobbies).

Good planning of single use areas such as kitchens, baths, stairs, halls, and storage areas leaves as much space as possible for social areas. Another alternative is to make typically single-use rooms serve more than one purpose: living-dining, living-family, kitchen-family, bath-laundry, hall-laundry, and garage-workshop. If the social area has limitations on the size and number of rooms, open space or open plans can overcome feelings of confinement or smallness.

The social area forms the core of the house. The bubble diagrams in Figures 5-1 and 5-2 show how the social areas typically relate to other areas in the house. A central location for the social areas lets traffic spread out to other parts of the house. Provide a separate entry in the social area connecting inside and outside living areas. If you entertain with outdoor cooking, have the kitchen near the patio door, screened-in porch, deck, or backyard.

Conversation Areas

Locations in which people can sit to relax and discuss the day's events are called conversation areas. These areas should be designed and arranged for people to sit comfortably and talk with minimal disruptions or distractions.

Room arrangement

Avoid cross traffic through the center of social areas. Notice the good and poor entrance locations in a

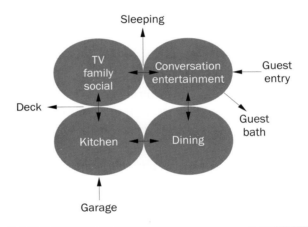

FIGURE 5-1.
Bubble diagram showing multiple social areas.

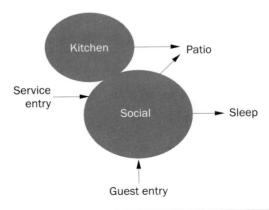

FIGURE 5-2.
Bubble diagram showing one large social area accompanying smaller social areas.

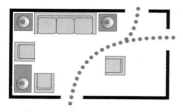

a. Poor pattern.
Poor doorway location creates
traffic lanes through the
conversation area.

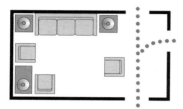

b. Good pattern.

**FIGURE 5-3.
Living room traffic.**

living room in Figure 5-3. In the
poorly planned pattern shown in
Figure 5-3a, people walking through
interfere with conversation or television viewing. It is better to group the
doorways at a corner or have the
traffic lane cross one end of the room.
Avoid through traffic in smaller living
rooms.

Room size

The ideal conversation circle for
seated people is about 10 feet in
diameter. In Figure 5-4a, the people
on the sofa and those on the chairs
will tend to form two small groups,
rather than one large one. If people
are standing, such as at parties, the
natural conversation circle is about 6
feet. With a room 12 to 14 feet wide,
furniture placed along each side of
the room maintains the proper
distance. Avoid living area widths
greater than 14 feet unless there is a
traffic lane along one side, or unless
the extra width has furniture that is
not part of the conversation circle.

Specific Activity Areas

Some areas of the house may have
specific functions so people can
watch television or play games. These
areas require special design considerations that depend on the level of
active functions.

Family room

Many houses have a family room.
It permits separating active (informal)
and passive (formal) activities.
Consider using the living room as a
place for conversation, reading,
listening to music, and studying while
keeping the family room for games,
dancing, hobbies, and active play. For
instance, a music system might be in
the living room and a television in the
family or media room, or a television,
music, and intercom system might be
installed in a media room with wiring
and speaker connections throughout
the house.

Family rooms can be much larger
than other rooms; for example, a
14- by 18-foot room is necessary for

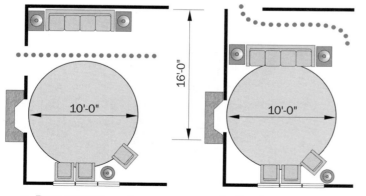

a. Poor arrangement.
Traffic through group;
seats too far apart.

b. Good arrangement
Traffic outside conversation area;
seats inside 10-foot circle.

**FIGURE 5-4.
Conversation circle.**

Table 5-1. Living room furniture areas.
Allow 18 to 24 inches between a sofa or
chair and a coffee table. Clearance needed
at a rocker or recliner varies.

Furniture	Dimensions
2 person sofa	32" or 34" deep 50", 55", 60" long
3 person sofa	32" or 34" deep 72" to 102" long
Straight back armchair	27" or 29" deep 27" long
Rocking chair	22" x 24"
Recliner/rocker	30" by 29" (66" to 75" open)

a pool table. The size of family rooms may vary greatly, but a space smaller than 12 by 16 feet is limiting and not recommended.

Great room

The term great room sometimes means living room, but more often it means a large living-dining-family-kitchen multipurpose area. Great rooms seem well suited for smaller families who entertain large groups in a smaller house (Figure 5-5). Some people like to keep contact with the family while working in the kitchen. Large families may find a great room too noisy for day-to-day living and too public for individual activities. Fireplaces and dividers can be included to help break the room into smaller areas.

Recreation and activity spaces

Ping-pong tables, billiards equipment, weight lifting and fitness equipment, extensive model train networks, and children's play areas are examples of activities that require larger spaces for equipment, storage, and movement. Finished basements often work well for these special interests. A well-planned activity area in the basement must have good lighting, good ventilation, and no moisture problems. See **Chapter 14, Foundation**, for additional information.

Hobby spaces

Some rooms serve particular hobbies or interests yet are considered a part of the social area. Special interests vary, so plan size and shape to fit your needs. As you plan your room for special activities:

- Avoid a traffic lane through the room.

- Avoid a line-of-sight view from the guest entry or living room, especially if this room may appear cluttered.
- Isolate the room by walls, dividers, or distance if noise or odors from your activities may be objectionable to the rest of the house or vice versa.

Arranging furniture is easier in rectangular rooms than in square ones. One conversation circle with extra space for circulation requires a room 16 to 18 feet long. A 22-foot long room can hold two conversation circles. Alter the suggested sizes to match each family's individual activities. A versatile living room can be multi-purpose.

FIGURE 5-5.
Multiple activity areas of a great room design.

- Plan for needed storage.
- Consider special floor coverings, an exhaust fan, separate temperature control, and other space and facility features to support the activities.

Dining Areas

Plan your eating space according to family needs and preferences. Eating patterns vary from family to family, but usually one will predominate. Sit-down meals need attention first since they require a larger, relatively permanent space. The area you use for these meals may be a separate dining room, a combination kitchen-family room, or a dining nook in a large kitchen. Quick meals and snacks usually call for areas emphasizing speed and convenience, with a minimum of interference from other activities. A kitchen counter snack bar, a small dining table and chairs in a corner of the kitchen, or even portable folding TV tables serve the purpose adequately. Since dining

activities take up a small part of the day, many families prefer dual-purpose dining rooms.

Provide adequate dining space for the style of eating and the number of people you want to serve at one time. In keeping with the concept of universal design, allow space for the table and other furniture and for moving around the room while people are seated.

These are the minimum recommended space allowances from the table to the walls or other furniture:

- 32 inches to push a chair back and rise.
- 36 inches to edge past a seated person.
- 44 inches to walk past a seated person.

For eating family meals in the kitchen, locate space outside of but convenient to the food preparation area. A snack bar or eating counter may be convenient if there is enough room for both the counter and the chairs. Figure 5-6 shows three typical

Use chairs with counter at table height on a base cabinet. Use stools or taller chairs with counters that are more than 30 inches high. Stools are less safe and less convenient for children and older people. Provide at least 24 inches of counter frontage width per seated diner.

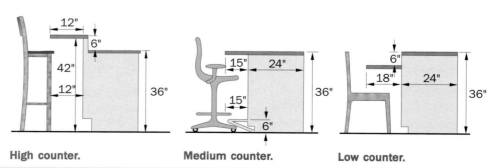

High counter.　　　Medium counter.　　　Low counter.

FIGURE 5-6.
Eating counters.

designs for eating counters. A counter is not as flexible as a table but may take less floor space. A low counter may best meet the needs of universal and adaptable design.

Many families prefer a separate dining room (Figures 5-7 and 5-8), but if space is limited, a combined dining-living area (Figure 5-9) allows expansion of the table yet reduces the space set aside specifically for dining. Provide adequate room length and width for tables and chairs plus access to them.

FIGURE 5-7.
Formal dining area.

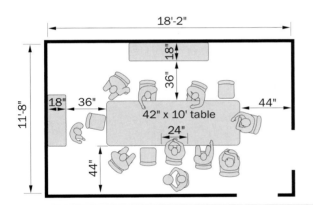

FIGURE 5-8.
A dining room for twelve.

A hutch or buffet is typically about 18 inches deep. To allow space for serving dishes and center pieces, a 42-inch wide table is common. There is space behind the chairs to edge past one side and one end, and to walk past on the other side and end. Table space is 24 inches per person, the minimum place setting zone. With armchairs at the ends, allow an extra 2 inches for each, and 4 inches to the room length.

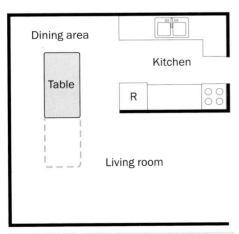

FIGURE 5-9.
Dining space expanding into the living room.

Figures 5-10, 5-11, and 5-12 illustrate various configurations for less formal dining spaces such as dining alcoves or kitchens.

If the space for dining is limited, consider a round or oval table (Figure 5-13). A round table usually does not save space, but it may fit a small space better than a rectangular table does. Also, seating an additional person around a circular table is easier than seating an extra person at a square or rectangular table. Table 5-2 shows typical dimensions for round tables.

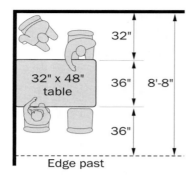

8'-8" for 36-inch wide table, 32 inches on one side to rise from the table and 36 inches on the other side to edge past. A 48-inch long table seats 4 and requires 34.6 square feet.

FIGURE 5-10.
Minimum width for table and chairs in a dining alcove.

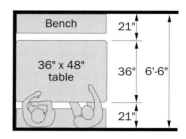

6'-6" for benches on both sides of a 36-inch table. A 48-inch long table seats 4 and requires 26 square feet.

FIGURE 5-11.
Dining space with benches.

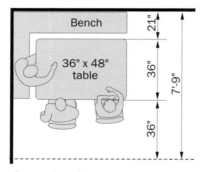

Corner bench.
Benches on one side and one end, and two chairs on the other side, seat five at a 3- by 4-foot table in 44.5 square feet.

FIGURE 5-12.
Bench and corner dining.

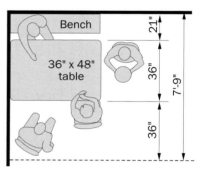

Bench on one side.
7'-9" for a bench on one side and chairs on the other. Seating for four requires 31 square feet.

Table 5-2. Round table seating.

Diameter of round table (inches)	No. of seats
36	4
42	5
48	6

A 36-inch round table with four swivel chairs fits in a 5'-10" x 5'-10" or 34-square foot corner space.

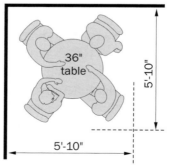

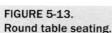

FIGURE 5-13.
Round table seating.

Outside Living Areas

Exterior living spaces, such as patios, porches, and decks, are natural extensions to indoor social areas. Gazebos are an increasingly popular addition for outdoor social activities. For most efficient use, these areas should be located next to and with easy access to kitchens, living rooms, family rooms, and/or dining rooms. Meditation gardens, flower or butterfly gardens, birdbaths, and birdhouses can be located away from the busier outdoor social areas to provide more serene views from the sleeping and retreat areas inside the home.

Planning

When planning outdoor living areas, consider the amount of sun or shade desired, the wind direction, the amount of privacy the space affords, the availability of water and electrical outlets, and other fixed conditions. Generally, the southwest and southeast corners of a house offer the best combination of sun and shade. The durability and dryness of the underfoot surfaces, protection from weather, privacy given by fences or hedges, safety for young children, ease of movement between interior and exterior areas, and the comfort with which some can rest while others play all affect the amount of use these outside areas receive.

Adding a deck

Adding a deck can be like adding another family room to your house. Plan your deck just as you would an interior room. Decks should be conveniently located next to the kitchen so that long trips back and forth can be reduced. The size should accommodate the type of activities planned, such as food preparation, a table and seating for dining, conversation, or lounging. Design the deck on one level or in multi-levels to suit the architectural design of your home or the lay of the property. Depending upon the size of deck and your family needs, options might include an outdoor entertainment area, complete with a weather resistant bar top, refrigerator and sink, grilling center, relaxing spas or hot tubs, shade shelters, privacy screens, built-in benches and planters, or a work center for potting and gardening activities and supplies.

Keep zoning and building codes in mind as you plan the details you want to incorporate into the design. Consider lumber spans, railings, planters, and built-in benches. According to most building codes, a deck railing should extend from 36 to 40 inches above the deck surface. If you are planning a bar or sink area or plan to entertain extensively, be sure to allow for water lines, additional outdoor electrical outlets, and adequate lighting. Consider durability and on-going maintenance, and select a finish that contains a water-repellent, a mildewcide, and a UV ray inhibitor.

Other Considerations

A house can have features, such as a fireplace and special lighting, that can make the social areas more enjoyable. Having high quality and durable walls, floors, and surfaces will increase the satisfaction derived from the area because of reduced maintenance and upkeep. Also, having adequate storage nearby will help reduce clutter while at the same time keeping necessary items handy.

Screened porches effectively extend your living space and provide a buffer and shade to the adjoining walls and windows. Planting trees, along with the use of ceiling fans designed for outdoor conditions, provides added comfort during warm weather. Sunrooms and enclosed all-weather porches are other options that make these social areas into all-season rooms.

For satisfactory performance fireplaces should be built with a few simple design principles in mind. For the sake of efficiency and appearance, the size should suit the room in which the fireplace is to be used. For example, the fireplace opening should be approximately 10 to 12 times the flue area. Therefore, an 8- by 12-inch flue would require about a 960-square inch opening. Also, the width of the opening should always be greater than its height. The depth, based on this example, can be 2 feet or more.

Fireplaces

Many types of fireplace designs and materials are available. Since they are most often a focal point in a room, keep possible furniture arrangements and logical traffic patterns in mind as you are planning the location of a fireplace. Try to avoid having a large television or entertainment center adjacent to a fireplace because each by itself can be a featured item in a room. A room with two feature items can make it difficult to arrange furniture that highlights both. The other problem that can exist is that one of the items will overshadow the other in a room. Figure 5-14 shows how a fireplace and a television can compete for attention.

While a fireplace provides an attractive, cozy feature in a home, it is among the most inefficient heat sources available. It literally sends energy dollars right up the chimney along with volumes of warm air. A roaring fire can exhaust as much as 24,000 cubic feet of air per hour, which must then be replaced by the same amount of air coming into the house. Although the fire is heating the immediate area by radiant heat, it is cooling the rest of the house by expelling warm air up the chimney. If you operate the heating system and set the thermostat at 68°F, a fire in the fireplace can cause the heating system to use more energy than it otherwise would by pulling in cold, outside air for combustion. Lowering the thermostat setting can reduce energy losses somewhat, as can closing the doors to the rest of the house while the fireplace is being used.

A fireplace can be made less inefficient if it has a properly sized duct directly to the outside. Installing glass doors in front of the fireplace is also an effective way to reduce heat losses. Some fireplaces are manufactured with a double wall that allows room air to circulate behind and around the fire. These can be very energy efficient if coupled with an outside air source.

Lighting

Natural, built-in, and portable lighting are important considerations in developing a flexible, comfortable home plan that suits your family

FIGURE 5-14.
Having the television and the fireplace next to each other is visually distracting.

needs. Proper lighting enhances your living areas and provides convenience, safety, comfort, and dramatic effects. Natural lighting, such as that seen in Figure 5-15, can bring an added sense of comfort and warmth to a room.

Factors to consider in selecting and installing artificial lighting include the size of the room, the mood that you want to create, and most important, the types of activities that will take place in each area. To save money that would be spent with future installation and to have the most effective lighting possible, plan your lighting needs as you design your living areas.

A good lighting plan has general, task, and accent types of lighting to serve a variety of purposes. General lighting provides overall illumination by chandeliers, ceiling or wall-mounted fixtures, recessed lighting, or track lights. Task lighting provides illumination for specific activities, such as reading, cooking, studying, or hobby work. Track and recessed lighting, pendant lighting, and portable lamps can provide glare-free, shadowless lighting for performing these specific tasks. (Be sure to include adequate electrical outlets in locations where portable lighting is planned.) Accent lighting adds drama to rooms by spotlighting paintings or other prized possessions or by highlighting the texture of a wall, drapery, or outdoor landscaping. This is usually provided by track, recessed, or wall-mounted fixtures. A variety of lighting options within a room or space allows for flexibility for serving different occasions and needs.

Save on future energy bills by using energy efficient options whenever possible. Linear and compact

FIGURE 5-15.
Natural lighting can add warmth and comfort to a room.

fluorescent lamps provide high-quality and high-efficiency lighting. Fluorescent lights are 3 to 5 times more efficient than incandescent bulbs and can last up to 10 times longer. Use task lighting to focus light on specific work surfaces or activity areas instead of brightly lighting an entire room. Dimmer switches save energy as well as allowing maximum flexibility of light levels. See **Chapter 15, House Utilities,** for more information on lighting.

Noise control

In your planning, consider how to control noise. Plan spaces for both quiet and noisy activities. The *quiet* space can be a den or a small study. In a small house, it may be difficult to isolate noisy activities from quiet ones. Tight-fitting solid core doors and insulation in the walls reduce noise transmission between rooms. Avoid placing heat ducts and outlets back to back in the same wall. Carpeting, draperies, and acoustic ceiling tile and wall coverings help absorb sound.

Rethink activity areas to fit your needs and the space available. Bedrooms are quiet spaces that can fill other needs, such as television viewing, studying, or practicing musical instruments while a party is taking place in the dining-living-family area. Closets, bookshelves, and similar features can be sound buffers between noisy and quiet areas.

Dust and odor control

Don't allow social areas to become polluted by dust and odors from other parts of the house. Manage kitchen and bath odors and moisture with good exhaust fans. Plan adequate ventilation systems to provide good air circulation throughout the social areas. See **Chapter 15, House Utilities**, for more information on ventilation. Control dust from hobbies such as woodworking with isolation. If family members have allergies or asthma, use smooth rather than textured surfaces for interior finishes to help control dust and potential air pollutants.

Interior surfaces

Consider ease of maintenance, appearance, cost, and expected wear life when selecting finish materials for walls, floors, and other surfaces within the social areas. Look for healthy choices whenever possible.

For example, low emitting VOC (volatile organic chemicals) options are available in wallcoverings, carpeting, and other finishing materials. Such products as low vapor paints and wood finishes help family members who have allergies, asthma, or sensitivity to chemicals used in these products. In addition hard or smooth surfaces are recommended if family members have allergies or asthma. For example, use wood, vinyl, or tile floors instead of carpeting.

Since social areas receive a great deal of use, consider durability and ease of maintenance in addition to appearance and costs for floors and walls. In figuring cost, include the cost of the product and its installation and the cost of maintaining it over its expected lifetime. Refer to manufacturers' specifications, recommended use, and safety factors for additional information about these products. You can obtain these specifications from the retailer or directly from the manufacturer, often by toll-free telephone numbers or from a web site.

Storage

Effective storage makes a multipurpose room more usable. List all the room's uses and plan storage for all items needed. Hidden storage can be especially useful. Built-in storage is always ready for use and can be easily concealed by folding doors or shutters. See **Chapter 13, Household Storage**, for more ideas.

Resources

Many excellent references on space planning and design are available at bookstores and libraries. Also, you can contact your county extension office with specific questions or concerns about interior products, indoor air quality, and energy.

De Chiara, Joseph, Julius Panero, and Martin Zelnik. 1991. *Time-Saver Standards for Interior Design and Space Planning*. New York: McGraw-Hill, Inc.

Nissen, LuAnn, Ray Faulkner, and Sarah Faulkner. 1994. *Inside Today's Home*, Sixth Edition. Fort Worth: Harcourt Brace College Publishers.

Susanka, Sarah, and Kira Obolensky. 1998. *The Not So Big House: A Blueprint for the Way We Really Live*. Newton, CT: The Taunton Press.

The Small Homes Council/Building Research Council, University of Illinois. http://brc.arch.uiuc.edu/Pubcatalog.htm#council%20notes%20set

Kitchens

PLANNING A KITCHEN requires making many decisions. You will probably need to consult professionals, such as certified kitchen designers, kitchen planners, architects, or interior designers. Their expertise will help you clarify your needs as well as prepare plans and specifications. Ask them about their experience with universal design and whether they specialize in remodeling or new design. Some professionals offer their services if you buy cabinets or appliances through their business while other professionals offer their services for a separate fee. See **Chapter 2, Working With Professionals**, for more information on the type of professionals to choose to help design your kitchen area.

Also, you or your kitchen professional will need to work with the mechanical contractor to make sure that the cooking and exhaust equipment will be compatible with the house's energy system. See **Chapter 15, House Utilities**, for more information on how the cooking and exhaust equipment can affect a home's energy system.

Location

Locate the kitchen conveniently near indoor and outdoor dining and living areas, and avoid directing general traffic through the work area. Some other factors to consider when you choose the location of your kitchen are as follows:
- Ability of the cook to interact with family members and guests while preparing meals.
- Convenience to yard or outside work areas.
- Convenience for unloading groceries and disposing of garbage, trash, and recyclables.
- Accessibility to an exterior door.
- Need for window that looks out over the yard, for instance, to watch small children.

When planning the location of the kitchen, also assess the amount of natural light available. Good natural light (daylight) can eliminate the need for electrical lighting during the day. To prevent overheating in the summer, use exterior shading or overhangs on south- and west-facing windows. The square footage of windows and skylights should equal at least 8 percent of the total square footage of the kitchen. If the kitchen is part of a larger total living space, the square footage of all windows and skylights in the living space, including the kitchen, should be at least 8 percent of the total floor area. Brighten every

Kitchens are a major activity hub and frequently open to other social areas of the home. Because today's kitchens are so visible, they need to be aesthetically pleasing while also functioning as the space in which meals are prepared, food is stored, and cleanup occurs. Additionally, many members of the household participate in activities in the kitchen, and it is easier and safer for them if you choose accessible and adaptable features. To promote functional kitchen designs that serve these needs, the *National Kitchen and Bath Association* (NKBA) developed guidelines for kitchen planning. Many of these guidelines are the basis for the information in this chapter.

counter work surface and the sink and range with appropriate task and general lighting. At least one wall-switch for lights must be provided in the kitchen. A wall-switch must be provided at the kitchen entrance.

For more information on lighting, see **Chapter 15, House Utilities**.

Needs

When planning your kitchen, consider your lifestyle and your use of the food preparation areas. How often do you cook? How often do you entertain? The amount of workspace and storage you need will be affected by whether you cook extensively at home, use ready-to-eat foods, or eat out frequently. However, you also should consider resale value if you intend to build a small kitchen. Plan for special household needs by asking yourself the questions in Table 6-1 and checking the appropriate answer:

Work Centers

Work centers are the main functional stations of the kitchen and include the appliances and countertops and the storage and floor areas. For efficient kitchen planning, two or more of these work centers should be contiguous. The major work centers are the preparation center, the sink center, the cooking center, and the refrigerator center. A serving center is often combined with the cooking center. If a microwave

Table 6-1. Determining household needs.

Questions to Ask	Yes	No
1. *Will several people use the kitchen to prepare food?* If several people cook, you may need large or multiple work areas, storage areas, and appliances that all users can access.		
2. *Do more than two people live in the house?* Households with more people may need more eating and storage space.		
3. *Do you need space to eat in the kitchen?* If household members eat at different times, a snack counter or an attached table may be most functional. See the Dining Areas section in **Chapter 5, Social Areas.**		
4. *Is it important that the kitchen not require extensive time to clean?* If so, select durable and easy-to-clean countertops, floors, cabinets, and appliances. Textured surfaces (for example, grout lines of tile) and intricate cabinet moldings are difficult to clean.		
5. *Do the heights of the people using the kitchen vary?* If any cooks are much shorter or taller than average or use a wheelchair, incorporate some lower and higher work surfaces to accommodate them.		
6. *Must the kitchen accommodate other activities besides cooking?* Some people use kitchen space for socializing, using a computer, completing homework, running a household business, feeding a pet, or watching television.		
7. *Are there special storage needs?* Storage may be necessary for soft drinks and bottled water; recycling bins; canning, freezing, and food-drying equipment; and coats, boots, and brooms. Kosher kitchens need additional storage for a second set of dishes and silverware. For more information, see **Chapter 11, Household Storage.**		

Adapted from *Kitchen Planning*, NCR #497.

oven is used frequently, it can be part of the cooking center. The microwave oven also may be a separate center but should be placed close to the sink center and the preparation center.

Normally, most of the walking during meal preparation is between the sink and cooking centers. People also make many trips between the preparation and sink centers and between the preparation and refrigerator centers.

- If the kitchen has only one sink, locate it near the cooking and refrigerator center (Figure 6-1). The dishwasher should be no further than 36 inches from the edge of the sink.
- The preparation center should be next to a water source. Locate the preparation center between the primary sink and the cooking center, between the refrigerator and the primary sink center, or adjacent to a secondary sink, island, or other cabinet section.
- The cooking surface should not be located below an operable window (Figure 6-2.)

The walking distance between the primary sink, primary cooking surface, and refrigerator is called the work triangle and should total 26 feet or less, measured from the center front of each appliance. If two or more people cook simultaneously, plan a double work triangle; appliances may be shared or separate (Figure 6-3). Arrange the work centers to reduce the amount of walking and to allow work to flow easily from one center to another. Do not split the work areas by traffic lanes or separate the primary sink, refrigerator, preparation center, or cooking center by a full-height, full-depth tall tower such as an oven cabinet, pantry cabinet, or refrigerator.

Doorways should be at least 32 inches wide; walkways should be at least 36 inches wide. The distance between parallel work centers should be at least 42 inches wide in one-cook kitchens and at least 48 inches wide in multiple-cook kitchens.

Each work center should have adequate countertop workspace and countertop storage space, facilitating the completion of work and permitting the storage of items used at that center. The standard height from the floor to the surface of the countertop is 36 inches. The height of the counter should be 3 inches below the

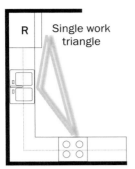

One cook.

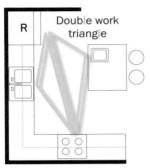

Two or more cooks.

FIGURE 6-3.
Work triangles.

Figures adapted from *Kitchen Planning,* NCR #497.

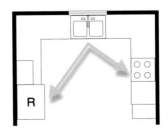

FIGURE 6-1.
Kitchen with one sink located near the cooking and refrigerator centers.

Figure adapted from *NKBA Kitchen Guideline #10.*

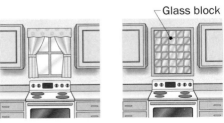

Unacceptable.   Acceptable.

FIGURE 6-2.
Do not locate cooking surface below an operable window.

Figure adapted from *NKBA Kitchen Guideline #20.*

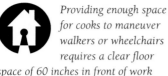

Providing enough space for cooks to maneuver walkers or wheelchairs requires a clear floor space of 60 inches in front of work centers (Figure 6-4), as well as adequate knee space below the sink, range, and preparation area so that one can remain seated while working (30 inches high by 19 inches deep).

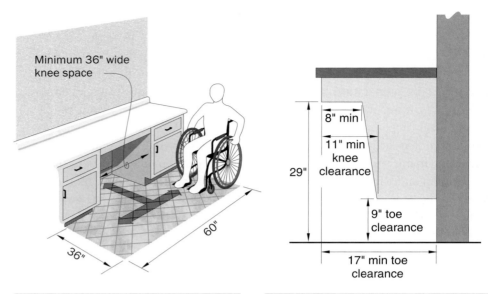

FIGURE 6-4.
Provide enough space to allow for easy maneuverability.

FIGURE 6-5.
Provide adequate knee space for sitting at counters.

elbow height of the worker and lower for tasks that require preparation such as kneading or chopping. A 30-inch high work surface is recommended for seated workers and may be useful for shorter workers. Offering additional work-counter heights, lower and higher than 36 inches above the finished floor, allows cooks of different heights to work in the kitchen more easily. The NKBA accessibility guidelines recommend seating areas to be 28 to 34 inches high, 30 to 36 inches wide, and 19 inches deep to accommodate different sizes, abilities, and mobility aids (Figure 6-5).

Regardless of kitchen size, counter work surface frontage (measured along the front of the counter) should measure 158 inches in total frontage, and the usable depth should measure 24 inches. Standard countertops typically measure 25 inches in depth with one inch of the countertop overhanging the base cabinet at the front and a vertical backsplash covering about one inch at the back, so the usable work area is 24 inches deep (Figure 6-6).

Countertops located adjacent to appliances and fixtures typically are used only as workspaces and not as storage spaces. These areas are called *landing spaces* because items removed from the nearby appliance and fixture are set on this area for only a short time. This area is not use for long-term storage. The minimum depth of a

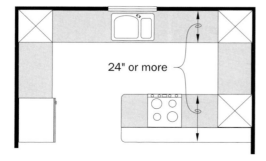

FIGURE 6-6.
Countertop space.

Figure adapted from *NKBA Kitchen Guideline #25.*

countertop that is used primarily as a landing space can be 16 inches in depth (Figure 6-7). Wall cabinets must be placed at least 15 inches above the counter, and most frequently are placed at 18 inches above the counter. Minimum lengths of counters recommended for different work centers are listed in the following sections. Whenever work centers are combined, the counter (or landing area required) should be equal to the longer of the countertops being combined plus 12 inches.

Preparation center

Plan at least 36 inches of continuous countertop for the preparation workspace. If two people are preparing foods simultaneously, two 36-inch work counters are recommended, either side by side or in separate areas of the kitchen. If not in a corner, a 60-inch work counter accommodates one full workspace and standing room

for a second person. In households with children, wider preparation areas are often needed to accommodate a teacher/student model of cooking.

Sink center

The kitchen sink is a major focal point for food preparation; it should have a minimum of 24 inches of counter on one side and 18 inches on the other side. If there is a second auxiliary sink, it should have 18 inches on one side and 3 inches on the other side. Allow a minimum of 21 inches of standing room (clear floor space) between the edge of the dishwasher and counters, appliances, and/or cabinets that are placed at a right angle to the dishwasher. Dishwashers may be installed to fit under a standard counter height or on a raised platform to be easier to use. To avoid water damage from a broken hose, the water supply to the dishwasher should be plumbed separately from other appliances. Other sink accessories requiring plumbing connections include a disposal and a water filtration system.

Cooking center

Cooking foods today may take place at various areas in the kitchen because cooking appliances can be separated by their functions, requiring more than one appliance. In purchasing and locating cooking appliances, it is important to understand the type and frequency of foods typically prepared.

Cooking appliances

Either gas or electric appliances can be selected as your main cooking source. Both gas and electric hookups can be installed if you choose a range

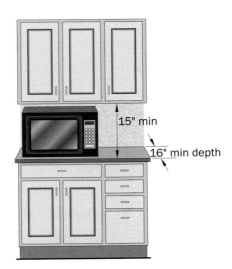

15" min

16" min depth

FIGURE 6-7.
Landing area for a microwave oven.

Figure adapted from *NKBA Kitchen Guideline #22*.

Unvented gas kitchen ranges vent combustion products from burning fuel into the space where they are located. Gas kitchen ranges produce carbon monoxide (CO), a deadly gas, and nitrogen oxide, a respiratory irritant. The amount of carbon monoxide produced can vary. Use a gas range or oven for cooking only; never use it to heat the house because extended use can increase CO concentrations to dangerous levels. Do not block the air vents to the oven or burners with material such as aluminum foil, and do not use the range and oven if the flames are uneven, orange, or yellow. Have the burners cleaned and checked for proper combustion. Read and follow all instructions in the operating manual. Discontinue use, contact a doctor, and have the unit inspected, cleaned, and adjusted if its use causes you to experience headaches, heart irregularities, or difficulty breathing.

Never use charcoal or other unvented, fuel-burning cooking appliances indoors. Charcoal produces large amounts of carbon monoxide that can cause headaches, vomiting, heart attack, coma, brain damage, and death. When using charcoal outdoors, do not use it in a confined area or near combustible materials, and avoid exposure to fumes.

with separate fuels for the cooking surface and the oven. Install and use a kitchen exhaust hood vented to the outside above cooking units to collect and remove grease, odors, smoke, and moisture.

Ranges and built-in cooktops

Counter surface on either side of the range or cooktop permits cookware handles to safely overhang the edge of the cooktop. A range or built-in cooktop should have 15 inches of counter on one side and 12 inches on the other. Vertically, there must be at least 24 inches of clearance between the cooking surface and a protected noncombustible surface above (for example, the top of an exhaust hood), or at least 30 inches of clearance between the cooking surface and an unprotected, combustible surface above (for example, a cabinet). If the protected surface is a microwave oven hood combination, follow the manufacturer's specifications to determine required clearances. Figure 6-8 provides a view of the space needed for ranges or built-in cooktops.

Major surface cooking appliances should to be paired with a hood or downdraft ventilation system of at least 150 cfm. Makeup air may be needed to ensure adequate air quality in the home. To remove moisture and combustion cooking gases, use a system that exhausts (ducted to the outside) rather than recirculates air (Figure 6-9). For more information on home ventilation, see **Chapter 15, House Utilities**.

Built-in ovens

Cooks make fewer trips to an oven than they make to other work centers in the kitchen because food placed in the oven does not require as much attention. The countertop required for the oven is primarily a landing space on which to place hot dishes removed from the oven. A built-in oven should have at least 15 inches of counter adjacent to it. If that is not possible and the oven does not open into a traffic area, provide a 15-inch counter no further than 48 inches from the built-in oven.

For safety reasons, in an island or peninsula situation, the countertop should extend a minimum of 9 inches behind the cooking surface if the counter height is the same as the surface-cooking appliance.

Include a minimum of 12 inches of landing area on one side of a cooking surface and 15 inches on the other side.

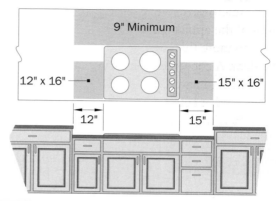

FIGURE 6-8.
Side space for a range or built-in cooktop.

Figure adapted from *NKBA Kitchen Guideline* #17.

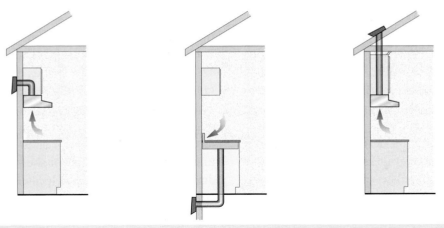

FIGURE 6-9.
Ventilation exhaust systems for a range or built-in cooktop.

Figure adapted from *NKBA Kitchen Guideline* #19. Ventilate at 150 cfm minimum.

Microwave ovens

The microwave oven is a major cooking appliance in U.S. homes and is commonly used by household members of all ages and abilities. Because it is a heating appliance and a central point in the flow of work in the kitchen, the microwave oven needs to be placed in a location that encourages safe and convenient use. A microwave oven should have a minimum of 15 inches of counter landing space adjacent, above, or below it (Figure 6-10). When mounting a microwave above the counter, position the microwave oven so that the bottom of the appliance is placed from 15 to no more than 54 inches above the floor. A convenient height for most cooks is to have the microwave oven placed at counter level or about elbow height plus or minus 6 inches. For safe use above the counter, the microwave oven should not be above a level that is 3 inches below the worker's shoulders. In-counter mounting of a microwave provides an accessible location for seated users.

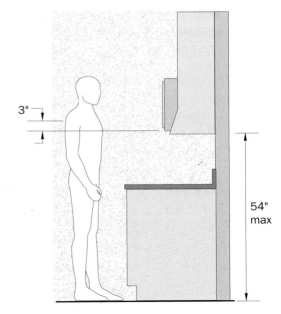

Above-the-counter mounting height.

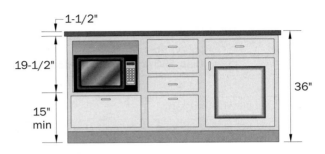

In-counter mounting height.

FIGURE 6-10.
Placement of a microwave oven.

Figure adapted from NKBA Kitchen Guideline #21.

People with physical limitations such as back problems, arthritis, or mobility impairments can function more easily if kitchens have more drawers, roll-out shelves, and D- or U-shaped handles on cabinets. Controls, handles, and door/drawer pulls should be operable with one hand, require only a minimal amount of strength for operation, and not require tight grasping, pinching, or twisting of the wrist.

Refrigerator center

A top or bottom freezer refrigerator should have 15 inches of counter on the handle side of the refrigerator. A side-by-side refrigerator should have 15 inches of counter on either side or at least 15 inches of landing space that is no more than 48 inches across from the refrigerator. Refrigerators with icemakers and water dispensers require plumbing and must be connected to a water source.

Storage space

A variety of types of storage is recommended in the kitchen. A useful method for determining adequate storage is to calculate shelf/drawer frontage using the Shelf/drawer frontage equation.

Equation 6-1.
Shelf/drawer frontage equation.

$$TF = \frac{(CW)(CD)(SD)}{12}$$

Where:

TF = Total frontage, inches

CW = Cabinet width, inches

CD = Cabinet depth, inches

SD = Number of shelves and drawers

The minimum total of shelf/drawer frontage recommended ranges from 1,400 inches for kitchens less than 150 square feet to 2,000 inches for kitchens greater than 350 square feet. The total storage should be distributed among base cabinets, drawers, wall cabinets, and pantry units. At least 400 inches of shelf/drawer frontage should be located within 72 inches of the center front of the primary food preparation sink; for large kitchens, there should be 560 inches. Table 6-2 summarizes the recommended frontage lengths based on kitchen size.

The sample calculation in Example 6-1 shows how the equation used in conjunction with Table 6-2 can help determine if a kitchen has adequate storage space. Homeowners can use the table and the equation to get a good estimate of how much cabinetry they will need to provide adequate storage. Knowing how much cabinetry is necessary also can help to determine rough estimates of how much the cabinetry will cost.

Drawers and pull-out shelves in base cabinets and pantry units provide easier access to storage than fixed shelves. Wall cabinets and pantry units should have adjustable shelves.

Table 6-2. Recommended frontage based on kitchen size.
Based on recommendations from NKBA Kitchen Guideline # 27.

Component	Kitchen Size Less than 150 sq ft	151 to 350 sq ft	Greater than 350 sq ft
Total shelf/drawer frontage (TF)	1,400	1,700	2,000
Wall	300	360	360
Base	520	615	660
Drawer	360	400	525
Pantry	180	230	310
Misc.	40	95	145

Interior vertical dividers, built-in bins and racks, and specialized drawers or shelves also increase the usefulness of the storage space. For a kitchen with usable corner areas, at least one functional corner storage unit should be included. Separate wastebaskets are needed for garbage and recyclables.

For more information on storage, see **Chapter 13, Household Storage.**

Other Considerations

The actual materials and appliances you choose for your kitchen should be considered as you are planning the arrangement. These can affect how easy it is to work and clean in your kitchen as well as contribute to its overall appearance and style.

Materials

Choose your materials carefully. For example:
- **Floor coverings** should be durable, resilient, and easy to maintain. Common materials are vinyl flooring (sheet, solid tiles, and composites), laminate, linoleum, wood, and ceramic tile. See Table 6-3 for comparisons.
- **Counter surfaces** should be easy to clean and able to withstand heat, cuts, and scratches. Common materials are laminate, solid surface, ceramic tile, butcher block, and stone. Some kitchens may have a different counter surface material in different areas of the kitchen. Select countertops that complement your design, are

Example 6-1. Determining the shelf frontage for a wall cabinet.

A small kitchen (less than 150 square feet) has five wall cabinet sections. The shelf widths (CW) are 12, 17, 24, 24, and 30 inches. All shelves are 12 inches deep (CD). Each wall cabinet section has three shelves (SD). Does this design provide enough wall cabinet frontage space?

Solution

Using Equation 6-1, the total frontage is:

$$TF = \frac{(12 \text{ in/shelf})(12 \text{ in})(3 \text{ shelves})}{12} + \frac{(17 \text{ in/shelf})(12 \text{ in})(3 \text{ shelves})}{12}$$
$$+ \frac{(24 \text{ in/shelf})(12 \text{ in})(3 \text{ shelves})}{12} + \frac{(24 \text{ in/shelf})(12 \text{ in})(3 \text{ shelves})}{12}$$
$$+ \frac{(30 \text{ in/shelf})(12 \text{ in})(3 \text{ shelves})}{12}$$
$$= 321$$

Table 6-2 shows a recommended wall cabinet frontage of 300 for a small kitchen. The frontage calculated for this kitchen is slightly greater than the recommendation; therefore, it has adequate frontage space.

Locate a fire extinguisher visibly away from cooking equipment, near the exit of the kitchen, and install smoke alarms.

durable and easily maintained, and meet your budget.

For areas around sinks, choose waterproof materials, such as plastic laminate, tile, stone, and solid-surface finishes. Matte finishes reduce glare.

When purchasing countertop materials, certain tradeoffs must be made. For example, plastic laminate comes in a variety of colors and requires minimal upkeep but can be prone to burns, scratches, and other marring. Tile and stone make attractive countertops but can be expensive to purchase and install. With tile, maintenance and repair of grout can be time consuming. Finally, solid-surface materials are extremely durable and come in a variety of colors but can be expensive to purchase and install. See Table 6-4 for comparisons.

- **Sinks** should be easy to clean and able to withstand scratching and chipping. Sinks come in a variety of materials such as stainless steel, porcelain enamel, acrylic, or quartz resin. They may be installed so they rest on top of the counter or mounted underneath the counter; some solid surface countertops include a sink integral to the countertop.
- **Kitchen cabinets** are made of wood, laminate, plastic, or steel. Sometimes glass is combined with other materials. The method of cabinet construction, the cabinet material and finish, and type of hinges and hardware will affect their quality, use, price, and durability. Cabinets

come in a variety of styles, qualities, and price ranges. Choosing cabinets that are made in standard sizes or are semi-custom is considerably cheaper than custom-made cabinets. Cabinets should be within easy reach of most users. Hardware should be easy to manipulate, requiring little grasping or twisting. Loop handle hardware, sometimes referred to as C- or D-handle hardware, is a good choice.

Appliances

The appliances and equipment you choose will greatly affect your kitchen's character and convenience. The size and type of appliances will affect available storage, amount of counter space, and the utilities you will need to install (plumbing, electrical service, gas hookups, and venting). You will have to decide whether your appliances will be freestanding or built in. Freestanding appliances may be less expensive to purchase, but built-in appliances integrate more fully within workspaces and can separate functions of an appliance (for example, oven and cooktop), allowing alternatives to placement to improve storage and workflow.

Before purchasing any appliance, be sure to analyze your wants and needs, and research the types of features available that best fit your home. The Consumers Union is an independent nonprofit organization that tests many different types of appliances on a regular basis. The Union supports itself through the sale of product information and services, individual contributions,

Table 6-3. Comparison of materials for kitchen floors.
Based on University of Minnesota extension publication *Kitchen Planning*, BU-01392, 1993.

Material	Price Range	Sizes Available	Design	Durability	Maintenance	Ease of feet and sound absorption	Installation
Vinyl composite tile	Low to Middle	12" squares	Wide range of patterns, printed or embossed	Very good. Resists grease and moisture can be dented by furniture	Sweep, damp mop and periodically apply protective finish	Fair	Requires some skill
Vinyl tile and sheets	Middle	12" square tile 6', 9', 12' and 15'	Wide range of patterns and colors	Very good. Resists grease, moisture, and denting	Sweep, damp, mop and periodically apply protective finish	Good, softness varies with backing	Tile [a] Sheet [b] Large piece requires precise cutting
Ceramic tile	Middle to high. Product low but installation increases cost.	1/2" to 16" squares, rectangles, hexagons, etc.	Wide range of patterns and colors	Excellent, depends on the body and hardness glaze	Sweep, damp mop and occasionally scrub grout indentation	Poor	Tile mounted on mesh back or paper sheet. [a] Determining layout for patterns and spacing between tile [b]
Quarry tile, slate and brick	Middle to high	Variable	Limited range, more natural colors	Excellent	Sweep, damp mop occasionally scrub grout indentations	Poor	Determining layout and spacing requires skill [b]
Carpeting	Low to middle	12' widths	Soft and warm. Wide range of color and pattern	Good	Clean spills and and stains immediately. Frying causes grease buildup which collects dirt. Mold or mildew may occur in damp areas.	Excellent	Requires some skill
Wood	Middle to high	6", 9", and 12" squares; 3" X 6" and 3" X 9" pieces; and lengths and widths	Natural beauty, visually warm	Excellent if properly finished and sealed. Can be sanded and **refinished** if showing wear. Cannot take standing water or continuous **dampness.**	Clean spills and stains immediately. Must be sealed or waxed.	Good	Prefinished tiles [a] Planks and other on-site installations [b]
Acrylic (Poured floor)	Middle to high, product low but installation increases cost.	Covers any size without seams.	Wide range of colors. Limited patterns.	Excellent	Sweep and damp mop.	Fair	Requires professional installation. Takes time for layers to dry.

[a] Requires some skill
[b] Requires skill and experience

Continued

Table 6-4. Comparison of materials for kitchen countertops.
Based on University of Minnesota extension publication *Kitchen Planning*, BU-01392, 1993.

Material	Cost Range	Design	Durability	Cleanability	Resistance to Heat	Resistance to Stains	Resistance to Moisture	Resistance to Scratches and Cuts
High pressure decorative laminate	Low to middle	Many colors, patterns and textures	Good, if damaged must be replaced	Good, rough textures present a problem	Good, hot pans can scorch	Good	Good	Good, knives will cut surface
Solid Surface (cast acrylic/polyester)	High	Elegant, some have limited color range	Excellent, can be sanded to remove scorch and scratch marks	Excellent	Good	Excellent	Excellent	Good
Butcher Block	Middle	Adds warmth	Good, shows wear. Can be sanded and sealed with mineral oil	Good, needs sanitizing after contact with raw meats and poultry	Good, will scorch	Poor, shows stains	Good, if sealed. If not sealed, moisture causes warping, discoloration	Good, shows wear. Develops patina. Can be refinished easily
Ceramic tile Granite	Middle to high	Widest choice of color and patterns	Excellent	Good, seal non-epoxy grout periodically with a silicone sealer. Grout indentations need periodic scrubbing	Excellent	Excellent, if glazed tile. Grout stains if properly sealed	Good	Good
Granite	Very high	Natural, elegant	Excellent	Excellent	Excellent	Good	Excellent	Good
Stainless steel	High	Commercial look	Excellent	Excellent	Excellent	Excellent	Excellent, may show water spots	Good, brushed surface helps camouflage

and a few noncommercial grants. Consumers Union publishes the *Consumer Reports* ® publications and hosts the *Consumerreports.org* ® website. The Consumers Union analysis of kitchen appliances can be found at http:/www.consumer reports.org/cro/appliances.htm.

The *Consumerreports.org* ® website lists a "How to Choose" section for many different types of appliances.

This information is available for a nominal fee:

- *How to Choose Refrigerators* http:/www.consumerreports.org/ cro/appliances/refrigerators/ refrigerators/how-to-choose.htm
- *How to Choose Ranges* http:/www.consumerreports. org/cro/appliances/ranges/not-sure-what-to-buy/how-to-choose.htm

- *How to Choose Cooktops and Wall Ovens*
  http://www.consumerreports.org/cro/appliances/cooktops-and-wall-ovens/not-sure-what-to-buy/how-to-choose.htm
- *How to Choose Microwave Ovens*
  http://www.consumerreports.org/cro/appliances/microwave-ovens/microwave-ovens/how-to-choose.htm
- *How to Choose Dishwashers*
  http://www.consumerreports.org/cro/appliances/dishwashers/dishwashers/how-to-choose.htm

Electrical receptacles

Codes require that all electrical receptacles in a newly constructed or remodeled kitchen must be protected by a ground fault circuit interrupter (GFCI). GFCIs provide protection from electrical shock.

Each kitchen needs a minimum of two receptacles for 20-amp current protected by GFCI. Many small appliances are designed for 20-amp current. At least one GFCI must be installed within 24 inches of the outside edge a wash basin and in each wall that is wider than 12 inches. Receptacles must be spaced so that no point along the counter top wall is more than 24 inches from a receptacle, which in most cases means 48 linear inches following the counter along the wall (Figure 6-11). Receptacles must not be located more than 20 inches above the countertop. Each countertop island or peninsular countertop that is at least 12 inches wide and 24 inches long needs to have a GFCI.

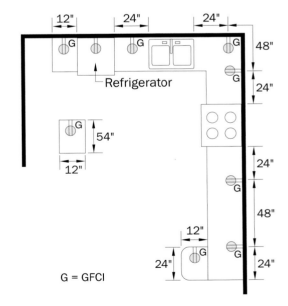

FIGURE 6-11.
Receptacle locations for a kitchen.

Figure adapted from *National Electrical Code Handbook*, 2005, Exhibit 210.26.

Resources

Center for Real Life Kitchen Design, Virginia Tech University: http://www.ahrm.vt.edu/
housing

Consumers Union: http://www.consumerreports.org/cro/appliances.htm

Galvin, P.J., with E. Cheever. 1998. *Kitchen Basics*. Hackettstown, NJ: National Kitchen
and Bath Association.

Hawks, L.K. 1995. *Kitchen Appliances*. Extension Publication: Utah State University.
(http://extension.usu.edu/files/homipubs/hi18.pdf)

Kitchen Planning. 1993. University of Minnesota Extension Publication, *BU-01392*.

Kitchens. 1991. Raleigh, North Carolina: The Center for Universal Design, North
Carolina State University. Publication number TP #5.00.

National Electrical Code Handbook (NFPA 70). 2005. *National Fire Protection Association*
(NFPA), 1 Battery March Park, Quincy, Massachusetts, 02169-7471.

National Kitchen and Bath Association Website: http://www.nkba.org/xconsumers/
index.asp

Olson, W.W., D. Ginthner, and B.L Yust. 1993. *Kitchen Planning* (NCR #497). St. Paul:
North Central Regional Extension Publication, Minnesota Extension Service.
(also at http://www.extension.umn.edu/distribution/housingandclothing/
DK1392.html)

CHAPTER 7

Bathrooms

THE BATHROOM IS TRADITIONALLY A FUNCTIONAL PLACE for the daily grooming routine. Recently, however, it also has become a place to relax and luxuriate. Many of today's bathrooms are multi-use, including dressing, exercise, and laundry areas. Each year, homeowners spend millions of dollars remodeling existing or adding new bathrooms to their homes. Similar to kitchen designs, the *National Kitchen and Bath Association* (NKBA) has guidelines for bathroom planning. Many of these guidelines are the basis for the information in this chapter.

General Planning Considerations

When planning a bathroom, consider the following issues:

- **Family size, age, and composition.** How large is your family? Will that size increase or decrease in the near future? Is this a home where one or more older persons might live, now or in the future? Is this a home where young children might live, now or in the future?
- **Individuals who will use the space.** Will the bathroom be shared? Will more than one person use the space at the same time? Will this be a private space, or will guests use it as well?
- **Family lifestyle.** How much time will you have for the maintenance and upkeep of the bathroom? Of more than one bathroom?
- **Family activities.** What activities other than toileting and bathing might take place in the space? For instance, will the space be used for dressing, applying makeup, exercising, or laundering clothes?
- **Budget or cost.** If remodeling, what is your budget for re-doing or adding a bathroom? If building or purchasing, will your budget allow you to build or buy a home with the kind and number of bathrooms you desire?

Location

General guidelines for locating bathrooms are as follows:

- Provide visual and sound privacy (do not open directly into social areas).
- Minimize plumbing costs by locating bathrooms, kitchens, and laundry areas close together (Figure 7-1).
- In multi-story homes, locate one bathroom above another to minimize plumbing requirements.

Even with the expanded use of bathrooms, they are still an area of the home where accidents can and do happen to people of all ages. Every year, more than 200,000 people are injured in the bathroom, primarily caused by falls on slippery surfaces. For this reason, bathroom design should emphasize safety as well as comfort. Careful planning, thoughtful selection of fixtures, and quality construction can make bathrooms attractive, convenient, comfortable, and safe for all users. See **Chapter 2, Working With Professionals,** for more information on the type of professionals to choose to help design your bathroom area.

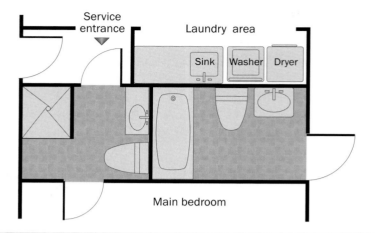

FIGURE 7-1.
Plumbing costs minimized by locating bathrooms and laundry areas close together.

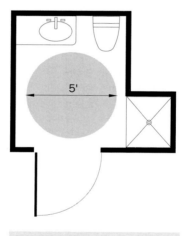

FIGURE 7-2.
Full-sized bathroom with a 5-foot turning circle.

Start with the location of the essential bathroom—a full-sized bathroom on the main level—that also will accommodate overnight visitors who might use wheelchairs (Figure 7-2). If there is only one bathroom in the home, it should be centrally located to serve all bedrooms and should have easy access from the entry without interfering with the living area. If there will be multiple bathrooms:

- To make it accessible to people unable to climb stairs, locate one full bath on the ground or entry level of a home.
- Have one bath centrally located to sleeping areas.
- Make one bath easily available for visitors to use from social areas.
- Locate other bathrooms for privacy in the bedroom suite, for dual purposes such as serving the bedroom suite and entry, and on other floors in a multi-story house.

Bathroom Size

The size of the bathroom should depend on the kinds of features in the space and the number of users. A bathroom should be large enough to accommodate two people and to maneuver a wheelchair, which requires a 60-inch diameter of clear space. Not every bathroom in a house needs to be accessible, as long as there is one accessible bath on the main floor that can be used by those visiting the home.

Figures 7-3 to 7-7 show basic bathrooms that do not have enough space available for a wheelchair bound person to adequately turn around. Figures 7-8 to 7-13 show dual dimensions. The smaller dimensions are for minimum bathroom size. The larger dimensions for increased mobility show the size needed to allow a wheelchair-bound person to turn around adequately. The doors shown in these figures should provide 32 inches of clear opening.

In Figures 7-3 to 7-13, if more than one person will be using the space at the same time, you may want to consider zoning or compartmentalizing your bathroom space. Zoning usually involves separating the bathroom into sections, allowing for privacy and multiple activities. Generally, the toilet and bathtub/shower are in one compartment, while the lavatory is separate. However, you may want to place the toilet in a separate compartment, depending on space.

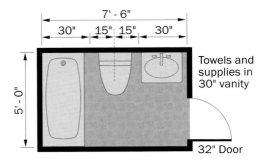

A small, three-fixture bathroom with limited storage in a built-in vanity meets basic bathroom requirements in a limited space. This bathroom is too small for a wheelchair. Area: 37.5 square feet.

FIGURE 7-3.
Small, three-fixture bathroom.

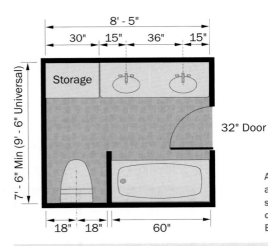

A two-lavatory bathroom with adequate room at the toilet and each lavatory. Note storage space under the lavatories and in a floor-to-ceiling unit. Not wheelchair accessible. Base area: 63 square feet.

FIGURE 7-4.
A two-lavatory bathroom.

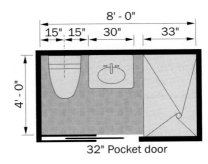

This bathroom features a generous 33- by 44-inch shower. Storage is in the 30-inch vanity and on shelves over the toilet. Not wheelchair accessible. Base area: 33.3 square feet.

FIGURE 7-5.
Bathroom with a large shower.

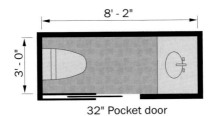

A wall-hung lavatory instead of a vanity squeezes in a 3-foot width. A 32-inch pocket entry door is used. Not wheelchair accessible. Base area: 24.5 square feet.

FIGURE 7-6.
Minimum half-bath in a 3-foot width.

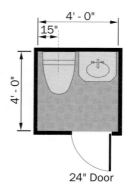

Minimum size for standard fixtures;
4'-6" by 4'-6" gives a more
spacious feeling. Not wheelchair
accessible. Area: 16 square feet.

FIGURE 7-7.
Minimum half-bath in a
4-foot width.

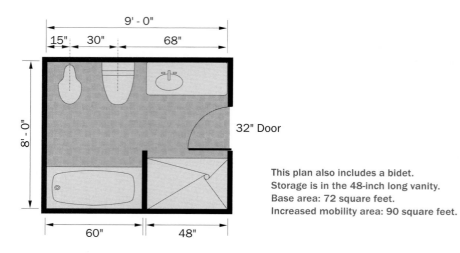

This plan also includes a bidet.
Storage is in the 48-inch long vanity.
Base area: 72 square feet.
Increased mobility area: 90 square feet.

FIGURE 7-8.
Bathroom with a separate tub and shower.

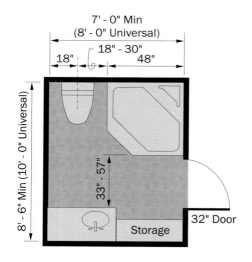

Although not usually a space saver, a square
tub fits some situations better than a
rectangular one. This three-fixture bathroom
has excellent storage. Base area: 59.5 square
feet. Increased mobility area: 80 square feet.

FIGURE 7-9.
Corner square tub.

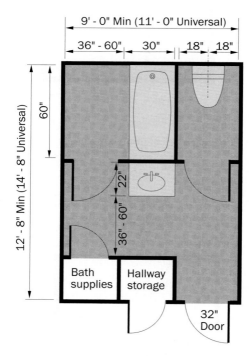

With fixtures in separate compartments,
this layout can replace a second bath by
accommodating more than one person at a
time. It is as large as two bathrooms but costs
less because of fewer fixtures and less
plumbing. Base area: 114 square feet.
Increased mobility area: 161.3 square feet.

FIGURE 7-10.
Large, three-fixture bathroom.

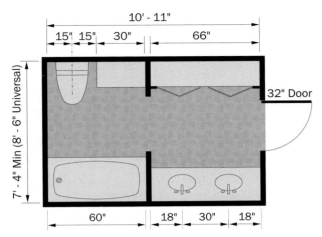

FIGURE 7-11.
Four fixtures, two compartments.

Three people can use this bathroom at the same time. Consider a pocket door between the compartments. Even with generous storage space, it takes only the same space as many non-compartmentalized bathrooms. Base area: 80.5 square feet. Increased mobility area: 92.8 square feet.

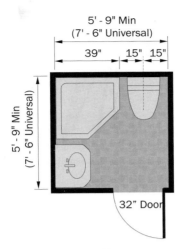

A corner shower and lavatory. Very little storage space. Base area: 33.1 square feet. Increased mobility area: 56.3 square feet.

FIGURE 7-13.
Bathroom with a corner shower.

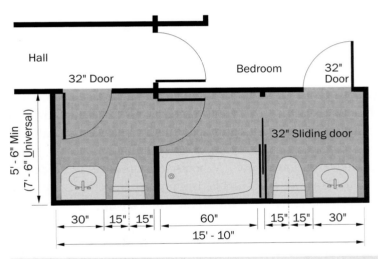

This bathroom acts as two full bathrooms. Two doors to each compartment are undesirable. Limited storage space is available. Base area: 87.1 square feet. Increased mobility area: 118.8 square feet.

FIGURE 7-12.
Bathroom with five fixtures, three compartments.

Fixtures

Base your selection of bathroom fixtures and materials on cost, durability, and ease of maintenance. For the most part, you will need to balance what you would like to install with what you can afford to install. Even though you may need to be conservative with your budget, the bathroom is not a good place to skimp. Installing materials that are not pleasing and durable simply because they are cheap would be a false economy. You want a bathroom to last for a long time and to look good for as long as it lasts. Because you will be confronted with a wide variety of products and finishes, you should consult with your plumbing contractor or a bathroom designer for help making good decisions.

Wall hung units have no tank attached. This can make them easy to clean. Wheelchair users may prefer to install a wall-hung toilet so that the height of the toilet seat will be the same height as the wheelchair seat, making it easier to transfer on and off the toilet. Special plumbing is required for this type of installation, and most wall hung units are not found in residential settings, but instead can be found in commercial and institutional buildings.

Toilets and bidets

Toilets account for the greatest amount of water use in a home: usually between 35 and 45 percent of total water use. Most older toilets use 5 gallons of water with every flush. Today's toilets conserve water, generally using slightly more than 1 gallon of water per flush.

The most common residential low-flow toilets are the gravity flush toilet, the vacuum-assisted toilet, and the pressure-assisted flush toilet.

The gravity flush toilet uses the force of gravity to move water. When the toilet is flushed, the flapper inside the tank opens, and gravity pushes the water out of the tank and into the bowl. The vacuum-assisted toilet, when flushed, uses a vacuum cavity inside the tank to pull air out of the trap below the toilet bowl. This allows the bowl to fill rapidly with water and clear the waste from the bowl. The pressure-assisted flush toilet contains a pressure vessel in the tank. This vessel contains both water and pressurized air. When the toilet is flushed, pressurized air pushes the water out of the tank and into the bowl at a high rate of speed.

Although more costly to purchase, the pressure-assisted flush toilet will perform better than the gravity flush toilet and thus will save water and operating costs over the long term. It's important to note, however, that the pressure-assisted flush toilet makes a loud noise when flushed and may not be appropriate in some spaces. The vacuum-assisted and gravity flush toilets have a quieter flush.

A toilet with an elongated bowl and seat shape is more comfortable than a toilet with a round shape. When designing a bathroom with an elongated bowl, though, be sure to account for the extra length of the bowl that will infringe on open space.

For most users, a toilet height between 15 and 19 inches above the floor is comfortable. A higher toilet usually makes sitting and rising easier, especially for people with bad backs or knees.

Toilets may be one piece units with the tank and bowl formed as one, or two-piece units with the tank separate from the bowl and usually supported by and attached to the bowl. One piece units are easier to clean.

While toilets are common fixtures in U.S. bathrooms, bidets may be a new item for most. Bidets, usually located next to the toilet, are fixtures designed to cleanse the perineal area. Like toilets, an elongated shape is preferable to the rounded shape. The bidet has hot and cold-water temperature controls and horizontal and/or vertical sprays.

When selecting toilets and bidets, make certain that all controls are within the user's reach.

Lavatories and faucets

Lavatories (bathroom sinks) are made of a number of different materials including enameled steel, vitreous china, cast polymer, glass, enameled cast iron, and solid-surface materials. They also come in a variety of styles such as pedestal, wall hung, or mounted in a vanity cabinet by one of several methods: rimmed, self-rimming, integral, above-mount, flush-mount, and under-mounted.

Pedestal lavatories are stand-alone units. The lavatory is mounted on top of a pedestal base. A wall-hung unit is mounted directly to the wall. Rimmed lavatories and self-rimming lavatories actually sit on top of the countertop. Rimmed lavatories have a metal rim that joins the lavatory to the countertop and is secured with a clip. On self-rimming lavatories, the detail on the lavatory's edge actually serves as a lip so that it hangs from the counter. Integral lavatories are formed from the same material as the countertop and are seamless. Above-mounted lavatories actually sit on top of the countertop. A flush-mount lavatory is mounted so that it sits flush with the edge of the countertop. Finally, an under-mount lavatory is mounted so that it sits under the countertop. The edge of the counter-top extends over part or all of the lavatory's edge.

Lavatories that do not require cabinetry, such as wall hung lavatories, are easier for those in wheelchairs to use as there is knee space below that allows them to roll up to and under the lavatory. Pedestal lavatories are not recommended for universal design because they rarely provide enough knee space for people in wheelchairs. If cabinetry is desired, but accessibility is a concern, a removable lavatory cabinet can be installed. These look like traditional stationary cabinets; however, they can be removed to provide knee space for wheelchair users. A wall-mounted lavatory and countertop must be used when installing this type of cabinet. The underneath edge of the counter should be at least 29 inches high and 30 inches wide to allow for adequate knee space below.

Cabinets come in a variety of styles, qualities, and price ranges, but cabinets that are made in standard sizes or are semi-custom are much more economical than custom-made cabinets. Whatever cabinetry style you choose, cabinet heights should be comfortable for most users. Hardware should be easy to manipulate, requiring little grasping or twisting. Loop handle hardware, sometimes referred to as U-shaped handle hardware, is a good choice.

Lavatory heights are traditionally between 30 and 32 inches from the floor; however, 34 inches or higher is actually more comfortable for most users. If possible, you may want to locate one lavatory at the standard height, and one between 34 and 42 inches.

Fittings, more commonly referred to as faucets, also come in a wide variety of styles, colors, and prices. When selecting your fittings, choose the best quality you can afford. Make ease of operation one of your most important criteria. Faucet handles should be easy to grip and control. A user should be able to distinguish clearly between the hot and cold settings. Single-lever mixing faucets are a good choice because they require only one hand to operate and adjust (Figure 7-14). Wide levers or single-handle faucets are also a wise selection for the lavatory because they require limited grasping ability. In addition, touchless electronic faucets are available that use motion sensors to turn the water on and off automatically.

Faucets come in a variety of finishes, but the most affordable are usually chrome. Styles and price ranges vary in chrome, polished brass, enamel, gold plated, or combinations of these materials. Faucets can have different mounting requirements. This is important to keep in mind if you are remodeling and expect to change the fittings. Some

 A popular option is to mount the lavatory on what looks like a chest of drawers, making the lavatory look like a bowl resting on a piece of furniture instead of a bathroom fixture.

FIGURE 7-14.
A single-handle faucet.

To save on water bills and help conserve water, use aerators on your faucets. Aerators are devices that mix water with air as the water flows out of the faucet, saving energy by reducing hot water usage and overall water usage.

Showering and bathing account for approximately 37 percent of the water use in the home. A low-flow showerhead can greatly reduce water usage. It usually releases water at a rate of 2 to 3 gallons per minute versus the usual 6 to 8 gallons per minute of a standard showerhead. Water-saving showerheads and aerators can minimize water use while saving on energy costs.

faucets are a single-hole design. Others require three holes. In addition, faucets come in both washer and washerless designs.

Tubs and showers

Tubs and showers come in many different sizes, shapes, and materials. The standard tub is 14 inches high and 5 feet long; however, tubs can come in other sizes for users of different heights. Some tubs are large enough to accommodate two users. The most common tub surfaces include enameled cast iron, enameled steel, and fiberglass. Fiberglass is generally the least expensive and perhaps the easiest to maintain, but it can be scratched easily with abrasive cleaners.

To reduce the likelihood of slips and falls, install a non-slip floor surface in your tubs and showers. The bottom of the tub and shower should be flat or nearly flat with no contours. Valve location also affects the safety of the tub or shower. Instead of placing the valves directly under the showerhead, offset them so they are closer to the edge of the tub and/or shower (Figure 7-15). This placement allows users to turn on the water without leaning into the shower and/or tub area. Another suggestion is to place the control valves on the wall opposite the showerhead and faucet.

One popular option for tubs is the whirlpool tub. Three types of whirlpool tubs are common: water jet, air jet, and combo. Jetted tubs require an additional electrical circuit for the pump motor and usually additional reinforcement for the floor.

Before buying a whirlpool, you might want to sit in the tub to see how much space is available. Bring a

partner if more than one person will be using the tub at the same time. The interior dimensions are what count, not the exterior. Look for removable sides to provide access to the pump and motor. Check the size of your water heater to see if it can supply enough water. Check the floor structure in the area where the tub will be located to determine if the floor will hold the weight of the tub when filled with water. A dedicated electrical circuit with an automatic shutoff is desirable to protect the tub when the water level gets too low for safe operation.

The smallest acceptable shower size is 30 by 30 inches. The smallest recommended size is 36 by 36 inches. Like tubs, showers should provide enough room for the user to maneuver. The most commonly used shower surfaces are fiberglass and ceramic tile. If shower doors are used, they should be made from safety glazing.

Showerheads vary from ordinary and efficient, to luxurious and massaging, and they come in a variety of price ranges. Three of the most commonly available showerheads are

FIGURE 7-15.
Offset bathtub valves.

the adjustable spray, the rain shower, and the shower tower.

Adjustable spray showerheads allow for the adjustment of both the force and style of water delivery. This showerhead may have a number of settings such as massaging or pulsating action, standard, stream, or a combination. Rain shower heads usually only have one setting and deliver a soft, quiet stream, much like a gentle rain shower. Shower towers have an overhead spray and vertical jets that deliver water to the bather. Showerheads do differ according to their installation methods and water pressure requirements. They also vary in their ease of adjustment. You will need to consider all these variables before choosing a showerhead.

An adjustable hand-held shower head is a great option for individuals who need to control and adjust the height or location of the shower spray. This is a particularly useful option for individuals who may be assisting others, such as young children or those with permanent or temporary disabilities, bathe.

Countertops

In selecting countertops, you will, again, find a wide range of material choices and price options. Choose your countertops based on how well they complement your bathroom design, their durability, their ease of maintenance, and their fit with your budget. Choose waterproof materials, such as plastic laminate, tile, stone, and solid surface finishes for areas around the wash basin. Matte finishes reduce glare. To promote safety for unsteady young children and seniors, select rounded countertop edges and corners.

Storage

Storage is a desirable feature in a bathroom. Storage is needed for personal grooming items and supplies, such as linens, soap, and cleaning supplies. Because space is usually limited, you will need to plan storage wisely.

Two common places for storage are above the toilet and below the wash basin. To prevent the toilet user from hitting his or her head, make storage above the toilet no more than 4 to 8 inches deep.

If storage is needed for cleaning supplies and medicines, consider providing a cabinet that can be locked to protect children from accidental poisoning. Medicine cabinets also may be recessed to prevent users from injuring themselves by coming in contact with sharp corners.

Storage also includes towel racks for bathers. Ensure that there are adequate towel racks for the number of bathers using the space and that they are in easy reach of the bather. Have at least one towel bar per bathroom for large towels and another towel bar for smaller towels. A towel rack near the lavatory is also important. People who use bath sheets will need an extra long towel bar. A heated towel bar is a nice luxury. See **Chapter 13, Household Storage,** for more tips on creating storage.

Mirrors doors, and floors

Mirrors in bathrooms are essential, allowing occupants to complete their grooming functions. Generally, you will find mirrors above the lavatory and over vanities. The bottom of the mirror should be between 36 to 40

Providing an area where users can sit and perform their grooming tasks is also a good feature for a bathroom. Sometimes cabinets are eliminated from beneath the lavatory and make-up area so that a seated person can use this area.

When using the bathroom exhaust system during a steamy shower, start the exhaust fan before starting the shower. The fan should remain in operation until the all the humid air is exhausted from the bathroom. You can tell if humid air has been exhausted by looking at the bathroom mirror. If the mirror is without condensation on it, then the humid air has been fully exhausted from the bathroom.

Sometimes water will drip from the fan, usually during operation. The most likely cause is a sag in the flexible exhaust duct that has allowed warm moist air to condense once it comes into contact with cold air. When the fan starts to operate, the vibration or air movement causes the water to drain slowly back down the flexible duct into the bathroom. This problem can be corrected be eliminating the sag and exhausting the warm, moist air outside.

inches from the floor. This position will enable most people to use the mirror, including those who may need to sit while grooming. If space allows, you may want to include a full-length mirror, particularly if the bathroom doubles as a dressing room. Tempered glass or a plastic, mirror-like finish is safer than glass.

Most bathrooms have doors that open inward. However, for safety reasons, the door to the bathroom should open outward, in case someone inside the space should fall against it. This will allow access to the person inside. Pocket or sliding doors also may be used.

Bathroom floors should be slip resistant. Purchase floors for the general bathroom floor, shower floor, and tub/shower bottoms that are specified for these types of uses.

Environmental Control

Bathrooms are one of the main areas in which moisture problems can exist. Hot showers can create steam that builds up in the room, and this moisture can make paint curl and lead to mold problems. Bathrooms usually are vented either by a window or by a mechanical ventilation system. A mechanical ventilation system is the most reliable method to exhaust moist air out of a bathroom. Figure 7-16 shows two types of mechanical exhaust systems. If you use a window to vent the bathroom, make sure that at least 3 square feet of unobstructed window opening are available to exhaust the moist air.

If you use a mechanical ventilation system to remove the moist air, size the fan to exhaust at a rate of 1 cfm for every square foot of space, with a

minimum rate of at least 50 cfm. It is important that the air be exhausted outside and not into the attic. Exhausting into the attic can lead to moisture problems with the insulation and rafters or trusses. Larger bathrooms may require two fans, one for the shower/bath area and one near the toilet.

Many bathrooms use supplemental heat to maintain room temperature. Heat lamps, floor heat, and toe kick heaters are the main methods used for supplemental heat in bathrooms. Some heat sources are included in a light and ventilation fan combination.

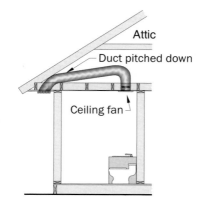

Venting out the eave.

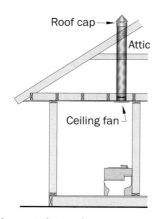

Venting out the roof top.

FIGURE 7-16.
Bathroom exhaust systems.

Figure adapted from *NKBA Bathroom Guideline #26.*

When heating a bathroom, your heat source should be able to maintain a minimum temperature of 68°F. See **Chapter 15, House Utilities,** for more information on ventilation and heating.

General Safety Concerns

The bathroom can either support or hinder an individual's independence. If a home owner/occupant cannot perform basic grooming routines, his or her independence is limited. Universal design—design for the lifespan of all people regardless of age, gender, or ability—makes the bathroom space accessible to all family members, both now and in the future. Because universal design concepts are not just specialized design but rather *good* design, they have been incorporated in discussions throughout this chapter, but they are especially important when considering bathroom safety

Grab bars

Grab bars are important safety features for the tub, shower, and toilet area. If you do not currently need grab bars, plan for their future installation (Figure 7-17). In new construction, reinforce the areas where grab bars are likely to be located. The best reinforcing is solid wood blocking. If reinforcing whole walls, use structural plywood panels. Shower stalls are available that have integral grab bars.

Grab bars should be mounted 1-1/2 inches from the wall. They should be 1-1/4 to 1-1/2 inches in diameter and mounted to withstand 300 pounds of force in any direction. Bars with a textured finish are prefer-

able because they can help prevent the user's hand from slipping. Horizontal grab bars should be installed at a height of 33 to 36 inches above the floor (Figures 7-18 and 7-19).

While grab bars are an added expense, they should never be substituted for with towel rods or other devices that are not specifically designed for bathroom assistance. Substitutes are not strong enough to support the weight or pressure of an individual leaning or pulling on them. Substitutions are dangerous and can lead to serious injury.

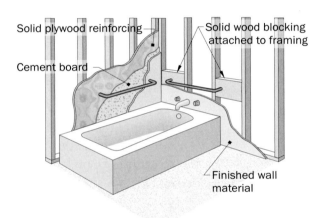

FIGURE 7-17.
Additional reinforcement needed for grab bars.

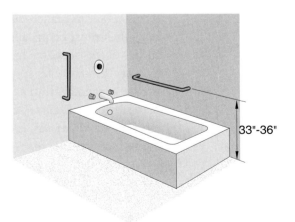

FIGURE 7-18.
Grab bar locations for a bathtub.

Adapted from NKBA Bathroom Guideline #14.

Common shower with seat and grab bars. Note the adjustable hand-held shower head with flexible hose.

FIGURE 7-19.
Showers with grab bars and shower seats.

Adapted from NKBA Bathroom Guideline #14.

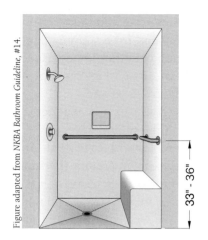

Figure adapted from NKBA Bathroom Guideline, #14.

33" - 36"

Grab bar locations in a shower.

functional area. Figure 7-21 shows an example of lighting and light switch locations. At least one wall switch needs to be provided at the bathroom entrance. Lights in a shower or tub space must be suitable for damp and wet conditions. No hanging fixtures are allowed within 3 feet horizontally, or 8 feet vertically from the top of the bathtub rim.

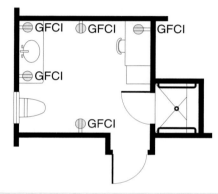

FIGURE 7-20.
Example of properly located electrical receptacles in a bathroom.

Figure adapted from NKBA Bathroom Guideline #24. GFCI = ground fault circuit interrupter.

Electrical receptacles

Codes require that all electrical receptacles be protected by a ground fault circuit interrupter (GFCI). It may or may not be present in the bathroom of an older home; however, building codes usually require them for newly constructed or remodeled bathrooms. Receptacle outlets must be supplied from a 20-amp branch circuit. At least one GFCI must be installed within 36 inches of the outside edge of the lavatory. Electrical receptacles must not be installed within a shower or bathtub space. Figure 7-20 shows an example of where GFCIs should be located in a bathroom.

General lighting should be provided in each bathroom. In addition to general lighting, task lighting should be located over or near each

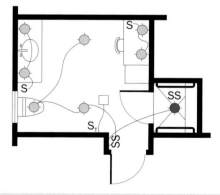

FIGURE 7-21.
Example of properly locating lights and switches in a bathroom.

Figure adapted from NKBA Bathroom Guideline #25.

Resources

Bathrooms. 1991. Raleigh, North Carolina: The Center for Universal Design, North Carolina State University. Publication number TP #1.00

Cheever, E.M. 1997. *Bathroom Equipment and Materials*: Vol. 3. Bathroom Industry Technical Manual. 2nd ed. Hackettstown, NJ: The National Kitchen and Bath Association and the University of Illinois Small Homes Council.

Consumer Reports August, 2005. Bathroom Makeovers: Relaxing retreats for less. Pgs. 20-35.

Frechette, L.A. 1994. *Bathroom Remodeling*. New York: TAB books.

Grab Bars. 1993. Raleigh, North Carolina: The Center for Universal Design, North Carolina State University. Publication number TP #1.10.

Jankowski, W. 1993. *Kitchen and Bath Designs for Living*. Glen Cove, NY: PBC International, Inc.

Joint Center for Housing Studies of Harvard. 2001. *Remodeling Homes for Changing Households*. President and Fellows of Harvard University.

Kicklighter, C.E. and J.C. Kicklighter. 1998. *Residential Housing and Interiors*. Tinley Park, IL: The Goodheart-Wilcox Company, Inc.

Kirby, S.D. 1995. *Accessible Bathroom Spaces*. Raleigh: North Carolina Cooperative Extension Service.

Mace, R.L. 1991. *The Accessible Housing Design File*. New York: Van Nostrand Reinhold.

Meredith Publishing Group. 1999. *Kitchens and Baths 1-2-3*. Des Moines, IA: The Home Depot and Meredith Books.

NAHB Research Center, Inc. and Barrier Free Environments. 1996. *Residential Remodeling and Universal Design Making Homes More Comfortable and Accessible*. U.S. Department of Housing and Urban Development.

National Electrical Code Handbook (NFPA 70). 2005. National Fire Protection Association (NFPA), 1 Battery March Park, Quincy, Massachusetts, 02169-7471.

National Kitchen and Bath Association. 908-852-0023. www.nkba.org

Peterson, M.J. 1996. *Universal Bathroom Planning*. Hackettstown, NJ: National Kitchen and Bath Association.

Philbin, T. 1992. *Costwise Bathroom Remodeling: A Guide to Renovating or Improving Your Bath*. New York: John Wiley & Sons, Inc.

The Center for Universal Design. North Carolina State University. 919-515-3083. 1-800-647-6777 info line. http://www2.ncsu.edu/ncsu/design/cud

U.S. Department of Housing and Urban Development. 1996. Residential Remodeling and Universal Design. Office of Policy Development and Research.

Bedrooms

EVEN IF WE USE IT ONLY FOR SLEEPING AND DRESSING, we spend about a third of our time in the bedroom. Many bedrooms, however, are used for other activities such as watching television, listening to music, studying, reading, and even exercising. Planning their bedroom allows family members to meet their personal needs as well as express their tastes through color, furniture, and accessories. The guidelines that follow consider bed sizes, door and window placement, storage needs, and health and safety concerns. If you plan to use bedrooms for activities other than sleeping and dressing, you may have needs other than those addressed here.

Number of Bedrooms

In 1984, only 18 percent of new houses had four or more bedrooms. By 1997, that percentage had grown to 31 percent (National Association of Home Builders). When planning the number of bedrooms needed, there are some generally accepted norms. Usually no more than two people share a room. Separate bedrooms are often provided for:
- Parents or a single parent.
- Each child over 18.
- Each pair of same-sex children (preferably with no more than 4 years of age difference).
- Each pair of different-sex children if both are under 9 (preferably with no more than 4 years of age difference).
- Each additional single adult or couple in the household.

Location

Locate bedrooms to provide both sound and sight privacy. Increase sound privacy with distance, sound-resistant construction and materials, sound-absorbing furnishings, finishes such as carpeting or acoustical ceiling tile, and barriers such as closets and baths. Achieve sight privacy by opening bedrooms off hallways rather than directly off other rooms. For privacy reasons, some family members may prefer having their bedrooms located on another level away from the rest of the family; for example, teenagers sometimes prefer a basement bedroom. If occupants will be playing music or pursuing other loud activities in their bedrooms, plan the proximity of their bedrooms to other bedrooms accordingly.

When planning bedroom spaces, consider these factors:
- How many sleeping rooms do you need? (For more information about floor plans, see **Chapter 3, Designing A Home.**)
- Where are the rooms located in relation to the other areas in the house as well as to the orientation of the lot? (For more information about building sites, see **Chapter 4, Selecting a Location or a Building Site.**)
- What activities will occur in each bedroom? What furniture and equipment is necessary for those activities?
- What are the personal needs of each family member? When do family members sleep? Are there special needs related to age or disability?
- Where are the doors and windows? (For more information about doors, see **Chapter 12, Entries, Doors, Halls, and Stairs.**)
- How much storage space is needed and where should it be located? (For more information about household storage, see **Chapter 13, Household Storage.**)

Continued

- Where are the bathrooms located? (For more information about bathrooms, see **Chapter 7, Bathrooms.**)
- How many generations are sharing this house? If three generations are living under one roof, for example, the need to provide privacy and facilitate care giving among generations will influence the location of the bedrooms. Also, young adults often live at home with parents for a period of time.
- How will bedroom space change in the future?
- How will rooms be used after children are grown?
- What additional members might be added to the household?

Also consider how bedrooms relate to:

- One another. Parents may prefer to be close to small children (Figure 8-1a) but separated from older ones (Figure 8-1b).
- The bath. You should be able to go from any bedroom to a bath without passing through a room other than a hallway.
- Work areas, particularly the kitchen and laundry. Placing the bedrooms near the laundry reduces the steps needed to take clothes and bed linens to and from the washer and dryer. It is quieter to locate the bedrooms away from the kitchen.
- Social, recreation, and family spaces. Maximize quiet for sleep, study, and privacy.

- Streets or major traffic areas. Minimize vehicle or pedestrian noises.
- The sun and breezes. (For more detail, see the section on doors and windows.)
- The supervision of young children and care of elderly or ill family members.
- Access by individuals with physical disabilities. On the first floor of two-story homes, have at least one room available that can be used as a bedroom for a sick or disabled person (Figure 8-2).
- Nearby storage of bedroom linens.

Main Bedroom

Many of today's homes feature a main bedroom suite that not only contains a traditional sleeping room but also includes one or more

a. Bedrooms grouped together.

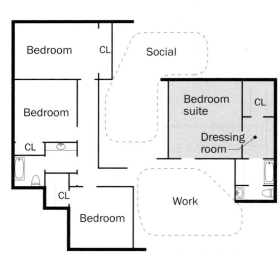

b. Main bedroom separated from others.

FIGURE 8-1.
Bedrooms on one floor.

bathrooms, walk-in closets, dressing rooms, hot tubs, and space for exercising, reading, watching television, or office work. According to the National Association of Home Builders (NAHB), a popular remodeling project is the addition of a 16- by 24-foot main bedroom with whirlpool and walk-in closet. Some main bedrooms function as mini-family rooms where family members watch television, read, play computer games, and snack together. Some main bedrooms have doors that open onto private outdoor balconies or patios. Sometimes the main bedroom occupies most of an upper level in a house.

Households will need to decide if the main bedroom is the domain of only the couple or individual that sleeps there or if the space should accommodate several family members engaging in leisure activities. Figure 8-3 shows a modest main bedroom area with a good circulation pattern to accommodate a bath area, and areas for sleeping, sitting, and dressing. Main bedrooms that include space for several types of activities may require wiring for phones, cable television, and Internet access. Extra plumbing will be required if the main bedroom has a hot tub, a snack bar with a sink, or an extra sink in the sleeping area for grooming use outside of the bathroom. If you opt for a large, multi-function main bedroom, you may be able to reduce family living space in other parts of the house. Plan your main bedroom carefully so that other activities do not interfere with sleeping if more than one person will be using the space.

If you plan to "age in place," that is, live in your house through your retirement years, you will want a bedroom that does not require climbing stairs. A bathroom should also be on the same level as the bedroom.

A separate guest room is ideal for guests and family members who often stay overnight. However, the guest area can be in a multipurpose area such as the family room or study. A built-in bed, rollaway, pullout couch, or sleeping bag requires little space.

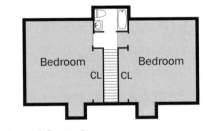

Second floor plan.

First floor plan.

**FIGURE 8-2.
Bedrooms on two floors.**

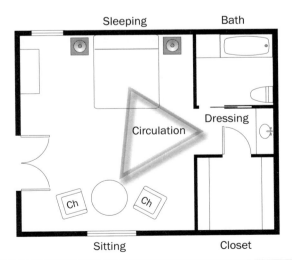

**FIGURE 8-3.
Main bedroom suite with circulation for sleeping area, sitting area, and dressing area.**

Figure adapted from *Housing by Lifestyle: The Component Method of Residential Design*, James W. Wentling.

Space Needs

At a minimum, bedrooms should provide space for sleeping, dressing, and clothes storage, but don't forget to allow wall space for items such decorations and a full-length mirror. The size of the bed is an important consideration in your planning. Table 8-1 contains typical bed dimensions for standard beds and waterbeds. The minimum size for a bedroom with only a single bed is 90 square feet; for a double bed with minimal furniture, 120 square feet; and for a king-sized bed with minimal furniture, 145 square feet. Allow at least 16 inches, preferably more, between the bed and wall for a person to make the bed. Persons using wheelchairs or with other mobility disabilities need at least 3 feet of space all around the bed to make it. Twin beds can be made from one side, so clearance is not needed for standing between a twin bed and the wall.

The number of pieces of storage furniture, such as chests or dressers, depends on the number of people occupying the room and the storage space inside the closet. To provide easy control of lamps from the bed, you may want a nightstand or table next to the bed for a lamp or for a clock or personal items such as books. A chair is convenient for putting on shoes and stockings. Provide at least 36 inches and preferably 48 inches of space (dressing circles) between pieces of furniture, for dressing, retrieving clothes from dresser drawers, and taking items from the closet (Figure 8-4).

Space requirements are different for other activities conducted in the bedroom. Table 8-2 offers a partial list of bedroom uses and the furnishings and equipment required for those uses.

Space for these needs can significantly increase the cost of the house, so compromise may be necessary. If

Table 8-1. Typical bed dimensions.
Lengths include 3 inches (1-1/2 inches on each end) for metal or wooden headboards and footboards; add another 7 inches of length for bookcase-type headboards.

Bed sizes: Based on common mattresses; some other sizes are available.

Type of Bed	Width (inches)	Length (inches)
Standard crib	27	54
Standard	36	78
Twin	39	78
Full	54	78
Queen	60	83
King	78	83

Waterbed sizes: Width includes 3 inches (1-1/2 inches per side) for the frame.

Type of Waterbed	Width (inches)	Length (inches)
Twin	42	87
Super single	51	87
Full	57	87
Queen	63	87
King	87	87

activity space in the bedroom replaces or reduces needs elsewhere, costs can balance out. As family members leave home, bedrooms can be put to other uses.

To save floor space for other uses, consider installing bunk beds or lofts. For children's bunk beds, allow at least 36 to 39 inches between the lower and upper bunks; for adult use, provide a minimum of 40 to 44 inches between bunks. Sleeping lofts provide space for such activities as studying at a desk beneath the loft, but it must be installed high enough above the floor to avoid head injuries. When planning the height of the loft, remember to consider ceiling height and headroom. Provide a safe ladder to an upper bunk or loft and a railing around an upper bunk and loft. Changing sheets on lofts and bunk beds can be difficult.

Doors and Windows

Door and window placements dictate furniture arrangement and traffic patterns through the bedroom. Doors into the bedroom should open against a wall to minimize space used by the door. For privacy, do not align the door directly with the bed or dressing area. The traffic path from the closet door to the chest of drawers should be short and direct so that you do not need to walk around the bed. Bedroom door widths range from 32 to 36 inches. Residents who use wheelchairs or other assistive devices need a clear opening of at least 32 inches; the door frame must be 34 to 36 inches wide to provide a clear opening of 32 inches.

Windows provide light, ventilation, and a means of escape in case of

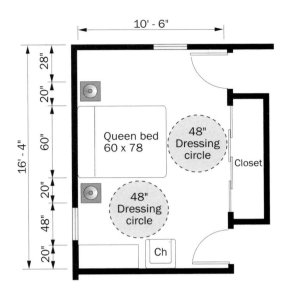

FIGURE 8-4.
Dressing circles.

Table 8-2. Other bedroom uses.

Bedroom Uses	Required Furnishings and Equipment
Study or office/work area	Desk, chairs, lighting, bookshelves, and computer storage
Play space for young children	Open area and storage
Audiovisual equipment	Television, stereo, VCR/DVD, tape/disk storage, and computer table, extra electrical wiring including cable
Private relaxation	Comfortable chairs, tables, and lighting
Exercise	Exercise equipment, audiovisual equipment, and equipment storage

fire. For these reasons, building codes usually dictate a minimum window area for bedrooms. Provide a minimum of 10 percent (20 percent is even better) window area in relation to the bedroom square footage. Placing two windows together on the same wall rather than separating them may provide more light as well as easier window treatments and furniture arrangements. On the other hand, windows on more than one wall allow cross ventilation. A door across from a window also helps air circulation throughout the house.

Most building codes require that at least one window in each bedroom be a potential fire escape. A 20-inch wide by 24-inch high opening is minimum for an escape window. The opening should be no more than 36 inches above the floor. Window sills 24 inches above the floor allow children, bedridden persons, and persons who are seated, including wheelchair users, to see out but can limit furniture arrangement. Clear floor space is needed in front of windows that will be operated by a wheelchair user. Double hung windows are difficult for many seated people and disabled people to open and close. Sliding and casement windows are easier to operate. High (strip) windows increase both furniture arrangement options and privacy but may contribute to a boxed-in feeling and limit air circulation.

Basement bedrooms also should have an easily accessible window for exiting the basement during a fire or other emergency. The window must have a minimum opening area of 5.7 square feet, be no more than 44 inches from the floor, and be at least 20 inches wide and 24 inches high. Windows that will serve as an emergency exit for a wheelchair user should be at least 30 inches wide and no more than 24 inches above the floor (Figure 8-6).

Closets

If possible, put bedroom closets near the door to the bedroom. Having a closet near the entry can be more

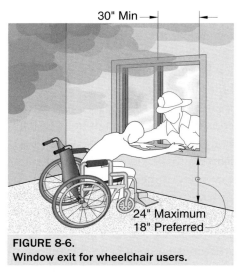

**FIGURE 8-6.
Window exit for wheelchair users.**

Adapted from *Windows*, Tech Pack #7.00, The Center for Universal Design. North Carolina State University.

convenient for clothing changes and for returning clean clothes to the room. Additionally, more usable bedroom floor space often results. You will probably want a closet light, especially for closets that are deep or located off poorly lighted areas. Automatic door switches are available.

Space arrangement and dimensions

Closet rods that are adjustable or installed as upper (81-inch) and lower (40-inch) double rods allow access to users of different heights and to both sitting and standing users. You will need at least 48 inches of linear rod space per person for hanging clothes, plus shelf and/or drawer space, either in the closet or in furniture storage pieces. Figure 8-7 shows different types of closets and some common configurations. Table 8-3 shows recommended closet dimensions.

To incorporate universal design into storage, have 50 percent or all storage less than 54 inches high.

Doors with lever handles (Figure 8-5) are easier to use, taking less strength to operate than doorknobs. For more information about doors, see **Chapter 12, Entries, Doors, Halls, and Stairs***.*

**FIGURE 8-5.
Lever handle on an interior door.**

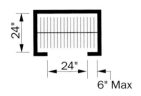

Reach-in closet.

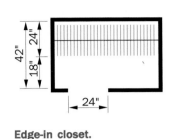

Edge-in closet.

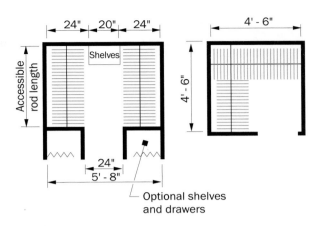

Optional shelves
and drawers

Walk-in closets.

**FIGURE 8-7.
Various closet types.**

Table 8-3. Recommended closet dimensions.
Provide at least 48 inches of rod space per person plus additional space for off-season storage. Reserve shelves above 76 inches for seldom-used items. Provide additional storage space for out-of-season clothes.

Dimension	Clear Interior Dimensions (inches)
Depth	24-28
Rod length, per person	48
Shelf depth	12-18
Rod height to center of pole	
Street clothing	62
Woman's evening clothing	72
Clothing for children 6-12	45 [a]
Universal design	54 or less [b]
Double rods	
Upper	81
Lower	40
Distance between rod and shelf	2
Distance between closet hooks	7

[a] Use adjustable rod heights.
[b] For 50% of the space.

Install adjustable height closet rods and shelves to add flexibility in storage. Motorized cabinets can be used to raise or lower cabinets.

Closet doors

Closet doors are usually 80 inches high. Large closet doors may take up more wall or floor space, but they do improve access to and visibility in the closet. Small closet doors may limit access to the closet, but conserve space.

Four types of closet doors—hinged, sliding pocket, sliding bypass, and bi-fold—are common. When you choose your doors, consider cost, appearance, and the ease and safety of operation. Make sure you will have enough wall and floor space for the door's projection or swing and for the net opening size.

A 1- to 2-inch space under the door allows air circulation in the closet and helps reduce mildew in humid conditions. Louvered doors further improve circulation and are useful when moisture condensation may be a problem, such as in closets

Persons with allergies or asthma have special health needs, and bedrooms can be problem areas for people with asthma and allergies. Dust mites are a common allergen and trigger for asthma attacks. People allergic to dust mites can reduce their exposure by eliminating carpeting, heavy draperies and bedspreads, stuffed toys, clothes storage under the bed, and upholstered furniture in the bedroom. Encasing pillows and mattresses with allergen-proof coverings also reduces exposure to dust mites. Wet cleaning the surfaces of wood, ceramic tile, vinyl, or plastic laminate helps control the dust mites, while frequent laundering of bed linens (at least weekly) in hot water kills dust mites. Keeping humidity levels low in the bedroom also reduces the incidence of dust mites. People with allergies to pets should not allow them in the bedroom

on outside walls, below grade, or where humidity is high.

Allow space for a hinged closet door (Figure 8-8a) to swing. These doors are 24 to 36 inches wide and

are single or in pairs. You can hang closet accessories on the inside face of the door. Fasten closet hardware to the side or top rails of a flush door with a hollow core.

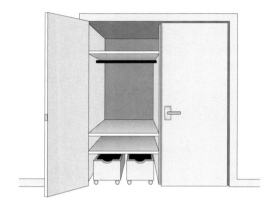

a. Hinged door.
Hinged doors do not block the closet opening but do project into the room. When using hinged doors, you must allow wall and room space for the door to open.

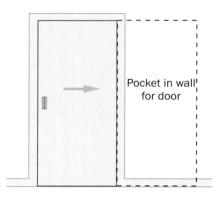

b. Sliding pocket door.
Sliding pocket doors do not interfere with access space or passing traffic; however, wall space must be available for the pocket. Avoid hanging heavy shelving, etc., on the walls along the pockets.

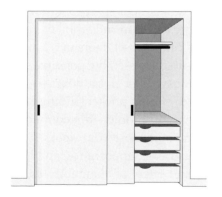

c. Sliding bypass door.
Sliding bypass doors do not interfere with wall or access space, and they do not impede traffic in front of the closet. They do, however, block part of the closet opening, which is unhandy with narrow doorways.

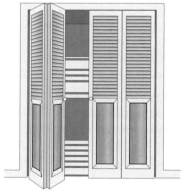

d. Bi-fold door.
Two panels, 12 to 18 inches wide, make a bi-fold door. One or two bi-fold doors close openings up to 72 inches wide. The door panels project into the room less than hinged doors, so they need less clearance, but the door blocks part of the opening, which is unhandy with narrow doorways. Bi-fold doors are often louvered.

FIGURE 8-8.
Closet doors.

Alarms and Electricity

Planning where to locate smoke detectors, fire alarms, and security alarms should be part of the process of planning bedrooms. You also need to plan for sizing and locating electrical receptacles. Decide where to incorporate these items into the bedroom during planning and design, not as an afterthought. Dealing with these necessary items early in the process rather than waiting until construction has begun will save time and money.

Alarms

Safety and security devices should be installed in the hallway or stairway near the sleeping rooms. The alarms on these devices should be able to wake sleeping occupants. Smoke detectors should be installed on or near the ceiling, while carbon monoxide detectors can be installed at any level. Smoke detectors that operate a strobe light to wake hearing-impaired occupants are available; they should be installed inside the bedroom. Nightlights are a safety feature for persons who often get up during the night. For people whose sleep is disturbed by light, motion- or sound-activated nightlights that can be plugged into an outlet near the bed are available.

Bedrooms can be located in basements or attics. Occupants should take steps to ensure that radon levels are low in basement bedrooms and that there are no contaminants from furnaces, water heaters, or sewers. Do not place emergency exits near furnaces or water heaters. Make sure to use smoke and carbon monoxide detectors near basement or attic

bedrooms. Install fire escapes for attic bedrooms.

In homes that have security alarm systems, the main bedroom is often designed to have a *panic alarm* to activate the system, may have switches to activate outside security lights, and may have a lock to serve as a refuge in event an intruder is feared. Also, the alarm system may be activated or deactivated from the main bedroom as a chore to perform each evening or the first thing to do each morning.

See **Chapter 15, House Utilities**, for more information on carbon monoxide and smoke detectors, nightlights, and alarm systems.

Electrical receptacles

Bedrooms can use 15- or 20-amp circuits. Receptacles must be spaced so that no point along the wall is more than 6 feet from a receptacle, which in most cases means 12 linear feet following along the wall. Any space 2 feet or more in width that is unbroken along the floor line by doorways or similar openings must have a receptacle. Receptacles are often located 12 inches from the floor, but locating them 18 inches or higher off the floor will make them more accessible.

At least two receptacles in a bedroom must be readily accessible. To reduce the risk of fire, any receptacle located behind a bed must be protected from the bed contacting any attachment plug. Receptacles located in children's rooms should be protected from the children inserting items into them. Many hardware, children's specialty, and building supply stores have child-safety protection devices for receptacles.

Resources

Bedrooms. 1991. Raleigh, North Carolina: The Center for Universal Design, North Carolina State University. Publication number TP #6.00.

Creating Accessible Homes. 1996. Manhattan, Kansas: Cooperative Extension Service, Kansas State University. Publication number MF-2213.

Healthy Air at Home–A Checklist for Parents. 1995. Ames, Iowa: Iowa State University Extension. Publication number PM 1622.

Home modifications for the disabled. 1992. Ft. Collins, Colorado: Colorado State University Cooperative Extension. Publication number 9.529.

Life-Cycle Housing: Evaluate Before Buying, Building, or Remodeling. 1995. Stillwater, Oklahoma: Oklahoma State University Cooperative Extension Service. Publication number T-5135.

National Association of Home Builders (NAHB). *Characteristics of New Single-Family Homes: 1975-1997*. Retrieved January 29, 1999 from the following website: http://www.nahb.com/sf.html

National Association of Home Builders (NAHB). *Popular Remodeling Projects: Costs vs. Value*. Retrieved January 29, 1999 from the following website: http://www.nahb.com/most.html

National Electrical Code Handbook (NFPA 70). 2005. National Fire Protection Association (NFPA), 1 Battery March Park, Quincy, Massachusetts, 02169-7471.

The DoAble Renewable Home: Making Your Home Fit Your Needs. 1991. Washington, D.C: American Association of Retired Persons.

Wentling, James W., *Housing by Lifestyle: The Component Method of Residential Design*. 1990. McGraw-Hill Publishing Company.

Windows. 1991. Raleigh, North Carolina: The Center for Universal Design, North Carolina State University. Publication number TP #7.00.

Home Offices

AS YOU DESIGN YOUR HOME OFFICE, consider your work habits. The tasks you perform and the way the space relates to the rest of your home, your family, and your lifestyle dictate which of the following three types of home office you need:

- An office for a home-based business.
- An office for occasional work at home.
- An informal office.

A home-based business needs a specialized area in which you can carry on normal business activities; this probably will require a space fully separated from other areas of your home. A work-at-home office is an office in which you occasionally telecommute, where you work after hours in your home, or where you sometimes see clients. An informal office is an office where you conduct family business such as menu planning, bill paying, organizing the family's social calendar, and e-mailing.

Your work activities define the location and work area needed, the furnishings required, and the arrangement of the work area. Home offices also vary depending on whether you use the office for full- or part-time work or if more than one person will be using the office. If two workers are sharing the home office, make sure you consider each individual's work habits and needs. Your budget also affects the location of your home office. Are you planning to use existing space in a bedroom or dining room; convert a loft, porch, attic, garage, or basement; or are you including space for a home office when building a new home? With recent advances in desktop technology, even the smallest home office can have advanced capabilities that match those found in traditional corporate locations.

Before using your house as a location for a home-based business, check with local zoning and city ordinances that may dictate whether you can conduct a business out of your home. Some cities have limitations or special business taxes on home-based businesses. Also check with a tax accountant to determine the limitations on federal and state income tax deductibility for home offices.

To qualify as a home office and as a deductible expense against federal and state taxes, IRS regulations require that an entire room be designated exclusively as a home office. You may want to consult with your accountant about claiming your home office as a deductible expense on your taxes. Generally, if your employer provides an office for your work and you have a home office primarily for your convenience, the IRS will not allow a tax deduction for a home office.

A home office needs to meet some basic requirements to be useful and inviting. To ensure that you have thought about these minimum requirements, use the following checklist as you plan your home office.

- ❑ Sufficient electrical outlets, including outlets for phone/ fax/modem connections
- ❑ Acoustics and privacy satisfactory for you
- ❑ Window coverings that minimize glare
- ❑ Good quality lighting and ventilation
- ❑ Adequate work surface
- ❑ Proper ergonomics with adjustable components
- ❑ Necessary seating/ conference space
- ❑ Ample cabinet and file storage space
- ❑ Healthy and safe interior environment

*Clients coming to your
house will need access
to a bathroom. Decide
if you want them to use
your private bathroom where they
may walk through your house or if
you want to them to use a bathroom
installed near the office*

Note that under certain circumstances
you may trigger a tax audit if you claim
your home office as a deduction. Also,
you may be subject to the alternate
minimum tax if you claim your home
office as a deduction for tax purposes.

Office Configuration and Location

Many home-based workers need
offices that are accessible to an entry.
Some want to be able to hear their
children while others want privacy
with minimal interruptions. If your
home office has an outdoor entry and
clients come into your home, make
coat storage available. Consider

adding hooks, a coat/hat rack, or a
separate closet. If the location is
convenient, the family's coat closet
can provide coat storage for clients.

If you have a large number of
clients coming into your home office,
you might consider having a separate
entrance for their use. If clients come
to your office, security may be an
issue. You may want a locking door
between the office and the rest of the
house, or between the house area and
where the client might wait.

Choose a configuration for a work
area that makes your home office
functional and inviting. Figures 9-1
and 9-2 show examples of typical
office configurations.

Wall or strip office layout.

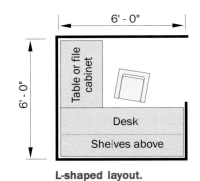

L-shaped layout.

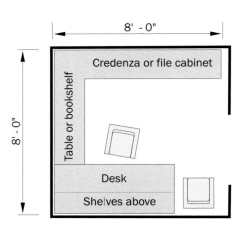

Horseshoe or U-shaped office layout.

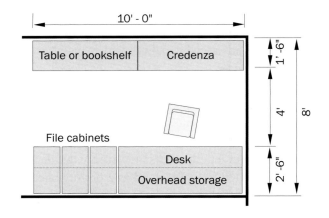

Parallel or corridor office layout.

**FIGURE 9-1.
Office layouts.**

- Wall or strip.
- U-shaped.
- L-shaped.
- Parallel or corridor.
- Double L-shaped.

The U-shaped work area works well because it allows you to keep everything within reach on three surfaces. The wall layout or the L-shaped work area takes up less room and may be easily created from existing space in your home. The parallel or corridor work area could provide more work surface. For dual workers, Figure 9-2 illustrates a double L-shaped office with a shared peninsula layout.

To determine required floor space for a home office, inventory your activities and equipment as well as your files, books, and supply storage needs. Do you require space for clients to sit? Do you have equipment or projects that require table surfaces so you can spread out in comfort? Some home workers want plenty of walk-around space that requires a separate room while an informal home office can be part of another space such as the kitchen, the living or family room, a bedroom, or even a closet area. Room arrangement has been made easier with the use of laptop and notebook computers and through the advent of wireless

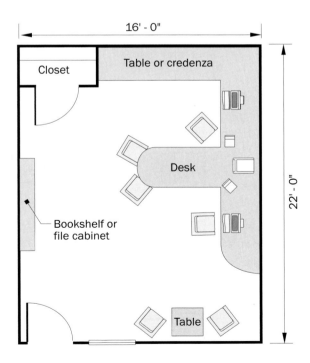

FIGURE 9-2.
Double L-shaped area for two workers.

technology. Figure 9-3 shows a variety of office layouts. Figure 9-4 shows a well organized, two person work area. For more information about floor planning, see **Chapter 3, Designing a Home**.

An efficient home office might be a desk with a file drawer under a stairway, a workspace incorporated into the kitchen, or a self-enclosed furniture unit. To help you determine how you want to arrange your office, ask yourself questions like the following: How much work will you want to hide at the end of the day? How much area do you expect to need for future work and storage expansion?

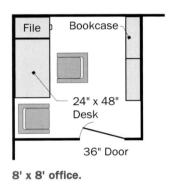

8' x 8' office.

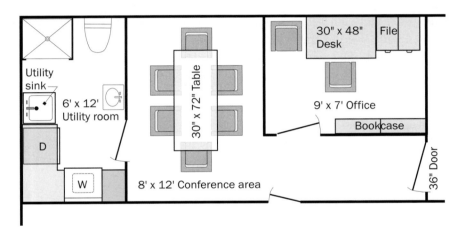

12' x 24' office.

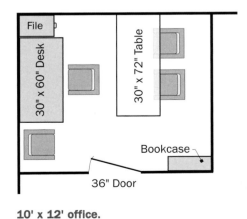

10' x 12' office.

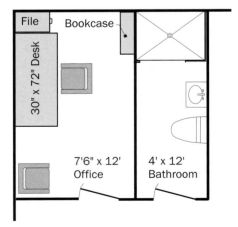

12' x 12' office and bathroom.

**FIGURE 9-3.
Various office layouts.**

FIGURE 9-4.
Work area in a two-person office.

Furnishings

Function and ergonomics are key criteria for choosing office furnishings. Fit furniture and office tasks to your body measurements (Figure 9-5). Adjustable furniture is desirable, especially seating that adjusts for height, angle, and back support. Select comfortable heights for equipment on the desk, table, cabinets, and shelves. Keep in mind that functional furniture is more crucial than appearance. Consider ready-to-assemble home office furniture and adjustable modules. Many desk-type units that store computer equipment and supplies are available. Match storage space to your needs—consider height, amount, and arrangement. Make your office flexible by using modular furniture that can be rearranged and added onto as needs change. A portable cart with wheels offers efficient storage and additional work surface area.

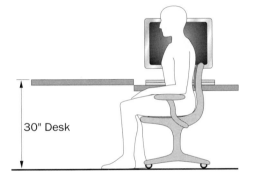
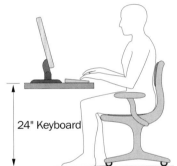

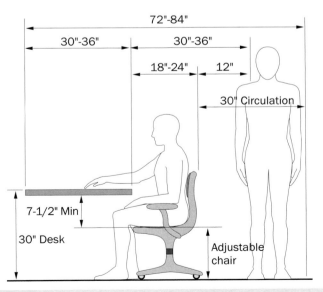

FIGURE 9-5.
Using ergonomics to choose home office furnishings.

Consider having space for bulletin boards or a dry erase board to track projects and post important business reminders. Placing screens, bookshelves, or plants in any room can define your work area, hide supplies, and muffle outside noise. Your home office should include accessories that express your personality: pictures, wall hangings, or a favorite special collection.

Since most work performed in the home office is from a seated position, the most important piece of furniture is the chair. Seating should be adjustable to the user's body and to the opening and height of the desk. An adjustable chair fits your body size and height and allows multiple home office workers to use the same chair if needed. Seating and a conference area for clients, workers, or family members also may be needed. Remember, it is appropriate to include a comfortable, homey chair or sofa in your office, because inspiration does not always occur behind a desk.

A file drawer in the desk may be adequate for filing records and resources. For additional filing, choose vertical (allow 24 inches to open) or lateral (allow 18 inches to open) file drawers. To meet your needs, you can select file cabinets that are two or more drawers high. File cabinets can double as an efficient room divider and as extra surface for office equipment. Additional drawers provide a great deal of storage and can be combined with other units for a storage wall.

Shelves for books and materials can be freestanding, built in, or wall hung. Shelving can be adjustable or fixed. Modular or component storage systems are also available. If you plan for future needs, units can be mixed and matched as desired and added later. To use space efficiently, think vertically, and place shelves as high as possible on the wall. Use stacking bins to hold magazines and papers. You can place these bins next to or under your desk. Before you purchase additional cabinets, toss out unnecessary papers. For more information about storage, see **Chapter 13, Household Storage**.

The Work Area

When you organize your office work area, incorporate ergonomics, thus increasing your convenience and comfort and improving orderly workflow. Consider all home office tasks and the corresponding items needed to perform each of them. Be sure to account for universal design concepts, and plan for adaptability. Take into account required clearances. An office chair should have about 39 inches of floor space between its desk and other furniture. Place frequently used items within easy reach, or within 30 inches, of your sitting position (Figure 9-6). Identify the items that you use most often and select the most convenient place for each. To reduce repetition or prolonged one-sided movements, arrange materials and equipment in their order of priority. Place largest items first and then smaller ones, leaving space to use each piece of equipment and to move around it. If you arrange items neatly, you will not have to hide them. To avoid writing over the phone cord, place your phone on the left-hand side if you are right-handed and vice versa. Use a long cord or a cordless phone so you can reach information or supplies you may need while on the phone. A cellular phone might be an even better choice.

Computer workstation

If you use your computer every day, first consider the best placement of the computer monitor. Set it in a location that minimizes glare and is on a surface height appropriate for your body. Then arrange your monitor, keyboard, printer, and papers in a flexible configuration (Figure 9-7). A desk for a

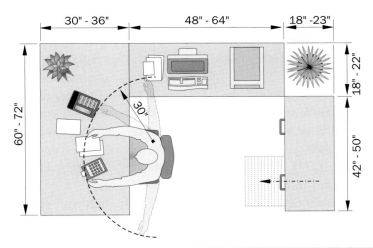

FIGURE 9-6.
Arranging your work area in a home office.

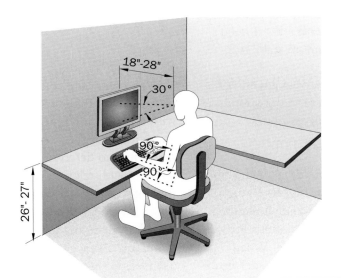

FIGURE 9-7.
Arranging computer workstation in a home office.

computer requires different work surfaces and heights than does a writing desk. Save space with all-in-one office equipment that includes the printer, scanner, fax, and copier. Plan for appropriate grommets, or holes in the work surface, that allow wires to pass through to power and/or connect the office equipment.

Some workstation features that promote comfort and convenience are these:

- **Work surface:** at least 30 inches deep and 5 feet wide with leg room at least 23 inches wide, minimum height from floor: 20 to 28 inches depending on the user's body build and need for

The environment in your home office—including color, airflow, and noise—influences its comfort. An appropriately selected color of paint on your office walls can improve your mood and senses and can make the office area more comfortable and productive. Use an open window or fan (portable or ceiling) to circulate fresh air around the office and diffuse heat from equipment. Control noise with carpeting and acoustical ceiling tiles. To absorb sound, you may also consider various types of wall coverings or partially covered wall panels.

accessibility. Being able to adjust the height would increase the workstation's universality and adaptability.

- **Monitor:** correct height is the top line of the screen at or below eye level with an adjustable tilt to reduce reflections and increase user comfort.
- **Keyboard and mouse:** position 2 to 4 inches from the front edge of the work surface; consider a wrist rest for comfort.
- **Document holder:** adjustable to position work at eye level.
- **Desk chair:** adjustable so thighs are horizontal and feet are firmly on the floor with a five-footed base for maximum stability.

Visit http://www.osha.gov/SLTC/etools/computerworkstations for additional recommendations.

Lighting

Light comes from the sun and from artificial light (light bulbs). Natural lighting is beneficial and should be one of the first considerations for locating your home office. When using natural sunlight, consider how the office is used most frequently. Take into account the use of computers and how glare from the sunlight can affect working conditions. To control glare, select appropriate window treatments, and ensure that your computer screen is either facing a wall without a window or at a right angle to a window.

Artificial lighting for your home office area can come in the form of ambient (such as overhead fixtures), task (such as a desktop lamp), or general (overall lighting from fluorescent tubes). A combination of lighting

prevents eyestrain and heavy shadows. Select glare-free ambient or general lighting. Provide task lighting on document areas without it shining directly on your monitor.

People spending time in front of a computer monitor find that a low-level mix of natural and artificial light with some brighter task lighting for writing is best.

To help with your choices for lighting your home office, consult a lighting specialist or the appropriate literature for the best amount and placement of lighting. For more information about lighting, see **Chapter 15, House Utilities**.

Planning

When planning your office, consider how the office will fit in with the overall home environment, and be sure to check with local authorities to determine how your plan fits with relevant codes such as those governing parking, traffic, and usage. Having a checklist can make the job of planning your office or evaluating a space to convert to an office easier. Most offices need access to the internet. Make sure to have sufficient capacity for the number of computers, phones, fax machines, and other communication lines that may be needed for the office. Be sure to make allowances for future expansion. Having wireless Internet capabilities can allow you to move a laptop computer to other locations in your home.

When planning your home office, consider these strategies:

- To make your office affordable, use existing space that can be converted for your office needs.

- By designing an attractive workspace, you can make your work more enjoyable.
- To ensure that your office is convenient, identify all office tasks and the space you will need to accomplish each.
- Make your office efficient by placing items used the most (computer, phone) within reach.
- Be sure your office has a healthy work environment by determining proper levels of window light, heating and/or air conditioning, and airflow and by selecting furniture that is ergonomically comfortable for your body.

Resources

Ergonomic design and equipment dimensions: http://www.osha.gov/SLTC/etools/computerworkstations

Rosenbaum, A. 1999. *The Complete Home Office*. New York: Viking Studio Books.

Zelinsky, M. 1999. *Practical Home Office Solutions*. New York: McGraw-Hill.

Laundry Areas

NEARLY EVERYONE LIKES TO WEAR FRESH, CLEAN CLOTHING, but it does not stay that way long. It is estimated that every person in the United States generates about a quarter ton of dirty clothes each year, and as a whole, Americans wash 35 billion loads of laundry annually. Thus, every family is faced with clothing care as a continuing challenge. Well-planned space to do the work makes life easier.

This chapter will suggest some points to consider in planning or evaluating a home with regard to clothing care needs. Just think of the processes required for care of clothes and household textiles as well as the equipment and supplies needed! Your list may look like Table 10-1.

Laundry Locations

Now that you have outlined the clothing care tasks, think about where you want to do them. In most 21ˢᵗ century homes, the space devoted to laundering is minimal. No matter how large or small, laundry space can be provided in

When planning for laundry facilities, think about the following:
- Locating laundry facilities close to the hot water and dirty laundry saves energy—both electrical or gas and human.
- The basement may be the least desirable location for a washer and dryer, since all dirty laundry will have to be carried downstairs and up each time it is washed.
- Washers and dryers in a small kitchen (or adjacent closet) may aid multi-tasking of homemaking jobs.
- In some homes, a back or utility entrance includes a "mudroom." In this case, it is handy to have the washer and dryer close by, along with a countertop, hamper, closet, and cabinets for storage.
- Appliance salespeople cannot be certain that appliances will fit unless they have visited your home and measured the space available. Since this is unlikely, it is important that you obtain accurate measurements before you purchase laundry appliances.
- Allow clearance space to open and close appliance doors as well as laundry space (room or closet) doors after the appliances are installed.

Table 10-1. Example of a plan that identifies task, equipment, and supplies needed for the laundering process.

Tasks	Equipment and Supplies Needed
√ Storing dirty items	Hampers, baskets, bins
√ Storing laundering products	Cabinets for detergent, bleach, stain removers, pretreatment sprays, fabric softeners, starch, and water conditioners
√ Sorting clothes before washing by color, soil level, and fiber content	Floor space, baskets, bins, counter space
√ Pretreating stains or presoaking before washing	Sink or basin, counter space, diaper pail
√ Washing	Washing machine; sink or basin to hand wash
√ Drying	Dryer, indoor and/or outdoor lines, drying racks , counter space
√ Iron or steam pressing	Ironing board, iron, distilled water
√ Hanging or folding clean clothes	Garment rack or closet, counter space

Water heaters are often set at 120ºF or 130ºF for the safety of infants and elders, but they may be set higher (140ºF to 160ºF) to allow a greater range of warm temperatures when mixed with cold water. Washing machines usually use a higher proportion of cold than hot water for the "warm" setting. When setting water heater temperatures, consider how cold your water supply is in winter.

many locations in the house or apartment. Frequently laundry space is provided back-to-back or next to the hot water heater, or next to kitchen or bathroom plumbing and electrical wiring. However, utilities can be provided in nearly any location. So, think about the location that will best suit your needs and floor plan. See **Chapter 3, Designing A Home**, for more information on floor plans.

Facilities planned close to the source of hot water and dirty linens and clothes saves energy—both electrical or gas and human. Carrying laundry from one end of the house to another for laundering is a waste of human time and energy. Although water pipes should be well insulated, the less distance the hot water has to go from the water heater to the washer, the warmer the water can be for soil removal.

Basement

The basement may be the least desirable location for a washer and dryer, since all dirty laundry will have to be carried downstairs and up each time it is washed. A laundry chute (16 by 16 inches) in a central hallway will be helpful, especially if the home is two-story, but it must be designed safely and located so that small children and/or pets cannot fall into it (Figure 10-1). The chute helps get the clothes downstairs quickly, but if it is not emptied regularly, clothing may seem "lost" until it is washed and returned to wearable condition. Also, permanent press items that are crushed in the chute are less likely to remain wrinkle free. Furthermore, there is a risk of mildew if damp or sweaty

items are put down the chute, and it is not emptied promptly. If you have a basement laundry, try using a basket for each family member's clothes. Each person can then easily carry his or her own laundered clothes back where they belong.

Bedroom or bath area

The advantage of locating laundry equipment in a bedroom or bath area is that soiled laundry usually is first collected in these places, and many steps and much time is saved. If the washer and dryer are nearby, soiled items do not have to be carried

Clothes are placed into the chute located in the sink cabinet.

Clothes drop straight down to the laundry area below.

**FIGURE 10-1.
Laundry chute.**

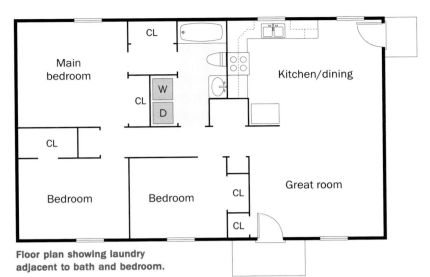

Floor plan showing laundry
adjacent to bath and bedroom.

Washer and dryer behind bi-fold doors.

FIGURE 10-2.
Floor plan with the washer/dryer located in a bathroom closet.

elsewhere for laundering, and family members may be encouraged to do their own wash. The bathroom basin may serve for stain removal and the tub or shower for drip-dry space. The disadvantages may be privacy concerns and the noise that may disrupt sleep when the equipment is running. However, new models are available that are nearly silent and without vibration, and a closet location can do a good job of concealing the appliance (Figure 10-2).

Family living area

Laundry equipment is attractive and does not need to be hidden out of sight. However, if the living area is the only social or public area of the house, you may prefer another location because of clutter that results with laundry tasks and supplies. Review Table 10-1 for space needs. One end of a living area may be designed to serve as a hallway to other areas of the house with laundry equipment installed in a closet there to conserve

space. Ironing tasks may be more pleasant if the ironing board can be set up in an area where family members congregate or watch television.

Halls and closets

Closeted washers and dryers can be installed almost anywhere–off hallways, bedrooms, and kitchens–in small homes or apartments (Figure 10-3). If so, space, such as an overhead cabinet or shelf, is useful to store laundry supplies. Having a full-length closet nearby is useful to hang up clothes after drying. In this situation, sorting may be done on the floor in the hall, but stain removal must be done elsewhere, such as in the bath or kitchen sink. The dining table or bed may be used for folding clean laundry. Think about how laundry tasks in these locations may clash with other family activities, and work on time management to avoid conflict. For example, it may be difficult to fold clothes on a dining table while a teen does school homework there.

FIGURE 10-3.
Floor plan with washer/dryer located in a hall closet.

Kitchen

Washers and dryers in a small kitchen (or adjacent closet) may aid multi-tasking of homemaking jobs, but care must be taken to keep dirty clothes away from food preparation areas so that food safety is not compromised (Figure 10-4). Clothes may be folded on countertops when they are clean. Laundry supplies should be stored out of the reach of small children, perhaps in an overhead cabinet, but safely separate from food.

Mudroom or garage

In some homes, a back or utility entrance includes a "mudroom" with a shower and space for changing out of heavily soiled clothing. In this case, it is handy to have the washer and dryer close by, along with a countertop, hamper, closet, and cabinets for storage. The lavatory or wash basin may serve for stain removal and the shower for indoor drip-dry. The garage may be an

FIGURE 10-4.
Washer/dryer and two closets located near the kitchen.

option for the location of a washer and dryer if the house is small and the weather is warm enough so the water pipes will not freeze. In this case, the water heater may be located right beside the laundry equipment. The garage may have shelves or cabinets for supplies and counter space for sorting and folding clean clothes, but, if not, space for these things and activities must be found elsewhere. Individual laundry baskets or bags for family members, a rolling laundry cart, or a clothes rack may be helpful in hauling items back and forth from where they originate in bedrooms or bath areas.

Measure Space Needs Carefully

Laundry appliances and equipment must fit the space available. Before making a purchase, carefully measure the size of the appliances and also the space in the home needed for installation and repair access. Remember to accurately measure entrances, halls, doors, and stairs as well; appliances may need to pass through them before being installed. If necessary, you can remove hallway or other doors to maneuver the equipment into place without damaging woodwork or walls. Table 10-2 shows typical appliance measurements.

Consider the space, or clearances, needed to open and close appliances as you use them. The design of appliance doors and openings varies greatly. Dryers may have reversible doors that can be mounted to open either right or left. Others have doors that open down and are the full width of the appliance. Washers may have lids on the top or front of the appli-

Table 10-2. Typical appliance measurements in inches.

Appliance	Width (inches)	Height (inches)	Depth* (inches)
Washers	26–27	36–44	25–29
Dryers	26–29	36–43	25–29
Combination unit	23–27	72–76	27–40

*Measurements are based on an average range of several manufacturers' brands and models.

ance and open up—right, left, or back. Allow clearance space to open and close appliance doors as well laundry space (room or closet) doors after the appliances are installed. Allow additional room for body space to bend and access the appliance. If appliances are installed in closets or hallways, bi-fold hallway doors may be needed to close off the area.

Storage cabinets should be installed with adequate clearance also. The space above top-loading appliances must allow clearance for the lid to open fully so that clothes and linens can be loaded and taken out easily. Cabinet doors should not interfere with hallway or other doors to the laundry area.

Dryer Venting

Allow space for dryers to be vented to the outdoors with metal ductwork (Figure 10-5). Venting to the attic or garage is unacceptable because the moisture and lint that is discharged in the drying process should not be trapped in the attic or garage. Exhausts from the clothes dryers may include residue that should not be breathed. For example, gas dryers may expel elevated amounts of carbon dioxide, carbon monoxide, nitrous oxides, and other products of combustion that should never be discharged indoors.

For the best venting, ductwork should not have sharp bends. If the ductwork has too many turns, it may accumulate lint, causing a fire hazard if the dryer continues to operate and emit heat.

The location of the vent on dryers varies, so check both the location of the dryer's vent outlet and the living space outlet to ensure that the ductwork can be installed without too many bends. Check the installation directions before you buy the dryer to ensure that your living space will accommodate the vent duct of the dryer.

Follow the manufacturer's and building code instructions on dryer installation. Dryers have powerful blowers that exhaust air from in-

doors to outdoors. Be sure there is adequate airflow to the dryer. For gas-powered dryers, additional air is needed to furnish combustion air to the gas flame. See **Chapter 15, House Utilities,** for more information about providing adequate ventilation to different areas of the house.

Lack of adequate make-up air can increase the drying time required or cause the clothes dryer or other vented appliances in the house to operate incorrectly. The most serious danger is backdrafting of vented fuel-burning appliances caused by blower operation. Check to make certain that all appliances vent correctly when the clothes dryer is operating.

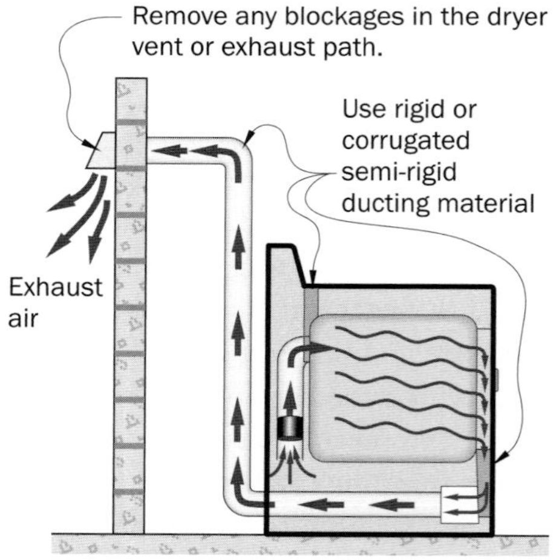

Equipment Selection

The consumer market for laundry appliances changes rapidly. Manufacturers frequently offer innovative products to stay competitive in an international marketplace and have detailed websites that compare features among the various models they offer at different price levels. Table 10-3 shows web addresses of major appliance manufacturers in the United States. Additionally, most of these websites have information on stain removal and other laundering questions.

It is important to compare features, costs, energy requirements, and space required before you buy appliances. *Consumer Reports* frequently offers a "best value" assessment and outlines differences in performance among brands. *Home Appliance Magazine* provides a summary of innovative features offered by various manufacturers.

Remove any blockages in the dryer vent or exhaust path.

Use rigid or corrugated semi-rigid ducting material

Exhaust air

**FIGURE 10-5.
Dryer venting system.**

Figure modified from a U.S. Consumer Product Safety Commission drawing on a dryer venting system.

Table 10- 3. Web addresses of U.S. laundry equipment manufacturers.

Amana:	www.amana.com
Frigidaire:	www.frigidaire.com
General Electric:	www.geappliances.com
Kenmore:	www.kenmore.com
Maytag:	www.maytag.com
Roper:	www.roperappliances.com
Whirlpool:	www.whirlpool.com

FIGURE 10-6.
Washing machine touch panel controls.

Washers and dryers are often purchased as a set, with matching control panels and coordinated design, but each can be purchased separately. The basic models have fewer cycles and settings than the top-of-the-line models. The latter are usually computer controlled with preprogrammed cycles, but also may let you create additional programs to suit your needs. When the "mother board" or main computer control panel fails, it is usually replaced rather than repaired. If a problem occurs shortly after purchase, have it checked promptly so that the replacement or repair may be covered by warranty.

Computer touch panel controls provide a variety of options for presoak, wash time, temperature, spin, cool-down, and rinse cycles, but similar options exist for models that use knobs or buttons for controls (Figure 10-6). Computer controls on some models may be set to delay starting time. When controls are knobs, notice if they can be turned either way without disrupting the machine cycles. When controls may only be turned one direction, they

may be damaged and require repair if they are turned the wrong way.

Most appliance models have sound signals (perhaps with adjustable volumes) to alert you to the end of the wash or dry cycle. The dryer signal allows you to hang clothing promptly, reducing wrinkling and avoiding the need for ironing, which saves energy and your time.

Washing machines

An important choice as you purchase a washing machine is whether it will be top or front loading. Top-loading machines are available in high-efficiency models that are designed to conserve energy at a level similar to front-loading or horizontal axis machines (Figure 10-7). Table 10-4 compares top- and front-loading machines.

Most washers have automatic timed or programmed cycles for

In accordance with U.S. Environmental Protection Agency and U.S. Department of Energy guidelines, appliances must be labeled to show their energy efficiency. Washers and dryers may earn the Energy Star label. To qualify for this label, appliances are compared using the Modified Energy Factor (MEF) that measures the energy used to heat the water, wash, and dry a load of laundry. The U.S. Federal Standard MEF is 1.04. The higher the MEF, the more efficient the equipment is. Energy Star washers use less water per load than conventional washers did before the U.S. energy standards went into effect; currently, only 18 and 25 gallons are common. The lower the Water Factor, the less water the machine uses. Energy Star washers extract more water during the spin cycle, reducing drying time. For detailed comparisons among models by various manufacturers, see http://www.energystar.gov/. Although the initial cost of appliances is related to features, cycles, and controls, the ongoing cost of the energy required to run the equipment should be a primary concern.

knits, permanent press, regular, and/ or heavy-duty washing, but some models offer a wider variety of combination settings. Wash and rinse temperature and water level controls help you to manage and reduce water use to fit the size and type of wash load. To aid in sanitation, newly designed washers can heat water up to 205°F.

Separate, independent soak and rinse cycles are convenient for cold-water soaking items such as diapers or other items with protein stains such as blood or mud on sports uniforms. Built-in bleach and fabric softener dispensers help maximize the benefit of the additives by automatically releasing them at the appropriate time in the wash cycle. The load capacity of washers, in cubic feet, is stated with the appliance specifications because the washing load weight varies with the fiber content of the fabrics in the wash load.

Front loaders may be placed on storage platforms so that you do not need to bend over to take clothes in and out (Figure 10-8). If so, they require more vertical space.

Table 10-4. Comparison of top- and front-loading washers.

Top Loaders	Front Loaders—Horizontal axis
Variety of brands, models; lower cost	Fewer brands, models; higher initial cost
Uses more water/energy	Uses least water/energy
Center agitator or wash plate*	Tumbler system
Soak cycles available	No soak option
Spin extracts less water; may go off balance	Spin extracts more water; shorter dry time
Uses regular detergent	Requires high-efficiency, low-suds detergent
Capacity = 3–7 cu. ft. (12–16 lbs.)	Capacity = 3–7.5 cu ft. (12–20 lbs.)

Sources: *Consumer Reports* and *Home Appliance Magazine*.
*High-efficiency top loaders usually cost more than other machines

**FIGURE 10-7.
Top-loading washing machine.**

Photo courtesy Maytag Corporation

**FIGURE 10-8.
Front-loading washing machine on platform.**

Photo courtesy Maytag Corporation

Most washers are durable but certain items like a heavy throw rug may be better to take to a commercial Laundromat to avoid repairs on your home washer.

Dryers

Both gas and electric-powered dryers are available in many brands and models of dryers, with gas often costing more. When deciding about a dryer, consider the utility costs in your geographic region because repeated cost of operation may be more important than purchase price. Energy consumption differences among dryers are less than among washers because water heating is not involved.

Dryers may have controls to set drying time, degree of dryness of the load, or a combination. Most have an air fluff or non-heating cycle that is useful for removing dust or lint. Some have a drying rack for items such as washable canvas shoes.

Drying centers include tumble dryers and a separate drying box or cabinet with space for hanging permanent press clothes or spreading dry-flat items on a horizontal screen. Vertical space required for these centers may be nearly double that of the ordinary dryer.

Combination units

Many apartments and condominiums have a *laundry center* or combination unit with a small washer that has a dryer stacked above it (Figure 10-9). These units can be installed in locations with less width but require about double the vertical space as a standard unit. Although the combination units usually have lower capacity, they may be sufficient for empty-nest families or single individuals.

All-in-one washer/dryer combination units are ventless and fit well in very small spaces. Using only nine gallons of water and a condensation drying system in which hot air is condensed to liquid that is pumped out a discharge hose, one model measures 33 inches high, 23.5 inches wide, and 24 inches deep.

Line drying

If you install a clothesline in your back yard or on a porch, be sure it is safely marked and high enough that people can walk under it. Outdoor drying lines can be mounted from a corner of the house to a tree or on special poles. If lines are left up at night, they must be identified with white or reflective materials, so that anyone who comes into the yard can see the line.

Many people prefer line drying to dryer drying because it costs less in utility bills. Even if you do not line dry all of the time, you can save energy by line drying rugs and heavy items. Some items, such as electric blankets, can only be line dried because the tumbling and heat of automatic dryers can damage the blanket's wiring and its insulation.

FIGURE 10-9.
Washer/dryer stacked combination unit.

In some areas of the country, particularly rural areas but also in areas where lawn chemicals are used, safety in laundry includes correct care of pesticide-soiled clothing. This clothing should be stored separately from family clothing in a "throwaway" box or bag until it is washed. It must be washed separately from family clothing. The storage box or bag should be disposed of with pesticide containers at the end of the pesticide-use season in accordance with hazardous waste guidelines for your area. If pesticide application is an annual or more frequent activity in your family, having a laundry area in a mudroom may be ideal.

Indoor line drying is also energy saving, if lines can be installed in dry, little-used large rooms. In space that is already damp or prone to mildew, indoor line drying probably is not a good choice. Drying time will be longer and clothes may sour. Indoor line drying may be good for small, quick-drying nylon or polyester items that will dry overnight and not require ironing. You can find small, foldable clothes drying racks at most discount stores.

Ironing

Thanks to synthetic fabrics and permanent press finishes, ironing clothes is not the chore it once was. However, natural fabrics like linen and cotton may still need to be *touched up*. If space permits, leaving the ironing board up all of the time is a very convenient practice. Do not leave the board up if young children are around on a consistent basis. At a minimum, a space for an ironing board is about 4.5 by 6 feet. Choose an iron with an automatic switch that turns it off if it sits a while. For safety, irons should be unplugged when not in use because most clothing and fabrics are flammable.

If your family has a lot of ironing, it may be more appealing to move the task into a room where other family members are likely to be. Fold-up ironing boards built into a wall are not very common, but if located in a convenient spot, they can be very useful and save space. Appliance manufacturers now offer ironing centers that can be built into cabinets

with storage space for the board, iron, spray starch, and distilled water.

Create Pleasant, Safe Laundry Areas

Laundry areas do not have to be dull, dreary, and characterless. You can add interest to your laundry space through use of lighting, color schemes, wall hangings, photos, or artistic prints even if the space is small. If you have a window, you can use colorful blinds or curtains to manage the light and bring cheer. Laundry baskets, bins, and clothes hampers are available commercially in countless colors and designs. They also can be fashioned from boxes spray-painted or covered with paper and lined with plastic bags. Shelves and cabinets for laundry supplies may be painted to fit your color scheme.

Plan to make laundering a family-centered activity. Organize space and tasks so that laundry equipment and supplies are in handy places and all family members can enjoy helping. Young children can bring their own dirty clothes to the washer and can learn to help sort dark clothes from light clothes before they are washed. Children can help match up socks and fold small items. Older children and teens need to learn to do laundry in preparation for being on their own, whether in college or elsewhere.

Remember that safety means storing all laundry supplies out of the reach of small children. Also, it is important to turn off irons when they are not in use.

Resources

Association of Home Appliance Manufacturers, *AHAM Guide to NAECA* (National Appliance Energy Conservation Act). Available for online purchase at: http://www.aham.org/ht/d/ProductDetails/sku/NAECA/from/706

Association of Home Appliance Manufacturers. *2003 Major Appliance Fact Book CD*. Available for purchase online at: http://www.aham.org/ht/d/Store/name/FACTBOOK

Association of Home Appliance Manufacturers, News Release: "*Historic Energy Policy Act Applauded By Appliance Manufacturing Industry.*" Available online at: http://www.aham.org/ht/d/Releases/pid/323

Consumer Product Safety Commission, *Overheated Clothes Dryers Can Cause Fires,* CPSC Document 5022, Available online at: www.cpsc.gov/cpscpub/pubs/5022.html

Consumer Reports, *How to Choose Washing Machines*. Available online at: http://www.consumerreports.org/cro/appliances/washing-machines/washing-machines/how-to-choose.htm

Consumer Reports, *How to Choose Clothes Dryers*. Available online at: http://www.consumerreports.org/cro/appliances/clothes-dryers/clothes-dryers/how-to-choose.htm

EPA and DOE, *EnergyStar Products, Clothes Washers.* Available online at: http://www.energystar.gov/index.cfm?c=clotheswash.pr_clothes_washers

Home Appliance Magazine, Washers, Dryers and Combination Laundry Appliances. Laundry– Clean and Simple. Available online at: www.appliance.com/laundry/editorial.php?article=780&zone=1113&first=1

Maytag Corporation, 403 W. 4th St. N., Newton, Iowa 50208. Information available at: http://www.maytag.com

Procter and Gamble, detergent and consumer product manufacturer. http://www.pg.com/main.jhtml

Ratcliff, K., K. Curroto, and R. Szczechowsxi, Red, White, and Sacre Bleu, *Mary Engelbreit's Home Companion,* June-July 2005, pp. 76-77.

Sears, retail source of many appliance brands http://www.sears.com/sr/javasr/vertical.do?BV_UseBVCookie=Yes&vertical=APPL

Soap and Detergent Association. Information available online at: http://www.sdahq.org and http://www.cleaning101.com/laundry. A free e-mail newsletter is available at: http://www.cleaning101.com/cleaningmatters/newsletter

CHAPTER 11

Garages

A GARAGE SHELTERS AND SECURES A FAMILY'S VEHICLES but also can provide multiple-use storage space. Some communities require garages for vehicles and have ordinances that prohibit parking on the streets overnight. Determine how you want to use the garage and plan the type, location, and size accordingly.

Garages provide shelter for a vehicle and its passengers, reduce time spent scraping frost and removing snow, and help maintain a vehicle's finish. Garages keep rain and dust off of a vehicle or other equipment stored in the garage, which reduces corrosion and deterioration. They extend the life of a vehicle by protecting the vehicle's finish and exterior and interior materials from ultra-violet light that fades and deteriorates plastics, fabric, and rubber. Besides protecting your vehicle, garages help protect your house against winter wind and snow as well as summer heat and rain. Garages also can provide storage space and room for shop and other hobby activities.

In parts of the U.S. where winter temperatures that fall below freezing are not a problem, it is common for furnaces, water heaters, and laundry appliances to be installed in the garage rather than inside the house.

Types

The two main types of garages are attached and detached. As the terms imply, an attached garage is connected to the house and a detached garage is not.

Most new homes are built with attached garages. Homeowners prefer the convenience, increased security, and weather protection afforded by an attached garage. However, carbon monoxide from vehicle exhaust and pollutants from fuel and other stored chemicals can leak from an attached garage into the house, affecting indoor air quality. Some building codes require garage floor levels to be several inches below the level of the house floor. The belief is that a step prevents the dangerous, heavier-than-air carbon monoxide fumes from passing through the connecting door into the house. In theory, this design could work, but it will not prevent fumes from passing from the garage to the house when a large amount of carbon monoxide has accumulated.

Air transfer from an attached garage into a house can be minimized by tightly sealing walls and doors to the house and by using an exhaust fan in the garage. Installing a carbon monoxide detector in the house is a good way to determine if fumes from the garage are seeping into the house and affecting indoor air quality. Never install carbon monoxide detectors in a garage because extreme temperature variations that can occur in a garage can cause the detectors to operate improperly.

Carbon Monoxide Poisoning

Carbon monoxide (CO) is a colorless, odorless, poisonous gas. It is produced by the incomplete burning of solid, liquid, and gaseous fuels. Running vehicles produce carbon monoxide.

Carbon monoxide is dangerous and can be fatal. Flu-like symptoms often accompany carbon monoxide poisoning, such as:

- Headache.
- Fatigue.
- Shortness of breath.
- Nausea.
- Dizziness.

A fever will not be a symptom of carbon monoxide poisoning. If you think you are experiencing any of the symptoms of carbon monoxide poisoning, get fresh air immediately; otherwise, you could lose consciousness and die. In addition, contact a doctor immediately. Tell your doctor that you suspect carbon monoxide poisoning.

To minimize the potential of carbon monoxide poisoning, **NEVER leave a vehicle running in an attached garage, even when the garage door is open.**

Continued

A running engine produces such high concentrations of carbon monoxide so quickly that people may become dizzy and collapse before they even realize they are being poisoned. When you plan to leave a vehicle running, always back it out of the garage, or connect a pipe or hose that will direct the emissions at least 10 feet outside the garage. Vehicle emissions tend to settle in the garage area and can eventually seep into the house. It can take several hours for carbon monoxide emissions to dissipate from a garage after a vehicle has been running inside of it.

Attached garages also can cause security concerns. Unwanted people oftentimes access a house through the garage. If you have an attached garage, be sure to install and use locks on doors to prevent entry into the house.

For health and security reasons, a detached garage may be desirable. When the garage is kept separate from the house, dangerous fumes cannot enter, and unwanted people cannot gain access to the house through the garage. A detached garage connected to the house by a covered, open air breezeway also promotes accessibility, because the garage floor, house floor, and connecting breezeway are on a common level.

Location

Whether attached or detached, the garage is usually placed near the service entry to the house. The garage area can serve as the entry court to the house, with both guest and service doors accessible from the driveway. When a driveway is long or merges into a busy street, a turn-around area not only may be desirable, it may be necessary. The driver needs to be able to see that the driveway is clear of people and obstructions. See **Chapter 4, Selecting a Location or a Building Site,** for more information about driveways and parking.

By considering the prevailing winds when you orient your garage, you can sometimes protect the house from winter winds without blocking summer breezes. Careful consideration of location also prevents you from inadvertently blocking a picturesque view from within the house.

You can use a garage to buffer your house from your neighbors, but do not locate the garage where it will take up a lot of valuable yard space. You may have to sacrifice some yard space so you can have a garage, but try to locate the garage to the side of the yard space that is available instead of in the middle of it.

Size

When determining the appropriate size for your garage, consider the number of vehicles that household members drive as well as large recreational or yard equipment, for example, boats, campers, bicycles, motorcycles, golf carts, lawn mowers, and snow blowers, that will be kept in the garage. Incorporate space for a shop, storage, and other planned uses. Nowadays, the third bay in a garage is often reserved for a mechanical or wood shop or for storing miscellaneous equipment and other items. Keep in mind that you may have a small vehicle now, but you may have a larger vehicle later. In addition, if you sell your property, having a large garage can be a good selling point. For these reasons, building a small, single garage that will accommodate only one vehicle is seldom advisable.

Figures 11-1, 11-2, and 11-3 provide dimensions for a one-, two-, and three-car garage. A minimum double garage is 20 feet by 22 feet, but a 24-foot by 24-foot garage is preferable to facilitate the opening of doors, maneuvering around the vehicle, and accessing the storage areas. Increase the size if more storage or work space is needed. The dimensions in the drawings are for typical, full-sized vehicles, which are usually about 6-1/2 feet wide and 17 to 19 feet long. As you are planning your garage, you would do well to check the exterior dimensions of your vehicles as listed by the manufacturers.

Storage and Work Areas

Garages can serve as storage areas for recreational equipment, garden equipment, outdoor furniture, and bulk chemicals. The storage area is generally on the side or back walls or suspended from the ceiling. Less frequently, garages contain a full attic or loft above the ceiling expressly for storage. Closets, shelves, cabinets, and hooks help organize the storage area. To simplify cleaning, you may want to keep cabinets off the floor. Limit garage storage to items that are

When constructing a garage, consider building in a floor stop for the front wheels of any vehicle. This helps to protect the rear wall of the garage.
Also, slope the floors slightly (1% or 1/4-inch per foot) toward the overhead door so water drains out of the garage.

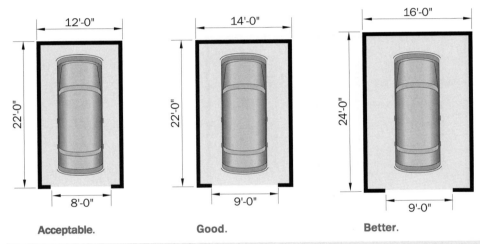

Acceptable.   Good.   Better.

FIGURE 11-1.
Dimensions for one-car garage.

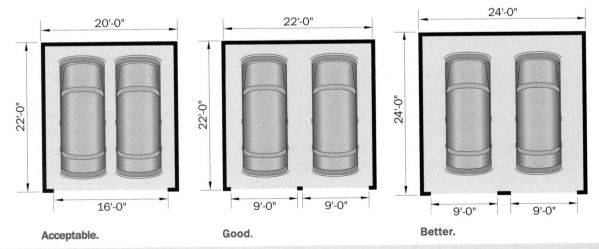

Acceptable.   Good.   Better.

FIGURE 11-2.
Dimensions for two-car garage.

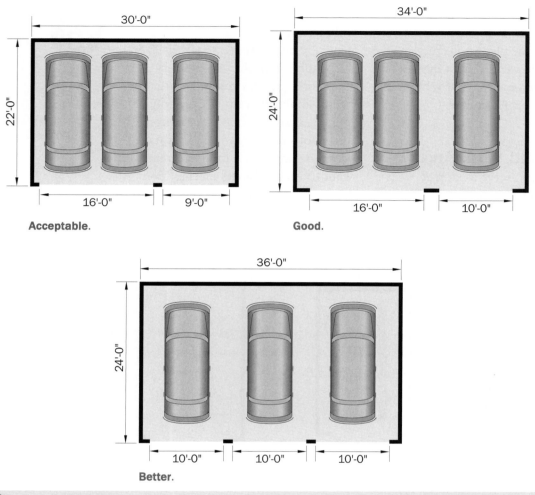

Acceptable.

Good.

Better.

FIGURE 11-3.
Dimensions for three-car garage.

used outdoors and that can handle dusty conditions. Avoid storing items that cannot tolerate extreme temperature and humidity variations in a garage.

Numerous configurations are possible for garage storage areas. Prefabricated storages are available that can be located either inside or outside the garage for yard and garden equipment such as lawn mowers, rototillers, and gasoline-powered appliances.

Garages can double as a workspace for people who like to do basic vehicle repairs and maintenance and fix small items. Some homeowners also use garage areas for woodworking or other hobbies. Consider your needs and the possible needs of future owners when considering whether or not to incorporate storage and work space into your garage. If you do want to use part of your garage for a work area, be sure to allow sufficient space to maneuver between workbenches and vehicles. Workbenches should be designed to be at least 24 inches wide; preferably 30 inches. Allow for 24 to 36 inches of space between the bench and vehicle to allow for enough room to work at the bench.

Doors

In new double garages, install 16- or 18-foot wide overhead doors. In older garages, two 9-foot doors side-by-side are common. An electric door opener is very handy, especially in inclement weather and is a necessity to meet the needs of universal design.

For convenience, include at least one walk-in door, eliminating the need to open the big door and providing access to a rear yard. Select doors that blend with the style of the house. If you draw attention to a walk-in door, it may encourage visitors to use it instead of the guest entry. Keep in mind that an overhead door may not meet code exit requirements. To ensure accessibility, make sure walk-in doors have a clear opening width of at least 32 inches.

Carports

Carports, which can be low-cost alternatives to garages, provide overhead shelter for vehicles but are not enclosed, offering garage-like space that does not completely block light or breezes (Figure 11-4). Like garages, carports also can serve as storage areas. Note that carports are good alternatives to garages in areas of the country where winters are not severe; however, they do not provide the same level of cold-weather protection and convenience as a garage does.

Wheelchair Accessibility

To make your garage wheelchair accessible, consider the following variables:
- Floor size.
- Overhead clearance.
- Changes in garage floor level.

Fully accessible garages require power-operated overhead doors. Accessible garages may need to be larger than standard garages if space

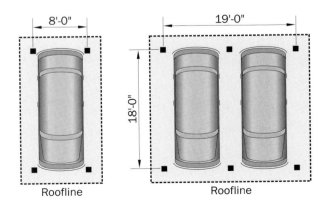

FIGURE 11-4.
Dimensions for one- and two-car car-ports.

is allotted for a ramp and for an access aisle to accommodate lifts or open vehicle doors. Depending on the lift and type of vehicle, plan to incorporate a 5- to 8-foot wide access aisle beside or between vehicles.

Provide more overhead clearance, that is, extra height, for a van fitted with a lift. Likewise, vans equipped with raised roofs may be as high as 8 feet and not fit in garages having standard ceiling heights and entrance doors. If you allow at least 6 inches for clearance, the ceiling height and/or door opening height may need to be as much as 9 feet. Before establishing a minimum overhead clearance, first determine the dimensions of the vehicles likely to be used.

As an alternative to a ramp, consider sloping the entire garage floor from the vehicle entrance door up to the house floor level. This continuously sloping floor provides a more uniform, gently sloping surface. With a sloping garage floor, you will need to install through-the-wall vents at the bottom of the slope to release any fumes that might accumulate in the garage. Before building a sloping floor, check this solution with local authorities to be sure that it conforms to local building codes.

Resources

Ideal Garage Plans —Tips: http://www.askthebuilder.com/B271_Ideal_Garage_Plans_-_Tips.shtml

Designing for garages and pantries: http://www.closetsmagazine.com/0408/designdirections.cfm

Vehicular Transportation and Parking. 1991. Raleigh, North Carolina: The Center for Universal Design, North Carolina State University. Publication number TP #8.00.

CHAPTER 12

Entries, Doors, Halls, and Stairs

THE PLACEMENT AND DIMENSIONS of entrances and hallways help direct traffic flow. Well-placed, adequate entries and hallways also allow convenient, efficient use of space. Careful attention to the placement and dimensions of halls, stairs, and doors influences construction costs and prevents safety hazards.

Entries

A well-designed house entrance should invite people into the house, provide basic protection from the weather, and allow for safe entry into the house (Figure 12-1). Pathways to house entrances should be smooth, well lit, and

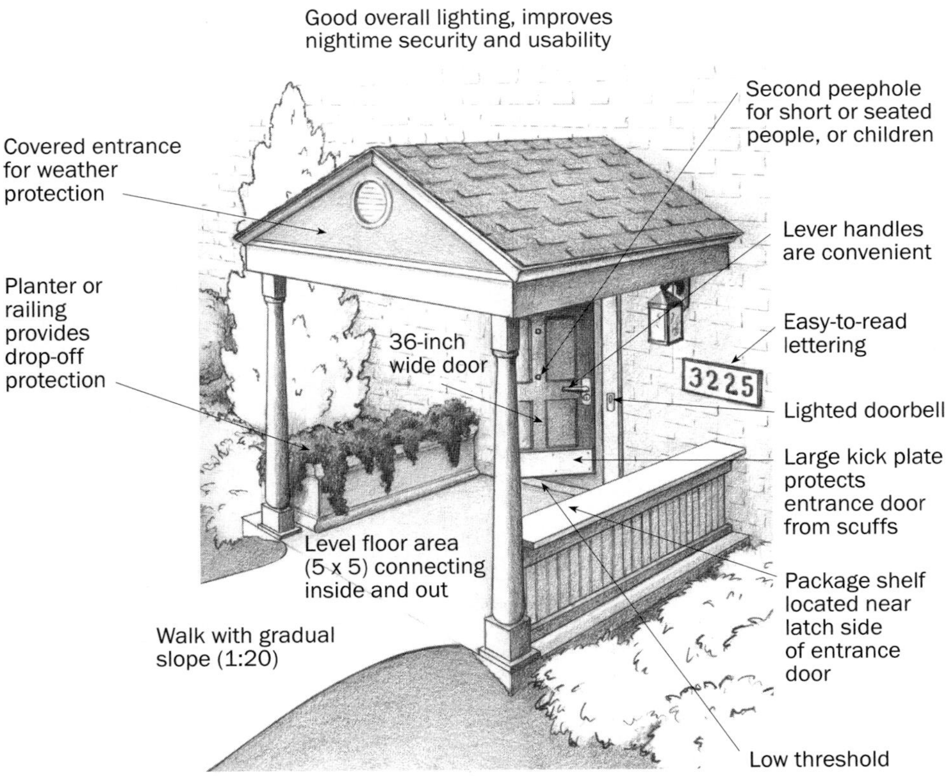

Good overall lighting, improves nightime security and usability

Second peephole for short or seated people, or children

Covered entrance for weather protection

Lever handles are convenient

Planter or railing provides drop-off protection

36-inch wide door

Easy-to-read lettering

3225

Lighted doorbell

Large kick plate protects entrance door from scuffs

Level floor area (5 x 5) connecting inside and out

Package shelf located near latch side of entrance door

Walk with gradual slope (1:20)

Low threshold

FIGURE 12-1.
An inviting, safe, and accessible home entrance.

Based on *A Welcoming Home* (PM1804) http://www.extension.iastate.edu/Publications/PM1804.pdf.

Sometimes planners get so wrapped up in thinking about the larger social and work spaces in a home that they forget about the equally important smaller spaces that make a home function well. As you plan your house, don't neglect to consider entries, doors, halls, and stairs. The basic concepts listed below may help you focus your thinking about these important areas.

- Guest entrances work best near rooms used for social activities.
- A service entrance close to the parking area with direct access to work areas is very convenient.
- In a typical house, exterior doors lose more heat in the winter and gain more in the summer than any other part of the structure. For this reason, they need to fit well and be tightly sealed in all seasons.
- Exterior entry doors should be selected on the basis of appearance and function, keeping in mind that they need to withstand the elements as well as protect the interior from leaks and drafts.

Continued

- When open, an interior doorway should have 32 inches minimum clear opening; 36 inches is preferable.
- For maximum energy efficiency, limit the total floor space used as a hall to between 6 and 8 percent of the total square footage.
- Local building codes regulate the construction of stairs.
- Use two light fixtures, one at the top and one at the bottom of stairs.
- For safety reasons, stair steps need to be a uniform depth and height.
- On stairways, the minimum headroom between the top of a step and the ceiling should be 6 feet 8 inches.
- Straight stairs with straight entries and exits are the easiest to climb.

gently slope away from the house at a 1-foot drop in elevation for every 20 feet of horizontal distance (1:20). The approach to the house should be landscaped and graded so the entrance does not require stairs. Entries need a 36-inch wide door with an easy-to-open lever handle. A minimum 5-foot by 5-foot staging area or porch outside the door needs to be covered, edge-protected, and well lit. A carefully and attractively planned entrance with these features welcomes everyone, provides a smooth transition between inside and outside, and safely shelters individuals waiting outside for transportation.

The entry into the house should:
- Provide protection from weather.
- Be well lit.
- Enable visitors to be seen without the door being opened.
- Have a sturdy door that is at least 36 inches wide.

- Have a lever handle on the door.
- Not have any steps or barriers that could result in tripping or falling.
- Be near a coat closet upon entry.

Sidewalks, steps, and porches

Make the approach to a house inviting and safe. To make a house accessible, provide at least one no-step entrance (Figure 12-2). The guest entry sidewalk should accommodate two people side by side, and the steps should be comfortable (Table 12-1). If an entry sidewalk is wheelchair accessible or designed to be used by people with disabilities, a closed, covered entry is a good option, especially in areas where inclement weather and rain or snow can severely limit access. The porch, or stoop, at the door should be large enough to accommodate people with canes, crutches, or wheelchairs and to

FIGURE 12-2.
No-step entry.

Table 12-1. Sidewalk, step, and porch dimensions.

Location	Dimension	
	Recommended	Minimum
Sidewalk to guest entry width	5 feet	4 feet
Other sidewalks	4 feet	3 feet
Steps*	7-inch rise, 11-inch run	6-inch rise, 12-inch tread
Porches	5 x 5 feet	4 x 4 feet

* Design steps based on: (2)(rise) + (run) = 25 ± 1. The rise and run measurements are in inches.

allow a screen or storm door to open out. If remodeling an entry requires installing a ramp for accessibility, experts recommend that a railing be installed on both sides of a ramp or sloped walkway.

Guest and service entries

Entries can be planned according to their intended purpose; two common types are guest and service. The guest entrance should be readily identifiable to visitors and be convenient, attractive, and accessible to all. A guest entrance located near the center of the house encourages efficient interior traffic flow. Guest entrances work best near rooms used for social activities, but keep in mind that furniture arrangement is easier with an entry at the end of a room rather than centered. The entry should provide enough space for a person inside the house to open the door and step back (Figure 12-3). A closet for guests' and family members' outerwear is handy near the guest entry; a closet just beyond the entry door is more convenient that one directly behind the opened door. Figure 12-4 shows how entry closets can relate to the entrance door.

A service entrance close to the parking area with direct access to

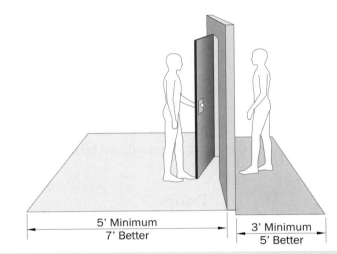

5' Minimum
7' Better

3' Minimum
5' Better

FIGURE 12-3.
Entry dimensions.

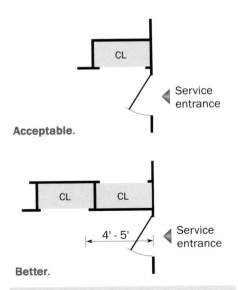

CL

Service entrance

Acceptable.

CL   CL

4' - 5'

Service entrance

Better.

FIGURE 12-4.
Closet-entry door relationships.

Wood doors may be manufactured in various grades of quality and/or performance. For example, flush wood doors can be obtained in "premium," "custom," or "economy" grades; the selection of the grade depends on the finish. An opaque painted finish can cover the wood grain defects in the surface veneer in an economy grade door; if you want a transparent finish or stain, select a higher-grade door.

work areas is very convenient for carrying in supplies. Ready access to bathroom facilities is important for children coming in from outdoor play and family members returning from work (Figure 12-5). Especially in cold climates, provide a room, (often called a mudroom or a family foyer) for putting on and taking off outerwear with a chair or bench for putting on boots and assisting children. This is also convenient place for a rack with a drip pan for shoes, boots, and umbrellas. Make sure air can circulate to dry damp coats and shoes. Having a storage area in this entry location provides a convenient place to store or keep in a safe location such items as sports equipment, school backpacks, car keys, outgoing mail, and recycling materials.

Doors

Door manufacturers may belong to one or more national manufacturers associations. The National Wood Window and Door Association, for

example, issues a label ensuring that the design and manufacture of products have been tested, and that performance of the product meets or exceeds the appropriate standard. The certification of quality is based on periodic inspection of manufacturing facilities, quality control at the facilities, and laboratory testing of the finished units. To make the best choice of doors for your home, become acquainted with appropriate industry standards and compare options. The following sections discuss the two main types of doors: exterior and interior.

Exterior entry doors

Exterior entry doors should be selected on the basis of appearance and function, including weather tightness, insulation, dimensional stability, sound privacy, fire rating, and security.

Exterior doors need to withstand the elements as well as protect the interior from leaks and drafts. A

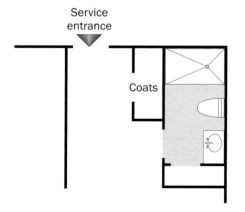

Service entry and bath.

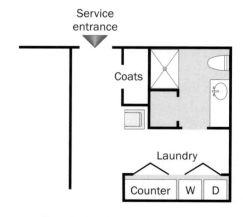

Service entry, bath, and laundry

FIGURE 12-5.
Service entries.

secure, energy-efficient door is made from solid heavy wood or insulating foam covered by metal or fiberglass with an equally sturdy insulated, sealed frame bolted into solid blocking with long screws. In choosing doors, select from doors with weather stripping systems that seal reliably over a wide range of temperature conditions. Unless a wood entry door is specifically rated as weather resistant, you will need to install a storm door for extra protection.

Using an airlock (Figure 12-6) will conserve energy in the home. Nonbreakable safety glass in door windows and sidelights floods the entrance with natural light. Two peepholes, one for standing adults and one for seated people and children, allow residents to identify visitors.

Install lever handles (Figure 12-7). They are easier to operate with one hand or an elbow. A solid kick plate at the bottom of exterior doors protects door finishes from moving dollies, strollers, and wheel chairs.

A mudroom or utility room might serve as an airlock at a service entry.

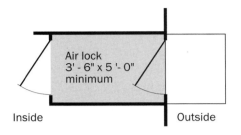

Air lock
3' - 6" x 5 '- 0" minimum

Inside   Outside

A mudroom or utility room might serve as an airlock at a service entry.

FIGURE 12-6.
Airlock to conserve energy.

FIGURE 12-7.
Door with a lever handle.

When planning or remodeling, consider including a low-threshold exit door in bedrooms to facilitate emergency egress.

Interior doors

Interior doors should be substantial to ensure privacy and to block out unwanted sound and light. Solid-core doors are durable and provide privacy and protection from fire. Hollow-core doors are economical and may be adequate for closets. Whenever possible, eliminate thresholds and install lever handles. If thresholds are installed, they should be less than 1/4 inch high with no beveled edges, or 1/2-inch high with edges beveled.

Wide interior doorways provide easier movement for everyone,

enhance interior circulation, and add a spacious, open feeling to rooms. Interior doors are most convenient when located at the corner of a room. They should open into the room and swing 90 degrees against the wall. When open, an interior doorway should have a 32-inch minimum clear opening; 36 inches is preferable. In older homes with narrow doors, consider installing swing-away hinges to allow the door to open past the hinge. Where there is not enough space for the door to swing open, a pocket door that fits into a cavity in the wall can be used instead of a conventional door, making a small room appear more spacious. See Figure 3-11 for examples of swing-away hinges and pocket doors.

In choosing interior doors, you will find that the most common and least expensive interior doors, by far, are hollow-core wood or wood composite doors. The traditional solid stile-and-rail door made of clear-grained lumber is attractive and durable, with good sound-reduction characteristics; however, the cost of such manufactured doors is much higher than the cost of alternatives. Consider engineered-wood doors (composite cores with wood veneer) that provide nearly the same appearance and all the functional advantages of stile-and-rail doors. In some applications, soundproofing may be a consideration for interior door selection. When this is

the case, remember that soundproofing requires reduction of noise transmission through air channels (all of the gaps among the door, the frame, and the floor) as well as through solid material.

Halls

Hallways need to be 36 to 48 inches wide (Figure 12-8). Wide halls accommodate strollers and wheelchairs, facilitate the moving of furniture in and out, and permit wall decorations. Good planning can encourage dual use of corridor space by locating storage and bookcases along hallways, preferably built-in storage and bookcases. Straight halls are preferable; long hallways that turn corners can waste interior space. A planning goal for space efficiency is to limit the total floor space used as halls to between 6 and 8 percent of the total square footage.

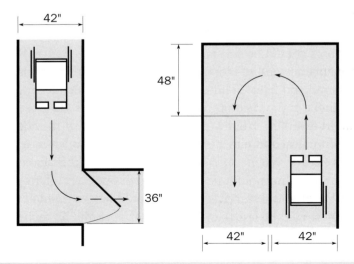

FIGURE 12-8.
Hall and door widths.

Stairs

Because stairs provide access between levels, the only homes without stairs are ranch-style buildings without a basement. Otherwise, all homes have stairs. Local building codes regulate the construction of stairways, so you will need to consult local building officials about code requirements for stairs while planning your new house or your remodeling project. The basic criteria for the design of safe, easy-to-use stairs include appropriate, consistent rise and run, functional handrails, good visibility, and excellent lighting.

Stairs require careful, prudent planning to ensure safety. Determine the actual opening after setting the ceiling heights. Set the actual dimensions for run and rise after the house is partially built and after measuring the exact story height and floor thickness. Cantilevered, open, and hanging stairs are often included in open-floor plans; however, some people may feel uncomfortable on open stairs.

For safety reasons, stairs need uniform riser heights and uniform tread widths (Table 12-2 and Figure 12-9). Safe, comfortable stairs match the strides of the residents. Risers should be sloped, or the underside should have an angle not less than 60 degrees from the horizontal. Stair treads should be no less than 11 inches wide from riser to riser. Smaller risers are easier to climb but require more floor space and larger floor openings to maintain headroom. The stairway should allow a minimum of 6 feet 6 inches (6 feet 8 inches is preferable) of headroom between the top of a step and the ceiling. If rise is increased, decrease tread width to avoid tripping over the nosing. The undersides of nosings should not be abrupt. Finally, nosings should project no more than 1-1/2 inches past the riser.

Avoid tapered treads; the outer portion needs to be wide enough for the user to feel safe and comfortable. Select dense, high-friction floor coverings for the treads, making them a color that contrasts with the risers.

These dimensions duplicate stair dimensions in public buildings. Consistency between public and home stair dimensions makes sense; the dimensions facilitate safe stair climbing for both young and older residents. The total floor space required for a stairway depends on tread width, riser height, stair opening width, headroom, and stair types. In general, during house planning, allow for a floor opening about 12 feet long and 4 feet wide to accommodate a stairwell, plus space for a landing if needed.

Straight stairs with straight entries and exits are the easiest to climb, especially when carrying objects. However, landings provide a resting place and reduce the distance a person could fall. If necessary, stairs can turn 180 degrees (a U turn) or 90 degrees (a right angle turn) at a landing (Figure 12-10. Doors that open onto a stair landing are safety hazards. Plan for doors to swing into rooms instead of onto stairs or landings.

All building codes require the installation of handrails and/or guardrails. Handrails help people steady themselves; they should be sturdy (1-1/2 inches in diameter) and easy to grasp (round or oval, no more than 1 1/2 inches from the wall). Handrails should be mounted between 30 and 38 inches above the

Table 12-2. Riser effect on stairwell size.
9'-0" total rise, 12" floor thickness, 6'-8" minimum headroom

Number of risers	Rise (inches)	Run (inches)	Total run	Minimum floor opening
14	7 3/4	9 1/2	10'-3 1/2"	9'-6"
15	7 1/4	10 1/2	12'-3"	11'-5"
16	6 3/4	11 1/2	14'-4 1/2"	13'-5"
17	6 3/8	12	16'-0"	15'-0"

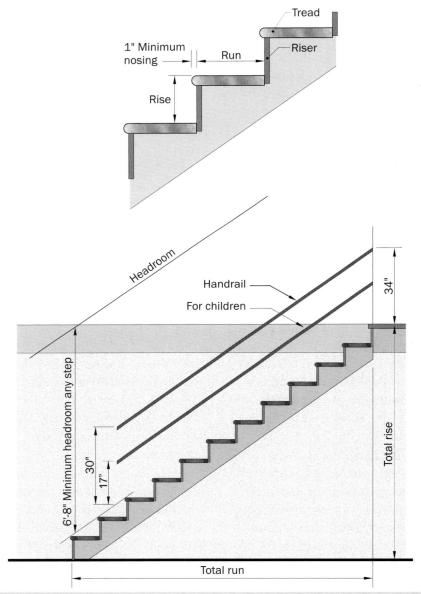

FIGURE 12-9.
Stair dimensions.

Stairs Terminology

Headroom:
Measurement of clear vertical space between the nosing and the ceiling.

Enclosed stairs:
Set of steps built between two walls.

Open stairs:
Set of steps with no wall on one or both sides.

Rise:
Distance between the top surface of one tread and the next.

Riser:
Vertical face of the step.

Run:
Horizontal distance from face of one riser to face of the next.

Nosing:
Portion of tread that extends beyond riser.

Tread:
Horizontal member of each step.

*Adapted from Kicklighter, Kicklighter, and Baird:, 2000 (pages 256–258).

floor or tread surface. Guardrails, a handrail supported by balusters, prevent falls over the edge of a balcony or stairs. Guardrails must be sturdy, with pickets spaced no more than 4 inches apart.

Lighting on stairways should be as intense as or brighter than immediately adjoining areas. Provide lighting that makes tread nosing (horizontal part of each step that extends beyond vertical face of step) distinct but does not create glare or strong shadows. Use two light fixtures, one at the top and one at the bottom of stairs (Figure 12-11). Unless the stairs are continuously lit or lights automatically switch on, provide rocker switches at both points of access. A permanently illuminated, small light source such as a nightlight can be useful in stairways.

To summarize, stairs should:
- Have treads and risers with uniform depth and height.
- Have treads and risers with contrasting colors.
- Have coverings or surface materials with good traction.
- Have a minimum headroom of 6 feet 6 inches.
- Have handrails mounted between 30 and 38 inches above the floor or tread surface.
- Have round or oval handrails, 1 1/4 to 2 inches in diameter, and 1 1/2 inches from the wall.
- Provide good lighting with a light switch at top and bottom steps.

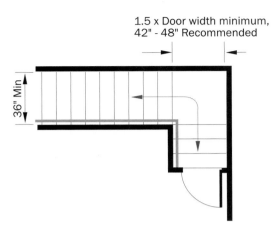

FIGURE 12-10.
90 degree or right angle turn.

FIGURE 12-11.
Stairs with lighting.

Resources

Bakker, R. 1997. *Elderdesign: Designing and Furnishing a Home for Your Later Years*: Penguin Books.

Bostron, J.A., R.L Mace, and M. Long. 1987. *Adaptable Housing: Marketable Accessible Housing for Everyone.* Washington, DC: U.S. Department of Housing and Urban Development.

Gill, T. June 18, 1999. The Role of the Home Environment on the Everyday Function of Community-living Seniors. Transcript from National Audio-Teleconference on Home Modifications. http://www.usc.edu/dept/gero/hmap/tran.html

Kicklighter, C.E., J.C. Kicklighter, and R.J Baird. 2000. *Architecture: Residential Drawing and Design.* South Holland, IL: The Goodheart-Wilcox Company, Inc.

U.S. Department of Justice, Civil Rights Division, Disability Rights Section, 2001. ADA Technical Assistance CD-ROM.

Entrances and Site Design. 1991. Raleigh, North Carolina: The Center for Universal Design, North Carolina State University. Publication number TP #2.00.

Doors and Doorways. 1991. Raleigh, North Carolina: The Center for Universal Design, North Carolina State University. Publication number TP #3.00.

CHAPTER 13

Household Storage

ADEQUATE, WELL PLANNED STORAGE SPACE makes daily living easier by helping keep the household organized and by making cleaning easier. Efficient storage allows the costly square footage of living space to be used for its intended purpose; however, lack of quality storage space is sometimes a shortcoming in today's homes. In an effort to create affordable housing, homes are being built smaller. In smaller homes, living space generally takes precedence over storage, but if the storage is not well planned and integrated, the space intended for living is often dominated by clutter. In other cases, when the house has been built to accommodate adequate storage, poor planning and space use can waste living space.

This chapter outlines some basic principles for planning and organizing storage and describes ways you can incorporate storage into a building or remodeling project. As you plan, remember that closet and storage design professionals can help you with your storage needs. If having adequate storage has always been a problem for you, then hiring a professional may help.

Storage Principles and Guidelines

Quality storage just does not happen. Creating good storage takes careful planning and consideration of every room. Since storage needs depend on the lifestyle of each family member, the entire household should be involved in the planning and implementation of a new storage system. Consider the following principles and guidelines.

As a rule of thumb, plan a minimum of 10 percent of your home's total floor area for storage. Include the floor space of closets and kitchen cabinets in your calculations. The square footage recommendation helps you decide the length and depth of your storage areas. Also consider the height of storage areas. Large items, such as oversized suitcases, golf clubs or skis, and folding chairs, may need especially high storage areas.

For each storage category (for example, foods, appliances, and linens), consider the length, height, and depth of space you will need. Table 13-1 provides the common depths of household items. To meet your changing needs, incorporate flexible features like adjustable shelves.

Accessibility to items is important for well designed storage. You will want to keep items for daily activities easily accessible in what is called *active storage*. Plan for adequate active storage first. Create storage so frequently used items and emergency medicines are within easy reach. Ensure that they can be

Holiday decorations, seasonal clothes, bicycles, fishing gear and other sports equipment, hobby supplies, and hundreds of other temporarily used items are common in most households. In designing household storage, the basic question to ask is how do we efficiently and safely store these items without taking up valuable living space? Begin the process of planning household storage by thinking about the following principles:

- Involve the entire family in planning and implementation.
- Allow about 10 percent of the living area of your home for storage.
- Keep items for daily activities easily accessible in what is called *active storage*.
- Provide storage near where an item tends to be used most often.
- If you use items together, plan to store them together.
- You will need to create storage to keep medicines, cleaners and other chemicals, guns and ammunition, and dangerous tools out the reach of children.

Continued

- Reduce storage needs. This idea is simple: the fewer items you have, the less storage you will need.
- Look for the opportunity to group and relocate common storage category items; you may find books, games, and hobby materials that could be stored in one location.

Table 13-1. Range of depths for storing common items.

Item	Depth (inches)	Item	Depth (inches)
Appliances, small kitchen	6-24	Food:	
		Boxes narrow side out	8-16
Bake ware	2-24	Staples	4-12
Bath linens	12-18	Footwear	10-12
Bath supplies and equipment	4-18		
Bed, folding	12-24	Games and toys	12-24
Bedding	12-24	Garden equipment	3-36
Beverages (6, 8, 12 packs)	12-16	Glassware	4-12
Books	8-16		
Business papers	12-16	Handicrafts	24
		Holiday decorations	12-48
Card table	4		
Cleaning equipment	18-30	Infant's equipment	24
Cleaning supplies	4-8		
Clothing:		Kitchen utensils	4-16
In drawers	8-16		
On hangers	24	Luggage	24
On hooks	16-20		
Cookware	12-24	Magazines	8-12
Computer equipment:		Medicines	4-6
Monitor	24	Musical instruments	12-36
Keyboard	8-12		
Computer	8-18	Radios	4-12
Dinnerware	4-12	Serving dishes	12-18
Drawer files	16	Sewing equipment	24
		Silverware	9-12
Electric fans	12-16	Sporting equipment	12-28
		Stereo equipment	8-24
Folding chairs			
Narrow side out	18-24	Table linens	16-20
Broad side out	4	Television	24
Food:		Tools:	
Bottled	4-8	Mostly hand-held	4
Canned	4-8	Power	12-36
Boxes broad side out	4-8	Trays, platters, bowls	8-16
		Vacuum cleaner, tank type	24

removed and returned without affecting other items. Space for infrequently used or seasonal items such as holiday decorations, garden equipment, and lawn furniture can be less accessible.

Another important accessibility issue is how easily something can be put into storage or retrieved after it is stored. Make sure that doors to storage areas are at least 32 inches wide. Wider doors can make it easier to move large boxes or items into and out of storage. Large storage rooms should allow for a 5-foot turnaround diameter. Motorized cabinets that can raise and lower will accommodate people of all heights and abilities, including children. In keeping with the concept of universal design and accessibility, at least half of all storage should be less than 54 inches in height.

In planning your storage, consider three other concepts:

1. **Selecting locations.** You will want to create storage that allows you to store items near where they tend to be most frequently used. Match activities and rooms so you can store items for a given room in or near that room.

2. **Making stored items visible.** Design storage so you can see stored items; items not seen are forgotten. Ideally, have some storage that allows you to keep items one row deep, if possible, or store similar items behind each other.

3. **Protecting stored items from environmental damage.** When planning storage, be alert to areas such as basements, attics, or garages where heat, moisture, fumes, vapors, insects, or rodents could damage stored items.

Before creating your storage areas, consider the types of storage devices and determine which ones best meet your needs. In your situation, is open or closed storage preferable? Would you be better served by having movable or built-in storage? Would a mixture of storage alternatives best meet your needs?

Closed devices hide clutter and conceal unattractive or unappealing items. Open storage can display valuable possessions, collectibles, and decorative articles. Open storage devices, however, do not protect items from dust, dirt, light, or grease.

Storage units that are portable or easily dismantled can be moved to a different room or house. But a finished appearance on all sides and extra strength to make portable units self-supporting may cost more than built-in storage.

Built-ins are logical for families planning to stay in their home for some time. Using space between wall studs adds storage as well as visual and actual floor area; both factors increase comfort in homes downsized to increase affordability. Finally, built-in storage may cost less by relying on the dwelling's structure for strength rather than on the storage device. To lower costs, only the front of many built-ins must be finished. If built-in storage is too costly to install during the original house construction, plan where it could be located in the future. As you plan, be aware that built-ins can change the shape of a room or create awkward traffic lanes.

Assessing Your Storage Needs

Having enough storage takes careful planning whether it is for a new, remodeled, or existing house. The following steps should help you assess your needs and develop a good plan for storage.

Step 1.
Call a household meeting to discuss the following steps and plan your storage strategy.

To ensure the most successful storage project, involve the entire family in planning and implementation. Individuals left out of the process may not appreciate your re-organization of their room or items. Children can offer many creative

Keep medicines, cleaners and other chemicals, guns and ammunition, and dangerous tools out of children's reach. Do not store cleaning supplies or medicines under a sink, on low shelves, or in low drawers unless the cabinet is locked. Install a security latch out of the reach of young children on closets where you will store cleaning products and other hazardous materials. To prevent a child from getting locked in a closet, select a fastener that is not self-latching.

If space is available, store duplicates in more than one place to save steps, for example, cleaning equipment and supplies in each bathroom. However, if space is limited, curtail duplicate storage. If you use items together, store them together; for example, keep cleaning equipment and supplies in one place. Store frequently used items about 25 to 59 inches off the floor for easy reach without bending or stretching. Put seldom used light items above and heavy items below these levels.

Many individuals do have difficulty getting rid of items they cannot use, do not need, or that may pose a health and safety hazard. Getting rid of items does not mean you have to throw them away. Remember, "One person's trash is another's treasure." Someone is likely to want or even need your items. Try these sources for finding a new home for your items:

- *Garage sale*
- *Salvation Army or Goodwill*
- *Antique shops*
- *Recycling center for magazines*
- *Used book store or library*
- *Hospital for magazines and books*
- *Child care center for used toys*
- *Senior center for used furniture*
- *Homeless shelter*
- *Vocational school for tools and motors*

ideas and are more likely to stick with the plan if their ideas are included.

Step 2.
Conduct an inventory of items that need to be stored.

This process can take several days. To keep it organized and simple, conduct the inventory room-by-room. Make sure you include all the hide-away areas in the attic, basement or crawlspace, the garage, and other out-buildings.

As you conduct the room-by-room inventory, create a list of storage categories that develops. Storage categories for a bedroom may include:

- Winter clothes.
- Books.
- Games.
- Give away items.
- Garage sale items.

For your inventory, you may want to consider inventory planners provided by your insurance company or one of several computer software programs.

Step 3.
Reduce your need for storage.

Before you begin building, reduce your storage needs. This idea is simple: the fewer items you have, the less storage you need. If you can reduce your needs before building, you may be able to cut construction costs and use space more efficiently.

Step 4.
Group common storage items and categories

Think about creating storage areas by grouping items by function. Look for the opportunity to group and relocate common storage category

items. Grouping similar items can help you define your storage needs. With your room-by-room inventory complete, you may notice that items found throughout the house could be grouped together in a single storage area. As an example, instead of taking up quality space in dressers and closets by storing winter clothing in each bedroom, create a safe storage area in the basement or in a guest-room closet and store all winter clothing in one location. Similarly, you may find books, games, and hobby materials from various loca-tions that could be stored in one location, again making space for other, more appropriate storage.

Some things do need to be in specific rooms, but other items can be put anywhere that is convenient, depending on room size, kind, number, and location. If the plan includes a hall, for example, cleaning supplies located in this central area may serve the family better than placing them in a utility room.

Step 5.
Inventory your storage assets and possibilities.

Each area of your house likely contains unrecognized options for quality storage. In this step, consider all possibilities for storage. Look at your building or remodeling plan, or walk from room to room, considering spaces such as closets and book-shelves as possible storage areas. As you examine and create your storage options, make sure you review the storage principles and guidelines described earlier in this chapter. Think creatively about how space can be used and consider all storage possibilities for an area.

Step 6.
Match existing storage space to items needing to be stored.

When you arrive at this step, you should know what items you will need to store (Steps 2, 3, and 4) and what storage options you have available (Step 5). Following the storage principles and guidelines and starting with items you use daily, create the active storage areas. Only after you have established your active storage areas should you begin planning storage for seasonal and less-used household items.

Step 7.
Filling the storage gap—creating additional space.

When you reach this step, you will probably have a good idea of what your storage needs are. However, even after planning and allotting storage space for expected needs, families often need extra storage for new or unexpected things. Ladders, bulky folding tables and chairs, children's toys, or sporting equipment, for example, may have been forgotten or their necessary storage space underestimated.

If you discover you will need more storage, you will have to return to the drawing board to come up with more space. Before you consider creating more storage, however, re-examine Steps 2 to 5 for options you may have overlooked. As you re-examine your storage options, make sure you apply the storage principles and guidelines described earlier in this chapter.

If you decide to create more storage, return to Step 5 to examine what new storage possibilities exist for the house. For example, could the washer and dryer be installed in a closet and the utility room be converted into a food pantry and kitchen appliance storage area? Do you have a crawl space that could be made dry and safe from insects and rodents? If so, could boxed seasonal clothing be stored there? Is there an inside wall cavity free from pipes or electrical wires that could be the spot for that knick-knack collection? Could a shelf be integrated above a window valance to display those antique family pictures and frames?

When looking for ways to develop additional storage space, be creative. Look at books and magazines, and when you visit friends and relatives, look at their use of storage. Do not be afraid to experiment with no- or low-cost ideas, and think multi-use and try to integrate living and storage space. Using ideas such as these you can find many new options for storage; in the end, you will probably be limited more by your pocketbook than by your imagination. Keep in mind that no plan should be etched in stone. Needs will change over time, and you should be able to adapt your storage systems to your changing needs.

Considering Your Storage Options

When it comes to storage devices, the options seem limitless. Books, magazines, and home centers offer many fun, colorful suggestions that you can research as you explore your storage options. The storage devices in this section illustrate many traditional choices. These devices are most useful if they are:

1. Flexible, for changing needs, such as pegboard, adjustable shelves,

After planning your storage areas, you may want to take your inventory one step further so it complies with your insurance contents inventory. This involves listing the age, purchase price, and manufacturer of the item. While assessing your storage needs, you also may want to videotape or photograph your stored items. If you are planning to use your inventory for insurance loss verification, you will need to keep a copy of the inventory and photos/videotapes in a fire- and water-resistant location, such as a home safe or safety deposit box. Some insurance companies will allow you to file your list with your policy records at their office. For future reference, try keeping an inventory list in an envelope taped to your main storage area. While open storage, like closets and shelves, makes items easy to see and access, you will want to keep an inventory close at hand for items stored in boxes and in difficult-to-locate areas.

adjustable or removable dividers, and adjustable closet rods for the clothing of growing children.

2. Capable of protecting and/or displaying stored items.

3. Efficient and able to use all available space but giving enough room to remove and replace items easily.

Alternatives

A variety of storage units are readily available for do-it-yourselfers to install with a few simple tools. Some alternative ideas for storage options that might help you decide how to incorporate storage devices into your house follow. The publication, *MWPS-21. Home and Yard Improvements Handbook*, also may be useful.

• Store folding table and chairs in a room divider.

• Recess a cabinet between interior wall studs for storage at the back of a counter; sliding doors work well. Avoid electrical outlets and wires, which must be protected by wallboard or wood. Recessed shelving increases noise transmission, unless there is a closet on the other side of the wall.

• Mount shelving over doors or high on walls.

• Provide storage under built-in seating in a family room.

• Extend kitchen cupboards to the ceiling or face soffits over cupboards with sliding doors.

• Install shallow shelves over a toilet tank.

• Use the space under beds or a loft and over or under stairs.

• Provide suitable access to a dry crawl space.

Devices

The following storage devices can be combined in unlimited configurations to create the ideal storage for you:

• Hooks, pegs, and racks.
• Shelves.
• Boxes, bins, and trunks.
• Drawers and trays.
• Storage furniture and cabinets.
• Closets.
• Room dividers and modular units.

Hooks, pegs, and racks. Hooks, pegs, and racks can support heavy loads such as bicycles or light items that need to be grasped easily, such as belts, ties, shoes, or the spices and measuring spoons in the kitchen cabinet (Figure 13-1).

An adjustable wire system is a popular option that allows for flexibility in arranging storage. This system is a good option for clothes storage because it allows for better air circulation, which is especially important in very humid climates. Clothes that lay on racks can get *wire marks*, but these marks often disappear after the item is worn for a little while.

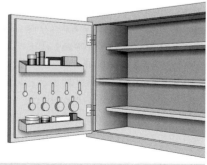

FIGURE 13-1.
Hooks, pegs, and racks.

Shelves. Shelving can be used to store a wide variety of items. Shelves may be fixed, adjustable, or pull-out and can attach to or hang from walls or ceilings. Variations include stepped and half-shelves (about 1/2 the height and width of fixed ones) to increase surface space.

Boxes, bins, and trunks. Boxes and bins store bulky items, such as boxes of food or dirty laundry (Figure 13-2). Dividers often make items more accessible. A storage trunk can be used to store bulky comforters and quilts.

Drawers and trays. Drawers are bins that pull out for convenience. Divide drawers, especially large ones, to improve usefulness. Sliding trays are pull-out shelves with the convenience of drawers (Figure 13-3). If storage is deeper than 20 inches, trays can be closer together than fixed shelves with the same access to stored items. Pop-up trays are particularly useful for small kitchen appliances that must be accessible without being kept on the counter.

Storage furniture and cabinets. Storage furniture, such as chests and dressers, usually has shelves and drawers. Furniture can be free-standing or built-in and comes in a variety of sizes to meet a wide range of storage needs.

Cabinets provide storage near the floor (base cabinets), on walls (wall cabinets), or to full wall height (pantries or closed bookcases). To be functional, cabinets usually include shelves, drawers, boxes, bins, hooks, pegs, and racks. A cabinet used as a food pantry is a good way to store a large quantity of non-perishable food items. A storage door with shelves, heavy hinges, and a support wheel can neatly store food items (Figure 13-4).

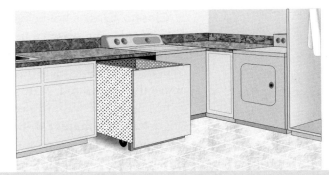

FIGURE 13-2.
Dirty clothes storage.

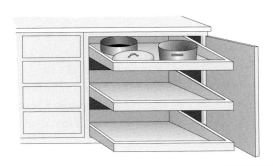

FIGURE 13-3.
Sliding trays (pull-out shelves).

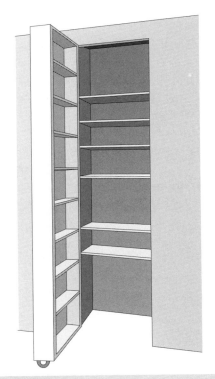

FIGURE 13-4.
Storage door.

Closets. Closets hold clothing, linens, and some seasonal items. Good closet design uses the space under shorter hanging garments and above the clothes rod. Many bedrooms now have walk-in closets (Figure 13-5). **Chapter 8, Bedrooms,** has more information on walk-in closets. For overall convenience and accessibility, all storage areas, but especially closets, should incorporate adjustable height rods and shelves, use power operated storage carousels where needed, have motorized cabinets that raise and lower to accommodate the height and reach of specific users, including children and people who might have trouble reaching items installed at standard heights.

FIGURE 13-5.
Walk-in closet.

Room dividers and modular units. Room dividers can be used to provide temporary and movable storage space that also helps separate living areas (Figure 13-6). Consider dividing large open plan spaces into more intimate areas: living room from guest entry, living room from dining room, dining area from kitchen, or sleeping from dressing or relaxation spaces in large bedrooms. To improve

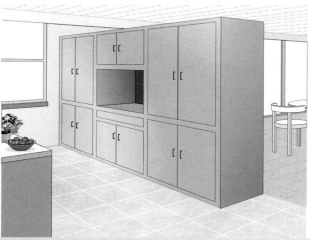

FIGURE 13-6.
Room dividers.

usefulness, a large room divider needs sub-dividers: shelves, drawers, cabinets, and bins.

Modular units have standard-sized components that can be combined as desired (Figure 13-7). Components include boxes, shelves, cabinets, drawers, desks, and closets. They can be stacked, hung, connected, or separate. Modular units are particularly appealing for remodeling or for expanding storage as needs emerge and resources permit.

FIGURE 13-7.
Modular units.

Resources

Home and Yard Improvements Handbook. MWPS-21. 1989. Ames, Iowa: MidWest Plan Service: http://www.mwpshq.org.

Using Space Wisely: http://edis.ifas.ufl.edu/pdffiles/HE/HE88100.pdf

Storage Solutions: http://www.thisoldhouse.com/toh/knowhow/tools/article/0,16417,220060,00.html

Storage Solutions for Your Home: http://www.mygreathome.com/indoors/organization/storage.htm

CHAPTER 14
Foundations

THIS CHAPTER PROVIDES YOU WITH INFORMATION about the various foundation types and their different requirements. While you probably will not be involved directly in constructing the foundation of your house, you will need to make decisions about the type of foundation you want. Additionally, you should be able to evaluate the strengths and weaknesses of various construction practices and to assess the quality of the foundation in any house you are interested in purchasing or remodeling. With the information this chapter provides, you should be able to make wise choices about the construction of your house and ensure that you have a safe, healthy home.

Foundation Types

The three principal types of foundations are slab-on-grade, crawl space, and basement. Which type is best suited for a new house is influenced by the surrounding topography, water table elevation (variation during wet and dry cycles), soil type, frost depth, depth to bedrock, and your preference. Table 14-1 located at the end of the chapter compares important attributes and features of the three foundation types.

Slab-on-grade

A slab-on-grade, also known as a floor slab or concrete slab, is a designed concrete floor located on a prepared base (Figure 14-1). Generally, concrete slabs should float independently of the building support foundation and not attach to or rest on footings or ledges of foundation walls. A wall ledger will not support a slab adequately.

Ideally, the top of the concrete wall foundation and slab should be at least 8 inches higher than the exterior soil level. This will protect the house from damage by isolating the wood framing from rain splash, soil dampness, and termites, and it should keep the sub-slab drainage layer above the surrounding ground.

Sometimes either supply or return air ducts are installed beneath the concrete floor. However, this is expensive and creates a potential serious problem for radon control. Air ducts below a concrete floor interfere with radon control and radon remediation, thus, this is not a good option for areas where radon may be found. Subsurface drains must be placed below the air ducts to prevent water from entering the ducts.

The primary functions of a foundation are to support the house and its contents, resist loads from the soil, and anchor the house against external forces. Secondary functions of a foundation are preventing excessive moisture (especially water) and radon gas from entering the house, minimizing heat loss, and resisting invasion by termites.

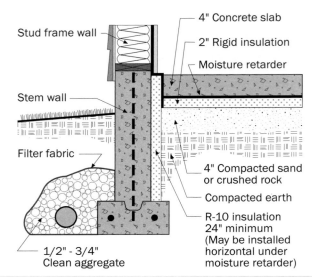

Stud frame wall

Stem wall

Filter fabric

1/2" - 3/4"
Clean aggregate

4" Concrete slab

2" Rigid insulation

Moisture retarder

4" Compacted sand
or crushed rock

Compacted earth

R-10 insulation
24" minimum
(May be installed
horizontal under
moisture retarder)

FIGURE 14-1.
Slab-on-grade floor and wall foundation.

Crawl space

A crawl space is a non-livable area located under the lowest floor level. The floor above a crawl space should be at a higher elevation than the surrounding exterior grade; often the floor is 3 feet or more above ground level. The crawl space must allow at least 30 inches of vertical clearance under all beams, ducts, and pipes to allow access to all areas in the space. A vapor retarder should be placed on the soil to limit the ability of soil moisture to create a damp crawl space (Figure 14-2).

There are two types of crawl spaces: vented and unvented. If not properly controlled, humid air accumulates in crawl spaces during warmer months. This moist air will make cool surfaces wet, which can lead to free water, mold, and wood decay problems. A vented and properly insulated crawl space allows the warm, moist air to exhaust to the exterior. The challenge of using a vented crawl space is that during cold weather there may be a problem with plumbing freezing and an increased heat loss from air ducts and the house floor. During warm weather, the crawl space is frequently cooler than outdoor temperatures. Warm outdoor air entering a cool crawl space through vents creates a damp environment in the crawl space. Therefore, limit ventilation unless the crawl space is warm and damp.

For vented crawl spaces, an insulation level of R-30 in the floor above the crawl space is optimal. The heated side of the insulation should have a vapor retarder that provides a perm rating of 1.0 or less, and a vapor retarder should cover the soil surface to slow the evaporation of soil moisture. All openings in the house floor need to be sealed to prevent air leakage from the crawl space to the living space. Crawl spaces should not be pressurized because pressurization might push poor quality air into the living space. Crawl space vents should be located as high as possible on each wall and no farther than 3 feet from each corner; they should be kept unobstructed (Figure 14-3). The total open vent area should be at least one square foot per 500 square feet of floor area. To prevent insects from entering the crawl space, vents should contain insect screening.

In unvented crawl spaces, insulation levels for the concrete foundation wall should range from R-5 for the middle United States to R-10 for the northern United States. Insulation levels for pressure-treated wood walls should be R-15 to R-20. Many closed-cell insulations limit moisture vapor flow and do not require the use of a separate vapor retarder. Extruded polystyrene insulation boards are

Sheathing panel
floor vapor
retarder

Insulation

Wood lath insulation
supports, 24"
on center

Foundation
vent

Vapor
retarder
sealed
to the
foundation

6 - 10-mil
vapor retarder

FIGURE 14-2.
Unheated crawl space

Adapted from *Keep Your Home Healthy*, Figure 6. K. Hellevang, North Dakota State University. (http://www. ext.nodak.edu/extpubs/ageng/structu/ae1204w.htm)

FIGURE 14-3.
Crawl space vent grate.

generally recommended. Rigid insulation boards should extend at least 3 feet in from the wall over the flat soil surface, with a vapor retarder on top of the insulation and soil surface.

Basements

In areas where foundation walls and footings must be several feet deep because of frost, you can add a full basement (Figure 14-4) for relatively little additional cost. A full basement doubles the available floor space in a single-story house for only 25 to 50 percent in additional costs. To provide a dry, energy-efficient area, basements require a considerable amount of care in both design and construction.

Two popular alternatives to a full basement are a walk-out basement and a garden level or daylight basement. A walk-out basement is an earth-bermed foundation that usually has two or three sides below ground with the remaining sides opening out to ground level. The main entrance for a house with a walk-out basement

Finishing the basement may cost as much as finishing above-ground space, but finishing the basement can be delayed until the space is needed.

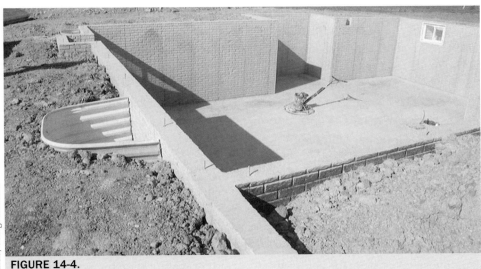

FIGURE 14-4.
Cast-in-place full basement.

is on the main floor, not on the walk-out level. This type of basement is typically restricted to a site where the house is built on a hillside.

A garden-level, or daylight, basement is a variation in which the basement's lower half is below the ground while the upper half is above ground, enabling the basement to contain large windows for adequate natural lighting and emergency egress. In areas with a high water table, the garden-level basement can minimize potential water problems because the basement is not as deep in the ground as in other basement styles.

A basement used as a living space needs to be heated, air conditioned, and ventilated along with the rest of the house. Insulating the walls during construction avoids condensation problems and will prevent you from having to oversize the heating, ventilation, and air conditioning (HVAC) systems because of heat loss and gains through uninsulated walls.

Plan specific use areas in your basement to meet current and anticipated needs. Plan similar room sizes, storage spaces, and privacy areas in your basement as you do for other floors. All states have specific code compliance requirements for bedrooms, living spaces, and bath areas located in a basement. (See **Emergency egress** for more details.)

Plan for windows, plumbing rough-ins, and electrical circuit needs and locations. Provide for reserve storage space for bulky, seasonal, and occasional use items. You may want to create space for hobbies and/or a home shop. Partition the basement lengthwise on or near the center line to support floor and/or ceiling joists

above. You can place rooms, hallways, and stairs on either side of this supporting wall. Be aware that any area that has an interior wall, column, or post needs a footing located below it.

As your family's needs change, the flexible use of space is as important in your basement as it is on the main floor of your house. If you use a beam for a portion of the support for upper levels, you can create a large recreation space with no supporting posts: a good spot for table tennis, pool, television, a home movie theater, or dancing. For a multipurpose recreation room, a width of 16 feet is a minimum. Depending on your plans, you may want a greater width, perhaps 20 feet or more. The length you need depends on the activities you plan. Placing a stairway near an exterior entrance gives direct access for teenage recreational activities or for a basement shop. Entry from a central hallway is convenient for access to family recreation and bedroom space.

In some large homes with multiple uses of the basement, two stairways may be desirable. An unobstructed straight entry from the outside or garage is ideal for moving bulky items like furniture or shop projects (Figure 14-5). The stairway width should be at least 36 inches, but 42 inches better accommodates a 36-inch door needed to pass large items.

Constructing the Foundation

To have a good foundation, careful planning, design, and construction are essential for the walls, footings, and floors. Also important are good site preparation before construction begins and proper landscaping to promote good drainage away from the foundation after construction.

Preparing the site

To prepare the site for the laying of the foundation, all organic material, vegetation, leaves, and highly organic soil must be removed from under the structure. Footings and floor slabs should be constructed on undisturbed soil, and if fill is required, it must be compacted. Any soil that has much void space or is not firm to walk on must be compacted using a vibrating compactor; typically, a pressure tamper is used for sands or for fine textured soils (silts and clays). The soil under footings and floors must be similar material and compacted similarly to avoid problems with differential settlement.

All footings and floor slab areas should have a layer of compacted clean, coarse sand, gravel, or crushed rock at least 4 inches thick under them. This layer serves as a bearing area, aids drainage of water, allows collection of radon gas, and is also a capillary break that prevents water from wicking up through wet soils. Fine textured soils may wick water up 10 feet or more. Large porous material keeps moisture from being drawn up into and through the concrete and also serves as a drainage layer to aid water flow to the footing drain system. If radon gas is present, the porous material allows it to be collected and easily remediated. (For more information about radon gas, see **Radon and other soil gases** later in this chapter).

Installing footings

Nearly all house foundations have footings, which are thickened concrete sections designed to sustain a heavy load from a wall, column, or post. Footings must extend below the frost depth or be insulated to prevent frost from forming beneath the footings. Make sure the footing is an adequate size to distribute the load of the building to the soil.

Generally, the foundation extends to below the frost depth to prevent frost heave, which occurs when frost forms under footings. Figure 14-6 shows a map that identifies frost penetration levels throughout the U.S. For the northern tier states, this is normally a depth of 4 to 5 feet, while in southern regions the foundation can be near the surface. The foundation does not need to extend below the normal frost level if there is adequate insulation between the ground surface and the footing to prevent frost from forming under the footing. Frost-heaving conditions exist where there are freezing temperatures, water, and frost-susceptible soils. Remove any one of these conditions and frost heaving will not occur. Frost-susceptible soils include any organic or finely textured soil that will hold water. Well-drained, non-organic soil materials such as crushed rock, gravel, and coarse sand are not frost susceptible.

The footing must support the foundation wall and be wide enough to contact sufficient soil to carry the load of the house and its contents. Most soils can carry a pressure of 1,000 to 2,000 pounds per square foot. The normal minimum concrete footing size for a load-bearing wall is about 16 inches wide and 8 inches thick. Compressible soils such as silts, clays, and organic soils may require that the soil be removed and replaced with engineer-selected

FIGURE 14-5.
A wide staircase entrance to a basement.

One inch of rain on a 1,000-square-foot roof deposits 625 gallons of water, so it is very important to direct this water away from the house foundation efficiently and quickly.

structural fill or that other options such as caissons or pilings be used to support the foundation.

Providing exterior drainage

Because water can cause serious damage that can be costly to fix, water problems are the source of many homeowner complaints about a house. In planning, remember that all openings to a basement should be several feet above the high water level to minimize the potential for water problems. Also, be sure to attend to the necessary details during design and construction to develop a system to direct water away from the house. To prevent outside water from entering a house, incorporate a

drainage system that includes the following characteristics:

- Collects roof rainwater with gutters and provides downspout extensions (leaders) at least 10 feet away from all sides of the house.
- Slopes the ground surface at least 6 inches in the first 10 feet away from the foundation wall on all sides of the house (Figure 14-7).
- Uses compacted, free-draining backfill, drainage board, or self-draining exterior insulation.
- Covers backfill around the foundation with a low permeability soil that has low shrink swell, a vapor retarder beneath the top layer of soil, or an impermeable surface.

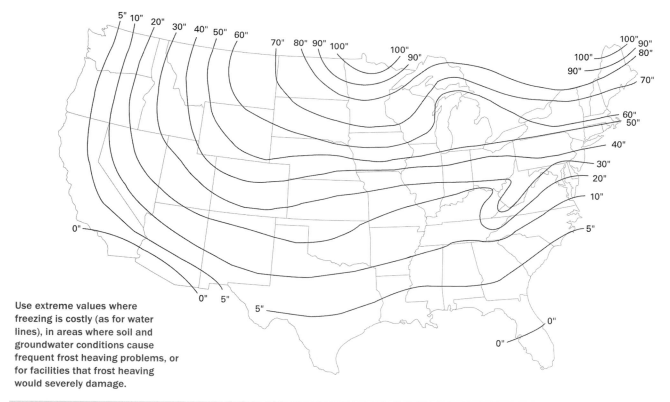

Use extreme values where freezing is costly (as for water lines), in areas where soil and groundwater conditions cause frequent frost heaving problems, or for facilities that frost heaving would severely damage.

FIGURE 14-6.
Extreme frost penetration.

- Has drains on the inside and outside of the footing below the bottom of the floor slab.
- Uses proper flashing where needed, and seals all foundation and floor penetrations.

Houses located in an area where wet basements are a concern should have waterproofing on the foundation walls. Waterproofing can prevent water from entering the basement due to intermittent water pressure, which can result from rainfall, irrigation, or snow melting. Waterproofing alone, however, will not prevent water or water vapor from entering through the basement wall due to constant water pressure, which can result from a high water table or saturated soils. The water needs to be removed from along the foundation wall with free-draining backfill such as coarse sand,

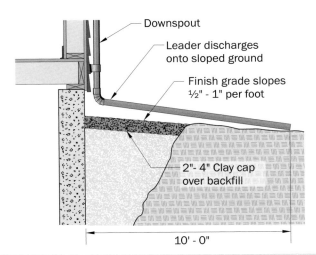

FIGURE 14-7.
Grading around foundation slab to promote good drainage.

a drainage board against the foundation wall, or exterior insulation with drainage properties next to the foundation wall (Figure 14-8). Figure 14-9 shows various configurations for locating drainage tile around footings.

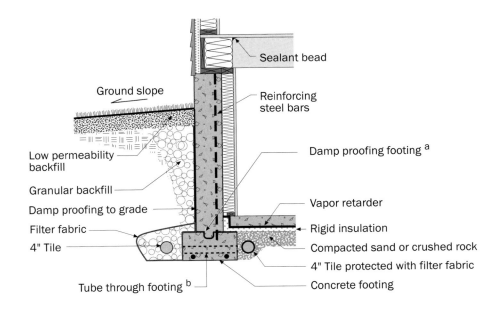

a Low perm or elasticmeric paint could be used in place of damp proofing

b Tubing allows water to drain from the tile located below the floor to the outside tile.

FIGURE 14-8.
Basement with a good drainage system and moisture control.

Adapted from *Keep Your Home Healthy*, Figure 7. K. Hellevang, North Dakota State University. (http://www.ext.nodak.edu/extpubs/ageng/structu/ae1204w.htm)

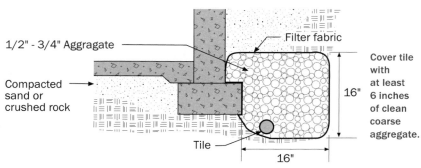

1/2" - 3/4" Aggragate

Compacted
sand or
crushed rock

Filter fabric

Cover tile
with
at least
6 inches
of clean
coarse
aggregate.

16"

Tile

16"

Tile below footing.

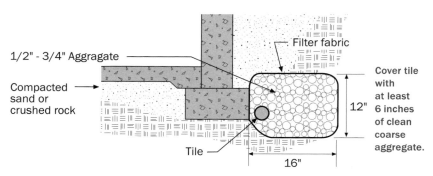

1/2" - 3/4" Aggragate

Compacted
sand or
crushed rock

Filter fabric

Cover tile
with
at least
6 inches
of clean
coarse
aggregate.

12"

Tile

16"

Tile at bottom of footing.

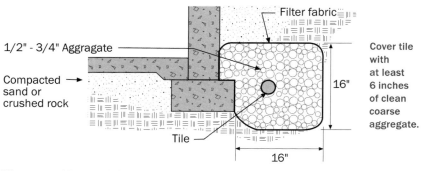

1/2" - 3/4" Aggragate

Compacted
sand or
crushed rock

Filter fabric

Cover tile
with
at least
6 inches
of clean
coarse
aggregate.

16"

Tile

16"

Tile even with top of footing.

**FIGURE 14-9.
Drainage tile locations around a footing.**

Adapted from *Foundation Drainage*, October 2002, Journal of Light Construction, *Concrete Floors On Ground*,
PCA EB075, and MWPS wall footing designs.

Basement walls should have porous backfill, consisting of at least a foot of coarse sand or 6 inches of gravel, against the walls to promote drainage, minimize the amount of moisture held next to the foundation, and reduce the pressure that expansive soils can exert on the foundation wall. If porous backfill is not available, drainage mat material placed against the foundation wall can facilitate drainage. The mat material, or porous layer, must extend down to the drain tubing (or drain tile) at the footing. The perforated, 4-inch diameter drain tubing surrounded with at least 3 inches of gravel to prevent fine soil particles from clogging the drainage area should be placed adjacent to the footing both inside and outside the wall. The drain tubing should slope 1 inch per 20 feet and lead to a gravity outlet or sump. The top of the tubing should be 2 inches below the level of the underside of the basement floor slab. Filter fabric should be wrapped around the outside of the gravel. A vertical clean-out pipe with an above-grade capped end serves as a flush-out for the drainage system.

For adequate basement drainage, a gravel layer at least 4 inches thick should be placed under the concrete floor slab. To reduce capillary and vapor moisture transmission as well as soil gas infiltration, a vapor retarder, or polyethylene membrane, at least 6-mils thick (10 mil preferred, especially for radon control) should be installed under the concrete floor slab and on top of the gravel. In areas with wet soils and high groundwater, a thicker gravel layer (6 inches or more) and more drain tubing should be placed under the slab. The basement sump—which can be concrete, plastic, or clay tile—should be at least 30 inches deep and either 24 inches in diameter or 20 inches square.

If water removal depends on an electrically operated sump pump, a duplex pump or a backup pump as well as a backup power source that can be used during power outages should be installed. The size and type of sump pump needed for a house depends on the frequency of use and the rate of water flowing into the sump. Talk to a plumber or a plumbing expert to determine the size and type of pump that is needed for your house.

Building foundation walls

Cast-in-place (i.e. poured) reinforced concrete and masonry block have been common materials used for foundation walls, and treated wood has been used successfully for many years for basements. One key to a successful foundation is to keep moisture out of the house or crawl space. If you live in an area where rainfall and soil conditions result in high water tables or seasonal surface water, consider waterproofing your foundation. Waterproofing is essential for basement walls where intermittent water (hydrostatic) pressure occurs due to rainfall, irrigation, or snow melting.

Concrete and masonry block walls

Cast-in-place concrete or masonry block are common materials for basement walls and for the stub walls that extend to the footings. Stub walls that have compacted soil on both sides of the walls may not need any reinforcing steel. Even though many codes do not require steel in the walls, basement walls should have reinforcing steel. Most basement walls that

need to be repaired do not have steel reinforcement, which indicates the advantages of using reinforcing steel.

The amount of steel reinforcement required for a basement wall depends on the wall height, height of the backfill against the wall, soil type, and wetness of the soil. Other factors that can affect the amount of reinforcing needed in a basement wall include a driveway and vehicle parked next to it, and vibrations due to earthquakes, trains, or heavy traffic.

For cast-in-place concrete basement walls, the reinforcing steel should be located towards the inside of the wall rather than centered in it. Steel reinforcement is needed in both vertical and horizontal directions. At least 2 inches of concrete should cover the steel bars. Some city codes will require a steel bar spacing of only 24 to 48 inches on center for a cast-in-place concrete basement wall. The American Concrete Institute in its *Building Code Requirements for Structural Concrete and Commentary* (ACI-318-05) specifies that the maximum allowable spacing for steel bars based on temperature and shrinkage is 18 inches without a major soil load against the wall. Work with an engineer to determine the proper steel bar spacing for your home's foundation. When masonry block is used for basement walls, reinforcing steel is even more important than it is for cast-in-place concrete.

Concrete will crack as it cures, but installing control joints in reinforced concrete and masonry walls will help minimize the negative effects of these cracks.

In wet or damp climates, waterproofing should be applied to the exterior wall surface and extended

If lumber is cut on the construction site, make sure that cut surfaces are thoroughly saturated with special-purpose preservative according to the manufacturer's specifications. Follow the specific requirements for fasteners as well. For more information, refer to the Permanent Wood Foundations Design and Construction Guide.

down to the drain tubing at the footing. Waterproofing materials include liquid-applied membrane, plastic and rubber vapor retarder, and a blanket containing bentonite clay. Keep in mind that waterproofing is only as good as the application process. At a minimum for dry climates, a thick, full-coverage damp proof coating of hot-applied bituminous tar, cold-applied coal tar, or an asphalt-based system covered by a vapor retarder to reduce vapor transmission from the soil through the basement wall should be applied. Giving attention to waterproofing and damp proofing materials and to the application process helps prevent later problems with moisture, high humidity, mold, and mildew in the basement.

Treated-wood walls

All-weather wood foundations have been used for basements for more than 20 years. They perform well when manufacturer's instructions are followed. Wood foundations are not suitable in areas that have problems with termites. Lumber suitable for use in preserved wood foundations will be individually stamped for that use.

The drainage system of a wood foundation is extremely important. A wood foundation should rest on a gravel layer with a thickness of at least three-fourths of the footing width beneath the basement walls. The gravel bed should extend out from the footing plate at least one-half the footing plate width. As with a concrete floor, a minimum 4-inch-thick layer of gravel with 3-inch plastic drain tubing sloped toward to a sump area in the middle of the

basement should be beneath the floor of a wood foundation. Concrete, plastic, or clay tile sumps at least 30 inches deep and either 24 inches in diameter or 20 inches square should be used.

Laying floors directly over soil

Concrete floors are commonly used for slabs-on-grade and basement floors. The concrete floor slab needs to be designed to minimize cracking, since large cracks can affect any flooring treatment applied to the concrete slab, especially tiles. Large cracks may occur when the soil or base material located below it settles, excessive shrinkage occurs during curing, or excessively heavy loads are placed on top of it.

Good base preparation, quality concrete, and steel reinforcing are used to minimize cracks in concrete. Concrete slabs need to be placed over a graded and compacted base material. An adequate base should consist of compacted-in-place natural soil covered with an evenly distributed 4-inch layer of compactible granular fill, such as clean gravel or crushed stone. The area must be level, and the soil part of the base must be free of vegetation and debris and should be of similar soil types for the entire area. Any wet spots in the soil area must be removed and replaced with new soil that is properly compacted. A vapor retarder (polyethylene membrane) at least 6 mil thick or rigid insulation with low perm value should be placed on top of the base before the concrete slab is placed.

The concrete slab should be at least 4 inches thick (5 inches preferred). Because the concrete shrinks as it cures, it will crack. Even a properly designed and constructed concrete slab will have many very small, almost invisible cracks. Crack size can be minimized by using quality concrete and proper steel placement. Concrete is ordered based on its compressive strength. Be sure that the concrete for your concrete slab has a compressive strength of 4,000 psi and that it does not contain too much water.

Reinforcing steel placement within the slab is important. The size and type of steel can vary depending on the size of the slab. Typically, steel reinforcement bars in a concrete slab are #3 or #4 bars spaced not more than 24 inches from center-to-center. If the steel welded wire fabric is used, the wire strands should not be placed more that 18 inches apart. Whichever type of steel reinforcement is used, it is not acceptable to lay the steel on the ground and pull it into position as the concrete is being placed. To be properly positioned in the middle of the concrete slab thickness, steel should be supported on chairs (special supports designed for this purpose) or by another acceptable method.

Water should not be able to accumulate and pond on the floor. To remove accidentally or intentionally released water, place at least one floor drain in the concrete floor, especially near appliances such as a water heater or clothes washer. Floors should slope slightly (about 1/4 to 1/2 inch in 10 feet) toward a floor drain so if water gets on the basement floor it will drain away. Be sure walls will not interfere with water flow to the floor drain.

To minimize moisture vapor and radon gas flow through the floor, the floor slab should be placed over a vapor retarder at least 6 mil thick that rests on a gravel drainage layer at least 4 inches thick. The joint between the concrete floor slab and basement wall should be sealed using a liquid joint sealant. All pipes and drains, the sump pit, and other penetrations of the basement floor or walls need to be completely sealed. The sump pit cover should be sealed and vented above the roof. If necessary, a fan can be installed to increase the ventilation rate.

Installing insulation

If not adequately insulated, houses lose or gain a large amount of heat through the foundation. The temperature several feet below the ground's surface is near the mean annual temperature for the area. The mean annual temperature is 40°F in Bismarck, North Dakota; 55°F in Topeka, Kansas; 53°F in Indianapolis, Indiana; 61°F in Charlotte, North Carolina; and 71°F in Phoenix, Arizona. Exterior placement of rigid, closed-cell insulation protects foundation damp proofing and reduces the freezing potential under and around the foundation. Make sure above-grade exterior insulation is protected from the sun's ultraviolet rays, rodents, and physical damage. Basement walls that are near grade or above grade need to be insulated the same as other exterior walls (usually more than below-grade insulation). The minimum recommended insulation values for a below-grade wall are R-10 to R-20 for the entire wall, from footing to the sub-floor above.

A house also loses heat through air leakage. Cold air generally enters the lower level of a multistory house

Carpets installed on a basement or slab-on-grade floor that does not adequately retard water vapor may absorb moisture coming through the concrete, creating an environment that fosters mold growth. Carpet pads are particularly troublesome because they readily absorb and even hold moisture. If you carpet your basement floor, install the carpeting without a pad, enabling the moisture to transfer through the carpet into the indoor air. If the floor includes a good vapor retarder and insulation, a carpet pad should be acceptable without causing a problem with mold.

Another concern with basement floors is water spillage that is quickly absorbed by a carpet or pad. In this case, a moisture-resistant pad may be an option; it gives the benefits of a pad but does not absorb and retain water. However, a moisture-resistant pad is not a good option unless a vapor retarder controls moisture transmission through the floor.

In rooms where a wheelchair is used, egress window openings should be at least 30 inches wide. The window should be located no more than 24 inches above the floor, preferably 18 inches.

because of negative pressures created by the tendency of warm air to rise and by air supplied to combustion heating equipment that does not have sealed combustion units. Also, the intake or suction side of the heating system is usually in the lower level of the house. The connection between the foundation wall and sill plate or joist header should be sealed so it is airtight. In most homes built before 1990, this connection has not been sealed properly.

Special Construction Considerations for Basements

Basements have special design challenges because they are located below ground level and because they usually provide a space for mechanical and electrical systems.

Emergency egress

Building codes require that all bedrooms located in a basement have an emergency egress, or exit, that opens directly to the outdoors. Egresses are important because they allow people to exit a house in the event of a fire. Depending on the size and use of the basement, more than one egress may be required. An egress window must have a minimum opening area of 5.7 square feet, be no more than 44 inches from the floor, and be at least 20 inches wide and 24 inches high (Figure 14-10). Occupants must be able to open the windows from the inside without using tools or keys.

Windows exiting from a wall below ground level must have a window well that provides a minimum opening area of 9 square feet

with a minimum dimension of 36 inches. Window wells with a vertical depth of more than 44 inches must be equipped with an approved, permanently affixed ladder or stairs accessible when the window is fully open.

Mechanical and electrical systems

Over the life of most homes, it is usually necessary to replace the furnace and air conditioner or the entire heating, ventilation, and air conditioning (HVAC) system as well as the water heater, water lines, and drain lines. Although some currently used materials last longer than in the past, many still will not last as long as the house structure. Expect to

Interior view of an egress window.

Photo taken by Brian Stauffer, University of Illinois, College of ACES.

Exterior view of an egress window.

**FIGURE 14-10.
An emergency egress window in a basement bedroom.**

upgrade the electrical system and even to add new systems, such as communication and computer systems. To facilitate repair and upgrade, it is important to have easy access to the various systems used in a home. Many of these systems are located within and below the main floor or above the basement ceiling. With basement space commonly used for living, the ceiling is often finished, and obtaining access can be difficult. To gain future access to components above the ceiling, plan to use a suspended ceiling with removable sections. This type of ceiling works best when the entire ceiling height is below the lowest component, usually the air ducts. To achieve the normal and desired 8-foot ceiling height, the basement walls need to be at least 8 feet 8 inches or 9 feet high.

Storm safety

Every year, tornadoes, hurricanes, and other extreme windstorms injure and kill people. Building a shelter or a safe room such as the one illustrated in Figure 14-11 near or in your house can help protect your family from injury or death caused by the dangerous forces of extreme winds. In hurricane-prone areas, do not build the shelter where it can be flooded during a hurricane. Design and build the walls and ceiling of the shelter so they are strong enough to withstand the impact of blown or falling debris. The Federal Emergency Management Agency publication *Taking Shelter from the Storm: Building a Safe Room Inside Your House*, FEMA 320, is an excellent resource that includes construction plans and cost estimates.

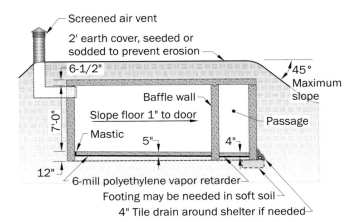

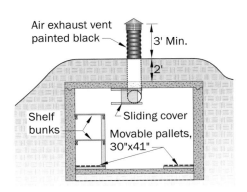

a. Below ground with reinforced concrete.

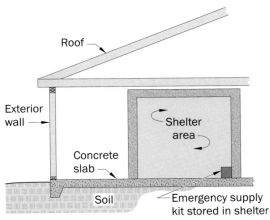

b. Inside a house.

Taking Shelter From the Storm: Building A Safe Room Inside Your House. FEMA 320. (http://www.fema.gov/pdf/fima/fema320.pdf)

FIGURE 14-11.
Storm shelters., below ground, reinforced concrete.

Other Design Considerations for Foundations

Radon and other soil gases, and termites are a concern in many areas of the country. Planning and controlling these problems before the foundation is constructed is usually the most cost-effective approach.

Radon and other soil gases

Radon is an odorless, tasteless, and invisible gas produced by the decay of naturally occurring uranium that is in soil and water. Radon and soil gases can have a negative effect on human health. Radon exposure is the second leading cause of lung cancer.

Radon and other soil gases, such as herbicides, termicides, and methane, can enter a house through cracks or openings in the foundation (Figure 14-12). All homes should be tested for radon. Houses located in the northern and western parts of the

U.S. have a higher likelihood of having radon problems.

Fortunately, these gases can be controlled with a foundation ventilation system called a radon control system. Installing a radon control system can be relatively inexpensive if installed in a new home during construction. The cost to install a radon control system in an existing house will be higher, but the health benefits will greatly outweigh the cost.

The basic method of keeping these gases out requires minimizing or sealing cracks and controlling the pressures that cause the gases to move. Refer to the section on concrete floors for information on minimizing cracks. Check out the EPA's Radon website (http://www.epa.gov/radon/) to find out more details about radon, radon zone maps, and other alternative radon gas control systems.

**FIGURE 14-12.
Common entry points for soil gases.**

Adapted from Building Radon Out: A Step-By-Step Guide On How To Build Radon-Resistant Homes, U.S. EPA, (http://www.epa.gov/radon/images/buildradonout.pdf)

Installing a pressure system to control soil gases is a job best left to professionals, but if a homeowner is interested in knowing how the system should be installed, the basic steps to installing a pressure system are listed below and diagrammed in Figure 14-13.

A. **Install a minimum** of a 4-inch thick layer of clean, coarse granular material (gravel or crushed rock) 1/2 to 1 inch in diameter underneath the concrete slab or flooring system of the house. This layer will allow soil gases to move freely underneath the concrete slab floor of the lowest level.

B. **Cover the 4-inch layer of clean granular material** with a vapor retarder at least 10 mil thick. The vapor retarder will help prevent the soil gas from entering the home. Note: the 10-mil thick vapor retarder needed for radon control is thicker than the one specified for vapor control. In crawl spaces, the sheeting is placed over the crawl space floor, as shown in Figure 14-14.

C. **Seal and caulk all openings** in the concrete foundation floor to reduce soil gas entry into the home.

D. **Install a 4-inch gastight or PVC pipe** with a 2-foot perforated extension on each end of a tee placed near the center of the house and extending into the basement from the layer of clean, coarse granular material. A single outlet extends upward through the vapor retarding membrane and is sealed to it. The concrete floor is poured around this pipe. Position the pipe so it can easily extend up through a wall or other space through the floors and above the roof. Extend the pipe up through the floors and roof to at least 2 feet above the roof. This pipe will safely vent radon and other soil gases above the house.

E. **In some cases** an exhaust or vent fan will be needed to create an adequate amount of pressure to exhaust the gases. Provide an electrical hook up (E) in case a fan is needed.

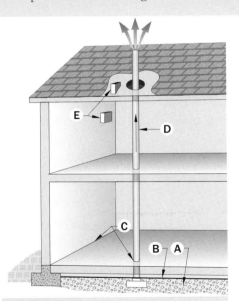

FIGURE 14-13.
Standard soil gas control system.

Adapted from *Radon-Resistant New Construction.* (http://www.epa.gov/radon/construc.html).

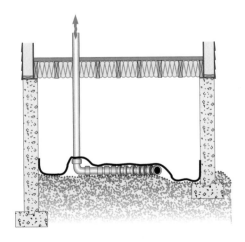

FIGURE 14-14.
Recommended method to collect and remove radon gas from a crawl space.

Adapted from the EPA publication *Building Radon Out: A Step-By-Step Guide for Building Radon-Resistant Homes.* (http://www.epa.gov/radon/images/buildradonout.pdf).

Subterranean termites

In much of the United States, techniques for controlling the entry of termites through house foundations are necessary. They include:

- Reducing soil moisture around the basement by using gutters and downspouts to remove roof water and by installing a complete drainage system around the foundation.
- Removing all construction wood from around the home and the building site.
- Placing a continuous bond beam or a course of solid cap blocks on top of all concrete masonry foundation walls, ensuring that no open cores are left exposed.

To resist decay and termites, make sure the sill plate is at least 8 inches above grade, and pressure treat it. Keep the sill visible for inspection from the interior. Place exterior wood siding and trim at least 6 inches above grade. Either pressure treat wood posts or plates on the floor slab, or place them on a concrete pedestal raised 1 inch above the floor. A bait system, a commonly used termite treatment, is very effective.

Summary

Table 14-1 compares important attributes and features of three foundation types: slab-on-grade, crawl space, and basement. Careful study of this table together with the preceding discussion will help you understand the differences in foundation types and choose the best type for your situation.

Table 14-1. Comparison of foundations and foundation features.

Features	Types of Foundations Slab-on-Grade	Crawl Space	Basement
Description	Foundation should extend at least 8" above the exterior ground level and at least 12" above natural soil level to ensure adequate drainage. Concrete floor is usual.	Lowest floor level is often 2 feet or more above ground level. There is no livable area in the crawl space; 30 inches of vertical space is needed below all parts associated with the floor and space above.	Below-grade earth contact for basement level. One or two floor levels above grade are typical. On a sloping site, one or more sides may be walkout or daylight. Concrete floor in basement is standard.
Advantages	Lowest cost ground connection option especially when the frost proof depth is shallow. A good choice for a site that has shallow ground water table. Ideal for families that need or want one living level. A choice where soil movement limits a basement.	Wide choice of exterior materials, finished space is more easily relocated than with other options. Good access to water, electrical, and HVAC systems. The best option for a site that has high groundwater.A common option in some areas.	More floor space with the same roof area. Low cost for additional space that can be finished later. Below floor plumbing is best installed when the house is built. A finished basement could be done initially and an upper floor added later. Easy access to water, electrical, and HVAC systems. Shelter from severe weather; ideal location for safe room.
Concerns or Limitations	Termite control is sometimes more difficult but is just as important for this option. To control drainage, floor level must be at least 15" above ground level. Perimeter insulation is difficult.	Same moisture control recommended as for a basement. Floor level must be a few feet above ground level. A no-step entrance may not be practical. Control of yard drainage is important.	Moisture, dampness, mold, and mildew concerns. Because of earth contact, plan to protect indoor air quality. Window and natural light limitations. Specific moisture control system must be installed when basement is built. Poor moisture control means wet or damp space. At least one egress window is required and one in each bedroom. Control of yard drainage is critical.
Heating, Ventilating, and Air Conditioning (HVAC) Systems and Ducts	Ducts are commonly placed in the attic. Under floor ducts can be installed before the floor is poured but this is expensive and may be a moisture and indoor air quality concern. Access to below floor ducts is quite restricted after construction.	In single-level homes, the ducts can be placed in the attic with return below the floor. A down draft furnace with under floor supply supply ducts is often used. When water is not a problem, furnace may be placed in a pit in the crawl space. Difficult to insulate below floor ducts.	Most easily accessible in unfinished basements. Easily accessible in finished basements with suspended ceiling. Furnace and air conditioning unit is always accessible. Ducts for a second floor are not accessible so initial planning is required. Lower external exposure means less energy needs when tight construction is used and foundation is insulated.
Water, Wastewater, and Electric Systems	Wiring is usually in attic space and has restricted access. Place water lines in walls or heated space to protect from freezing. Wastewater under slab floor is inaccessible.	Generally fairly easy access to main floor systems from crawl space or attic.	Has easiest access for main floor water, wastewater and electric systems with unfinished or suspended ceiling in basement. Wastewater under basement floor is inaccessible.

Table 14-1. Comparison of foundations and foundation features, *continued*.

Features	Types of Foundations Slab-on-Grade	Crawl Space	Basement
Insulation	Insulate inside surface of foundation to frost depth and under a few feet of floor on the exterior perimeter.	The floor above the crawl space should be fully insulated comparable to exterior walls for a vented crawl space. For an unvented crawl space, the foundation should be fully insulated as for a basement. Air ducts in a vented crawl space should be well insulated.	Fully insulate concrete foundation walls to R 5-10 for central U.S. and to R 10-20 for northern U.S. Insulation outside the foundation must resist weather, water, and rodents or must be protected from these damages.
Construction	Requires foundation and footing below the frost free depth. Use vapor retarder under concrete floor to control moisture in the home.	Requires foundation and footing to below frost free depth. Though not as critical to comfort in living space, moisture control is still important for a long structure life and prevention of damage to wood components.	Design for soil pressure with wet soil. Apply damp proofing or waterproofing to foundation walls and under basement concrete slab floor for moisture control. For a dry basement without mold or mildew issues, paying attention to moisture control details and external drainage is essential.
Radon Gas and Indoor Air Quality	Seal joint between foundation and floor slab and place at least 4" of porous material covered with a 10-mil vapor retarder under floor slab. Under floor air ducts may be an entrance route for radon gas.	Seal joints and penetrations of main floor and place a 10-mil vapor retarder over crawl space soil.	Carefully seal joints and penetrations of soil contact walls and floor, provide at least 4" of porous material under the floor, and install a vapor retarder of at least 10 mil under floor for radon control.
Moisture Vapor Control	Place at least 4" of porous material covered by a 6-mil vapor retarder under floor slab.	Damp proof soil contact walls and place 6-mil vapor retarder over a sand layer in crawl space.	Damp proofing of soil contact walls and a 6-mil vapor retarder under floor slab is essential to prevent water vapor from entering house through walls and floor.
Groundwater Control	Normally not essential except in locations of very high groundwater or in areas with springs. In this case, install drain tubing inside footing with surface outlet or a sump as used for a basement. Air ducts under the floor may flood on wet sites.	Same as for basements or earth contact. Water entrance does not flood the living space, but a wet crawl space creates an environment leading to structural deterioration and mold, which can affect air quality.	Install drain tubing with gravel envelope inside and outside of footing with drain to outlet or sump. In high rainfall areas and poorly drained soil, walls must be water-proofed to prevent water entrance. Consider backup sump pump and power supply. Air ducts under the floor may flood on wet sites.

Resources

Alaska Craftsman Home Program, Inc. 900 W. Fireweed Lane, Suite 201. Anchorage, AK 99503-2509.

Builders' Manual. 1995. Ottawa, Ontario: Canadian Home Builders' Association.

Canadian Home Builders' Association. 150 Laurier Ave. W., Suite 200. Ottawa, Ontario K1P5J4.

Closed Crawl Spaces: An Introduction for the Southeast http://www.advancedenergy.org/ buildings/knowledge_library/crawl_spaces/pdfs Closed%20Crawl%20Spaces_An%20 Introduction%20for%20the%20Southeast.pdf

Consider the Crawlspace, IBACOS, www.ibacos.com/pubs/CrawlspaceInsert.pdf

Farny, J.A. 2001. *Concrete Floors On Ground*. Portland Cement Association, 5420 Old Orchard Road, Skokie, Illinois, 60077-1083. Publication no. EB075.

Federal Emergency Management Agency: http://www.fema.gov Mitigation Directorate: http://www.fema.gov/mit/tsfs02.htm. 500 C St. S.W. Washington, DC 20472. 1-888-565-3896.

International Conference of Building Officials. 5360 Workman Mill Rd. Whittier, CA 90601-2298.

Labs, K., J. Carmody, S. Sterling, L. Shen, Y. Huang, and D. Parker. 1988. *Building Foundation Design Handbook*. U. S. Department of Energy, National Technical Information Service, U.S. Department of Commerce. Publication no. DE88-013350.

Lstiburek, Joseph. 2000. *Builder's Guide to Cold Climates: Details for Design and Construction*. Newton, CT: The Taunton Press, Inc.

Northern Comfort: Advanced Cold Climate Home Building Techniques. 1995. Anchorage: Alaska Craftsman Home Program, Inc.

Olin, Harold B., John L. Schmidt, Walter H. Lewis, and revised by H. Leslie Simmons. 1995. *Construction Principles, Materials, and Methods*. 6th ed. John Wiley and Sons, Indianapolis, IN.

Permanent Wood Foundations: Design and Construction Guide. 1998. Kenner, LA: Southern Pine Council, Southern Forest Products Association.

Taking Shelter from the Storm: Building a Safe Room Inside Your House. 1998. Washington, DC: Federal Emergency Management Agency (FEMA). Publication no. 320.

Uniform Building Code. 1994. Whittier, CA: International Conference of Building Officials.

CHAPTER 15

House Utilities

OPERATING SYSTEMS IN A HOUSE ARE SYSTEMS designed to provide comfort and safety. The most common operating systems in a house are:
- Heating.
- Cooling.
- Ventilation.
- Water and sewer.
- Electrical.
- Safety (smoke and carbon monoxide detection; security alarms, fire suppression).
- Indoor air quality (dust, gas, and humidity control).
- Convenience (sound and communication, entertainment, and vacuum).

Because a house will have several operating systems, you will need to have a well-developed plan so that one system will not interfere with another.

Planning Operating Systems

When planning any operating system for the house, work with your contractor and check with local building officials to determine the codes that apply to each operating system. Think about how the operating system will be used now, and envision how your house may change in the future. Be sure your design provides as much space as possible for these needs.

The two basic rules in planning for operating systems are:
1. Consider the house as one large operating system, and determine the effects each individual operating system has on the others.
2. Use high-efficiency components and sub-systems designed to operate properly in a new, tight house.

In your planning, consider the locations of heating and cooling ducts and registers. For example, ducts in the basement can interfere with finished space and remodeling; when possible, therefore, have the main duct run parallel to the support beams, and locate individual ducts between the floor joists. Using floor trusses is a good way to provide spaces for under-floor ducts. Plan to insulate ducts and hot water lines to save heat, and to insulate cold water lines to reduce condensation forming on them. Heat registers and radiators should be located next to outside walls where the greatest heat loss occurs, which is typically under windows. Have a plan for

A modern house has numerous systems that interact in complex ways. When planning a house, consider the effect each system has on the other systems, and design all of the systems within the house to function together correctly, making it comfortable, affordable, and safe. Neglecting to plan properly for the interaction of all operating systems can result in a system that fails and an unsatisfactory house. System failures might be small, such as a house that is expensive to heat; major, such as a house with excessive moisture; or catastrophic, such as an occupant who dies from carbon monoxide poisoning. You will need to rely on qualified professionals to install your house utilities, but you need to be aware of the operating characteristics of the various systems. You should understand the inherent strengths and weaknesses of your options so you can work with your contractor to make the choices that will result in a healthy, safe, convenient, and affordable home.

interior decorating that avoids blocking registers and radiators with furniture or draperies.

Houses with basements typically will have space in the basement for the furnace and hot water heater, but space also may be needed for appliances such as a refrigerator or freezer. In milder climates where basements are rare, the furnace and water heater are often located in the garage. Utilities occupy space and affect the use of the basement. For example, placing the water meter and water heater in one corner and the furnace diagonally across from where the gas line enters across the basement in another corner may prevent developing living space in either end of the basement. In planning for basement living space, keep plumbing lines serving the floor above concealed between floor joists. Where possible, cluster the entrance points for water, heating fuel, air conditioner refrigerant, and electrical services.

In most houses, whether or not a basement exists, the furnace and hot water heater should be located near the center of the house. Locating these units centrally helps to avoid long runs of ducts and pipes and results in more consistent and uniform performance. In houses that have heating and cooling systems or a water heater that services only part of the house, these units should be located near the point of use but not in a main room. Be sure to leave room for servicing the furnace and hot water heater.

Houses located on a slab or above a crawl space need to provide at least 3 by 6 feet of floor space in a garage or closet inside the house for the furnace or water heater. Most local codes require these units to be elevated above the floor to reduce the risk of fire or explosion. Provide plenty of clearance around a furnace or water heater to allow access for maintenance or future replacement and to provide fire safety. If a furnace or water heater is located in a closet or enclosed area, install a door wide enough to allow equipment to be removed. The electrical service entrance for these houses should be located in a utility room rather than in a kitchen or bedroom.

Heating Systems

The heating system that you select will depend on your climate, budget, specific needs, and the benefits and limitations of each type of system. Regional differences in fuel cost and availability also may affect the type of system that you install, but whatever the fuel type, two main issues are system efficiency and safety. In a cold climate, the best investment is to install the most efficient system available. It may cost more initially, but the lower operational costs will repay that investment over the lifetime of the system. When shopping for high-efficiency furnaces and boilers, look for the EnergyStar® logo (Figure 15-1). Buy a system with a good warranty and a reputable company to back it up.

FIGURE 15-1.
EnergyStar® logo.

Types

The most common modern heating systems are forced air furnace, pumped hot water, electric resistance, and heat pump systems. Less common systems include wood-burning stoves and unit heaters.

Forced air

A forced air furnace (Figure 15-2) draws cool air into its chamber (heat exchanger) where the air flows over a heating unit. The heated air is then blown through ducts where it is distributed to individual rooms in the house. The furnace can be fueled by natural gas, propane, fuel oil, wood, coal, or electric resistance elements. All but electric resistance elements produce combustion gases that need to be removed from the house through a chimney or vent system. All fuel-burning systems lose some heat through the chimney flue. The more efficient the furnace, the cooler the combustion gases and the less heat that escapes through the flue.

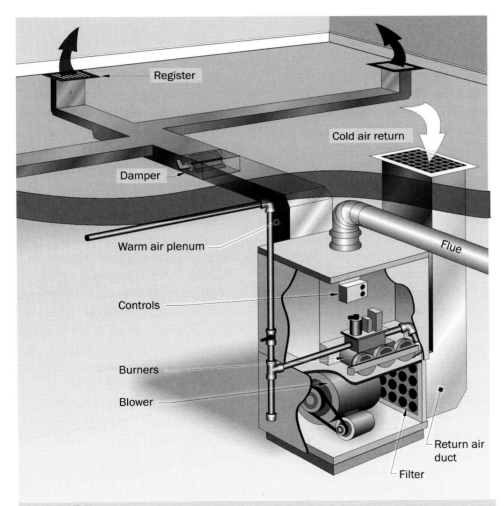

FIGURE 15-2.
Forced air furnace.

Adapted from Don Vandervort's Home Tips, *High-Efficiency Furnaces: A Buying & Care Guide*
(http://www.hometips.com/cs-protected/guides/forcedair.html)

The heart of the furnace is the heating unit or heat exchanger. The heat exchanger transfers the heat from the combustion gases to the circulating air stream but does not allow the circulating air to mix with the combustion gases produced during the burning process. If the heat exchanger is corroded, cracked, or has holes, carbon monoxide (CO) and other dangerous and sometimes lethal combustion gases may enter the house. If you are buying or remodeling a home, you would be wise to have a professional check the heat exchanger for cracks or holes to determine if you will need to replace the furnace.

A thermostat turns a furnace on or off when it reaches a temperature set point. When the thermostat signals the furnace for more heat, the furnace burners are ignited. Older, gas-fired furnaces use a small gas flame or pilot light that remains lit throughout the heating season. Newer units use electronic ignition; oil burners use an electric spark ignition system. Thermostats should be placed away from direct sunlight, drafts, doorways, skylights, and windows because they affect the sensors. Because a thermostat only turns a furnace on or off, increasing the temperature set point in a cold room to a very high level will not heat the room more quickly. It will only make the furnace operate longer so it reaches the higher set point, which wastes valuable fuel.

In older furnaces, a sufficient amount of replacement air must enter the house from outdoors to furnish the air needed for combustion (burning) of the fuel and to replace the air that flows up the chimney. New, sealed-combustion furnaces draw the combustion air from outside through a pipe. In addition to air exiting the house through the chimney, air also is exhausted out of the house through bathroom exhaust fans, clothes dryers, and kitchen range hoods. Each of these fans needs outdoor air to replace the indoor air that has been exhausted. In addition, new houses are being built tighter, and existing houses are being tightened up to restrict uncontrolled air from leaking into the house in an effort to save energy and reduce cold drafts. While tighter houses are easier to heat and cool and are more comfortable, they do not always provide sufficient replacement or make-up air for reliable operation of heating appliances.

When enough air is not entering the house through cracks and openings, a pressure imbalance can occur that results in air reversing and backdrafting through the furnace chimney or vent. Dangerous combustion gases can be forced back into the house. Some research reports indicate that up to 10 percent of gas-fired furnaces backdraft at least once during a winter. Backdrafting can be prevented by installing heating appliances that are made to operate in tight houses. You will want to choose a furnace with features that increase efficiency and safety including:

- A sealed combustion chamber.
- Powered exhaust flow.
- Sealed combustion air and combustion exhaust flow pipes.
- Safety controls.

A furnace should be sized to fit your home. Oversized equipment, which cycles on and off more frequently than a properly sized unit, shortens the life of the equipment. It can cause reduced comfort and excessive "air" noise. Undersized equipment, with airflow that is too low, can reduce the efficiency of the air distribution and accelerate wear on system components, leading to early failure. Good contractors will not size the heating equipment solely on the square footage of your house or assume that the existing unit was sized properly in the first place. During the house planning process or during an initial visit to your home, a contractor will calculate your home's heat loss during cold weather and heat gains during warm weather by taking measurements and asking you questions about your lifestyle and your comfort preferences.

The furnace should be installed in conditioned space, or a space that is well insulated. It should be located in an area that is easily accessible for maintenance and that provides plenty of room for airflow on all sides of the furnace.

Pumped hot water

In a pumped hot water or hydronic system, heat is produced in a boiler and is distributed throughout the house by hot water that is pumped to radiators or coils in the different rooms. Heat production in a boiler is similar to heat production in a furnace. A fuel is ignited and burned, and combustion gases must be vented outdoors. However, a boiler has a water jacket rather than a heat exchanger. Water propelled by a pump circulates through the jacket where it picks up heat from the combustion chamber.

Hot water heat uses no blowers or ductwork. Instead, circulating water is piped to individual heating units like radiators and convectors or to radiant floor heating systems. The air in contact with the heating units rises and circulates in the room. If the radiators and convectors are properly located (usually under windows), the heat from a pumped hot water system is silent and practically draft free. However, the system reacts slowly to changes in heating needs, and there is no air filtration element. Hot water heat is comfortable and may be cost effective, particularly if cooling is not required.

Radiant floor heating systems pump warm water through flexible plastic pipes embedded in the floor. Heat radiates from the pipes and through the floor, steadily warming the room from below. Since it requires no floor area, radiant heating allows complete freedom in furniture arrangement. Radiant floor heating systems are becoming increasingly popular, especially under tiled floors in kitchens and bathrooms.

Electric resistance

The simplest heating system is an electric resistance system, which is inexpensive to install and can provide room-by-room temperature control. It also lacks the hazards associated with fuel combustion and produces no indoor pollution. Heat is produced when electricity passes through a resistance electric element. There are no moving parts and very low energy losses in the house, making resistance electric heat nearly 100 percent efficient. The downside of resistance electric heat is that can be costly to operate where electricity is relatively expensive.

Different types of resistance systems include:

- Baseboard units.
- Individual, fan-assisted space heaters.
- Furnace with a resistance element as the heat source.
- Gypsum ceiling panels that contain resistance elements.
- Resistance elements installed in floor systems.

Electric resistance systems are controlled by a switch or thermostat. Room heaters can be floor- or wall-mounted heating elements and with or without fans. Other options include radiant heat elements in or below the floor or in the ceiling.

Electric resistance heating may require a larger electric service to the house, usually 200 amps. Qualified electricians should install the units, which must be located away from flammable items.

Heat pumps

The two main types of heat pumps used today are the air-to-air heat pump and the geothermal heat pump. The air-to-air heat pump uses heat captured from the outdoor air to both heat and cool a house, while the geothermal heat pump uses the earth's warmth to accomplish the same goal.

Like an air conditioner, the air-to-air heat pump has two coils: one indoors and one outdoors. In winter, the outdoor coil absorbs heat from the air and pumps it to the indoor coil. House air is circulated over the indoor coil, heating the air. During the summer, heat is absorbed from the air passing over the indoor coil and directed to the outdoor coil, acting just like an air conditioning unit.

A heat pump uses electricity to transfer heat between the outdoor and indoor coils. As temperatures get colder, there may not be enough heat available in the outside air to heat the house. A secondary heat source, usually an electric resistance element, is used with this system. In some areas, a gas-fired furnace is used as a back-up system. The heat pump is more economical when the outdoor temperatures are higher, but the COP (Coefficient of Performance) drops as the temperature gets colder, possibly making the gas-fired system less expensive to operate in very cold weather.

Heat pumps move refrigerant between an evaporator coil and a condensing coil. Heat is released at the condenser coil where temperatures are much cooler than at the furnace heat exchanger. The circulating air in a heat pump system is often only 90 to 100 degrees Fahrenheit, while the circulating air in a fossil fuel system is 100 to 140 degrees. For adequate heat to be delivered to the rooms, more air must be moved through the supply ducts than with a fuel-fired system. To prevent uncomfortable drafts, carefully consider where to locate the heat registers.

Like a furnace, the air from a heat pump is distributed through the house using a system of return grilles, ductwork, filters, blower, and supply ducts. Because the power source is electricity, no combustion gases like carbon monoxide are produced, and a chimney is not needed.

Geothermal heat pumps (Figure 15-3), one of the most efficient systems available today, can use the earth's warmth to heat in winter and cool in summer because the soil

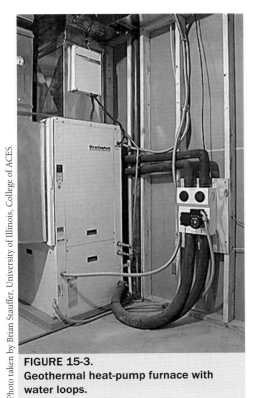

Photo taken by Brian Stauffer, University of Illinois, College of ACES.

FIGURE 15-3.
Geothermal heat-pump furnace with water loops.

temperature a few feet below the frost depth remains nearly constant, usually about 50 to 60 degrees Fahrenheit throughout the year. The temperature varies geographically, with the temperature being near the average annual air temperature. The most common system uses vertical loops of pipe in a well or horizontal loops of pipe buried below the soil surface to absorb or discharge heat. An anti-freeze solution circulates through the closed loop system to extract heat in the winter and cool in the summer.

The COP of geothermal systems is often in the 3.0 to 3.5 range, making them very economical to operate. Because of the constant temperature of the earth, back-up systems may not be necessary, except for an electrical power backup to operate the system. The installation cost is

higher than that of an air-to-air heat pump because of the additional cost of drilling the wells or cutting the trenches for the earth loops, the cost of the piping, and the cost of labor to install the piping. An experienced engineer or installer should design each geothermal installation.

Wood-burning stoves and unit heaters

In most modern homes, stoves burning wood are not used as primary heating systems but as backup heating systems or decorative elements. They provide economical comfort where firewood is readily available. Wood burning appliances can be messy. They require frequent cleaning, and large amounts of damp wood in a house can cause moisture and insect problems.

Older wood-burning appliances can have an efficiency rating of almost zero, but new wood burning units are nearly 80 percent efficient. They have tight fitting doors, a controlled draft, blowers, combustion air ducting, tight fitting dampers, and catalytic converters. Nevertheless, they can pollute the outdoors more than ordinary heating systems. In tight new houses, install only high-efficiency units with combustion air provided. The venting requirements for wood stoves are quite strict. Clearance must be maintained between the wood stove and flammable surfaces. To reduce fire risk, use approved heating units installed by qualified professionals.

Unit heaters are designed to heat a specific area only. They often are installed to supplement an existing system after a renovation or addition has been made to a house. All gas-fired units should vent outdoors.

Vented unit heaters can be satisfactory heat sources, but do not use unvented gas-fired or kerosene heaters as supplemental heating. They emit dangerous levels of carbon monoxide, carbon dioxide, nitrogen oxides, sulfur oxides, carbon particles, and water vapor into the air.

The climate, house size and structure efficiency (insulation level and air leakage) will affect the size of the heating system. System efficiency and fuel costs are variables to compare when evaluating heating systems. Fuel costs can vary considerably over time and in different locations. For instance, electricity costs in some part of the United States are ten times the electricity costs in other parts. Of course, electric heat will be much cheaper in those parts of the country where electricity costs less. To further complicate the matter, fuel suppliers will sometimes offer such incentives as lower prices or rebates. As you choose a heating system, consider your budget, the rising costs of energy, the availability of fuel, and your need for comfort.

Emergency heating

Modern furnaces and boilers require electrical power for operation. To ensure their operation during power outages, a back-up heating system is desirable in many climates. Assess the likelihood of a power outage at your house; consider the damage that could occur during a power outage, and think about the inconvenience a power outage could cause. You might conclude that the cost of providing a back-up heating source may be worthwhile.

Consider locating an emergency heating unit in a central location or a heat-specific area with several heaters that will prevent the plumbing from freezing. Emergency heating systems can increase the risks of fire and carbon monoxide so consider only heating equipment designed to safely heat houses. Wood-burning stoves and fireplaces can provide some emergency heat and may serve well for keeping a house livable for a short time, but normally, they will not be sufficient in extreme conditions.

Comparing heating systems

When comparing heating systems, people are most concerned about operating costs. In addition to fuel costs, operating costs are affected by:
- Heating system efficiency.
- Climate.
- House size.
- House structure efficiency.

Heating system efficiency

The most accurate way to judge the efficiency of a furnace, boiler, or heat pump is by its seasonal efficiency, because the efficiency varies with outdoor temperature: higher in cold weather for the furnace and boiler, lower for air-to-air heat pumps. The Federal standard for rating furnaces and boilers is known as Annual Fuel Utilization Efficiency (AFUE). The AFUE tells you how efficiently the furnace converts fuel into heat. An AFUE of 80 percent means that over the entire heating season, 80 percent of the fuel is used to heat your home, while the other 20 percent goes up the chimney. Federal legislation sets the minimum acceptable AFUE for new natural gas, LP gas, or oil furnaces or boilers at 78 percent. Higher efficiency furnaces up to about 95 percent are available but cost more to purchase.

Furnaces with AFUE ratings of 80 percent and higher are considered high efficiency. Some furnaces offer additional features that provide greater comfort (as well as additional energy savings). Two-speed furnace fans can run on low speed up to 90 percent of the time, so they operate more quietly and run for longer periods than do single-speed furnaces. Variable-capacity furnaces provide the ultimate combination of comfort, efficiency, and quiet performance. In addition to the benefits of two-speed furnaces, they offer "smart" motors than can monitor your home's comfort needs and automatically adjust the volume and speed of air to provide the most efficient heating or cooling. They offer added electrical efficiency as well: the smart fan motors on some variable-capacity furnaces use less electricity than a 100-watt light bulb. They operate so efficiently that they can actually increase the efficiency rating of your central air conditioning system and offer you added energy savings when you use continuous fan operation in any season.

Fuel cost comparisons

Estimating the cost of heating your house requires information about many variables. Table 15-1 shows a comparison between various fuels and efficiencies of heating equipment. You can use this table to compare the cost of your heating system with the cost of other heating systems.

Table 15-1. Comparing fuels and the efficiencies of heating equipment.

Adapted from *Heating Fuel Cost Comparison*, Greiner, T. 1984

Fuel	Quantity for one million Btu's	Fuel price	Annual efficiency	Fuel cost permillion Btu's
Natural gas	10.0 Ccf* x	_____ per Ccf	÷ (0.75 or _____)	= $ _____
Propane (LP gas)	11.11 gal x	_____ per gal	÷ (0.75 or _____)	= $ _____
Fuel oil (#2)	7.14 gal x	_____ per gal	÷ (0.75 or _____)	= $ _____
Electricity (resistance)	293 kWh x	_____ per kWh	÷ (1.00 or _____)	= $ _____
Electricity (air source heat pump)	293 kWh x	_____ per kWh	÷ (1.50 or _____)	= $ _____
Coal, hard	0.0417 ton x	_____ per ton	÷ (0.50 or _____)	= $ _____
Wood, hard	0.0357 cord x	_____ per cord	÷ (0.50 or _____)	= $ _____
Wood, medium	0.0476 cord x	_____ per cord	÷ (0.50 or _____)	= $ _____
Wood, soft	0.0714 cord x	_____ per cord	÷ (0.50 or _____)	= $ _____
Kerosene	7.41 gal x	_____ per gal	÷ (0.75 or _____)	= $ _____
Biomass (garbage, pulp, etc.)	143 lbs x	_____ per lb	÷ (0.50 or _____)	= $ _____

* Ccf = 100 cubic feet

If you were interested in comparing the cost of an existing propane system to any electrical system, there are several possibilities to select from Table 15-1. For example, if your furnace is 80 percent efficient, and propane sells for $0.75 per gallon and electricity is $0.05 per kWh, the comparable electric heat pump at an efficiency of 1.5 and electric resistance at an efficiency of 1.0 are:

Fuel	Quantity for one million Btu's	Fuelprice	Annual efficiency	Fuel cost per million Btu's
Propane (LP gas)	11.11 gal x	__$0.75_ per gal ÷	(0.75 or _0.80_)	= $ 10.52
Electricity (resistance)	293 kWh x	_$0.05 per kWh ÷	(1.00 or _____)	= $ 14.65
Electricity (heat pump)	293 kWh x	_$0.05 per kWh ÷	(1.50 or _____)	= $ 9.77

Cooling Systems

Most new home construction will include a cooling system. The system selected will depend on the house and the preference of the homeowner. To match the best system for your home, review the types of systems available, and install the most efficient system that will cost you the least money over several years, including installation, operating (energy) cost, and maintenance and repairs.

Types

The two main types of cooling systems that houses use are central or unitary. A supplementary cooling system called the whole-house fan system is being used to help save energy. The system you select will depend on your cooling goals, space availability, type of new construction, and remodeling constraints.

Central cooling systems

Central air cooling systems are the most common cooling systems used in houses because they typically use the blower and ductwork used for the forced air furnace. Examples of these systems are the central air conditioner and the air- and water-source heat pumps. The air- and water-source heat pumps can be used for both heating and cooling and are briefly described in the **Heating Systems** section.

Central air conditioners use the same operating principles and basic components as a home refrigerator. An air conditioner cools your home with a cold indoor coil called the evaporator. The condenser, a hot outdoor coil, releases the collected heat from indoors to the outdoors. The evaporator and condenser coils consist of looped copper tubing surrounded by aluminum fins. A pump, called the compressor, moves a refrigerant between the evaporator and the condenser. The pump forces the refrigerant through the tubing in the coils. The liquid refrigerant evaporates in the indoor evaporator coil, pulling heat out of the indoor air and thereby cooling the home. The hot refrigerant gas is pumped outdoors into the condenser where it reverts to a liquid, giving up its heat to the air flowing over the condenser's metal tubing and fins. Because of the noise of the condenser, plan to locate the air conditioning unit where its noise and heat will not affect outdoor living for you or your neighbors.

Unitary cooling systems

A unitary cooling system provides cooling to a room or section of the house. This system is used when ductwork is not present, installation of a more elaborate system is difficult, or when cooling is only desired in a room or section of a house. Examples of a unitary system are window, through the wall, and ductless split-system air conditioners and heat pumps (Figure 15-4).

Window and through-the-wall air conditioners can be noisy because the compressor and circulating fans are located within the unit. In ductless split-system air conditioners and heat pumps, the compressor is located separately from the fan. The compressor is located outside, usually mounted on the ground. The fan and cooling coil are located inside the house. A refrigerant line connects the compressor with the fan and cooling coil. Because the compressor is located outside, a ductless split-system is quieter than window or through-the-wall air conditioning systems.

Whole-house fan

Sometimes the inside temperature of a house is much higher than the outside temperature, which can occur during the late evening and early morning hours. Opening windows of a home often does not provide enough cross ventilation to cool the house, unless the wind is blowing in the proper direction with enough velocity. A whole-house fan system (Figure 15-5) is designed to draw cool outdoor air through open windows. Hot room air is usually exhausted through the attic to the outside by means of a high-capacity, attic or roof-mounted fan. This system can be used as the lone means of cooling a house, or it can help reduce the need for air conditioning. The fan can be located on an exterior wall or soffit.

This system uses considerably less energy than an air conditioner, and in moderate climate areas, it provides

FIGURE 15-4.
Window air conditioner.

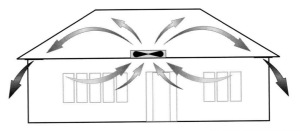

A whole-house fan pulls cool air in through the windows and exhausts hot air out of the attic vents.

FIGURE 15-5.
Whole-house fan concept diagram.

Adapted from *Whole-House Fans for Summer Cooling*, Tom Greiner and Shawn Shouse, Iowa State University. (http://www.extension.iastate.edu/Publications/PM1437.pdf)

adequate comfort except during periods of high temperatures or humidity. Manual switches or dehumidistats are available to control the fan's speed. Using variable speed controls or multiple fan speeds can help increase the efficiency of the system. Typically, a whole-house fan is installed to draw air out of a central location, such as a central hallway.

The disadvantages of this system are that it can only cool the house to the outside temperature; it does not dehumidify the house, and it allows dust and pollen to enter the house.

Efficiency rating

Air conditioners have an energy-efficiency rating that lists the number of British Thermal Units (Btu) of heat they can remove per hour for each watt of power they draw; higher ratings are more efficient. The efficiency rating for central air conditioners is the Seasonal Energy Efficiency Ratio (SEER). Select a unit that has a SEER rating of at least 12.0. Units can carry a rating of up to 18.0. The efficiency rating for room air conditioners is the Energy Efficiency Ratio (EER). Select a room air conditioner with an EER rating of at least 9.0 if you live in a mild climate and over 10.0 if you live in a hot climate.

Efficiency ratings are posted on an Energy Guide label, which must be clearly displayed on all new air conditioners. Many air conditioner manufacturers are participants in the EnergyStar® labeling program. EnergyStar®-labeled appliances mean that they have high EER and SEER ratings.

Make sure you buy the correct size of air conditioner. An air conditioner's efficiency, performance, durability, and initial cost depend on matching its size to the following factors:

- The area (square footage) of your home or room and number of windows it.
- The amount of shading provided to your home's windows, walls, and roof.
- The amount of insulation in your home's ceiling and walls.
- The amount of air leaking into your home from the outside.
- The amount of heat generated by the occupants and appliances in your home.

To be sure that you are getting the proper system for your home, take time to discuss energy efficiency ratings and system sizing with your contractor and system installer.

Ventilation Systems

A properly operating ventilation system will dilute and remove pollutants and moisture. Pollutants such as cigarette smoke, cooking odors, and out-gassing of composite and insulation materials can cause irritation and health risks. Moisture from cooking, bathing, cleaning, laundry, plants, aquariums, and below-grade basement floors and walls can cause mold, mildew, and rot problems. In winter, excess moisture can condense and freeze on windows and in leaky walls and attics.

Types

Ventilation systems can be either natural or mechanical. Natural ventilation can work well in moderate, dry climates but does not perform reliably when a house is closed during cold weather. New, tight houses can be wet and stuffy, leading to mold and rot. For that reason, experts recommend that new houses incorporate a mechanical ventilation system to reduce drafts, control moisture levels, and prevent mold and rot. Mechanical ventilation systems can be designed very precisely to eliminate over-ventilation that can increase energy costs and under-ventilation that can lead to problems, such as moisture condensation on windows. Some homeowners choose to supplement the mechanical system with natural ventilation when outside temperatures are moderate and relative humidity is low.

A well-planned mechanical ventilation system should have a general ventilation system for the interior or living area and a system for the attic of the house.

Living area

Generally, houses are constructed as tight as possible to minimize unwanted air leaking. The two most common methods to mechanically ventilate the living area of a house are by an exhaust-only fan or by a heat recovery ventilator (HRV). Ceiling fans are a third type of fan used to distribute the air within a room.

Some fans can be noisy, and a sone is the accepted measure of fan noise. Look for a fan with a sone rating of one or below if the fan is to be installed in the interior of a home.

Exhaust-only fan

Exhaust-only fans remove air from within the house living area directly to the outside. A fan that exhausts to the attic or into another room within the house is not operating as a true

exhaust-only fan. This system consists of a quiet, high-quality exhaust fan located in an outside wall or connected to an outside duct. These fans are inexpensive to install but expensive to operate and not as efficient as a heat recovery ventilator unit. Examples of exhaust-only fans are bathroom and oven/range hood fans. The fan in this type of system depressurizes the house and pulls fresh air into the house through leaks. Because the fan is exhausting air from the house and replacing it with outdoor air, operating costs depend on the size of the fan and the efficiency of the heating and cooling equipment.

Disadvantages include potential pollution of the air being pulled into the house by substances like dirt, pollen, and insulation particles. Such systems may lead to moisture problems in humid climates because moist air is pulled into the wall cavity. Because an exhaust-only system depressurizes a house, backdrafting of dangerous gas from vented appliances can be a result, or radon gas can be drawn in. Consult with a residential ventilation professional when sizing exhaust-only fans for a house. In general, you should plan to provide 100 cfm (cubic feet per minute) of ventilation for a kitchen and 50 cfm for each bathroom.

Heat recovery ventilator

An HRV system transfers heat from the exhaust air to the intake air during the heating season and from intake to exhaust during the cooling season. It reduces the energy costs associated with ventilation. An HRV ventilates the house with two fans. One fan brings fresh air into the

Moisture and Mold
Many activities in the home produce moisture that needs to be removed. Each person produces about 3 pints of water per day while breathing. About 1 pint of moisture is introduced during a 10-minute shower. Moisture coming through a concrete basement floor and walls due to moist soil on the outside may be as much as 100 pints per day. Excessive moisture can lead to mold in a home. Molds can damage building materials and cause respiratory problems. Children, the elderly, pregnant women, and people with existing respiratory sensitivities are at higher risk for adverse health effects of molds.

Moisture can be removed by ventilation when outside temperatures are cool and with a dehumidifier or air conditioning when the outside temperatures are warm.

Select a fan design and size that is appropriate for the room where it will be installed. Blades can be plastic, metal, or wood. Metal blades may be sharp and can corrode over time. Wooden blades that are designed for outdoor fans should come pre-treated to resist moisture and warping. For maximum comfort and flexibility, three-way motor speeds are preferable. Before purchasing a fan, run it on all settings to determine if it is too noisy. If it is, try a different brand or a model with blades made of a different material.

house while the second fan exhausts stale air. Within the heat exchanger, heat energy flows from one air stream to the other. In winter, air coming into the house is preheated by warm air blown out. In summer, air coming into the house is precooled by cool air blown out. The system offers excellent control of ventilation while recovering energy, thus reducing operating costs when compared to an exhaust-only fan.

Outdoor air coming in is filtered to improve indoor air quality by removing pollens and dirt. The system is balanced, so it does not affect pressures in the home or cause backdrafting. An HRV comes as a packaged unit with complete installation and operation manuals. The initial cost is considerably higher than for an exhaust-only interior ventilation system but may be well worth the investment.

Ceiling fans

Ceiling fans are popular both for comfort and as a decorative feature in a room. In warm weather, they move the air and create a breeze to give the sensation that a room is cooler than it really is. The thermostat can then be set at a higher temperature, reducing air conditioning costs. Since ceiling fans do not actually lower humidity or cool the air, they are most effective when used in combination with air conditioning.

Reversible ceiling fans help reduce heating bills in the winter by moving warm air (which rises up to the ceiling) down into the room, lowering energy costs and providing a more even, comfortable temperature distribution, especially in rooms with high ceilings.

Attic

Leakage through the top floor ceiling is a major source of air leakage out of houses and increases heating and cooling costs. Moisture in the air leaking from the house can collect in the attic insulation, reducing the effectiveness of the insulation and promoting mold growth in the attic. In addition, leakage through the ceiling depressurizes the house and can cause backdrafting of chimneys and vents. Careful sealing of cracks and openings to the attic and installing a continuous vapor retarder across the ceiling will help prevent the leakage of air and moisture into the attic. Avoid recessed lights, or use sealed recessed light fixtures in ceilings adjoining the attic.

The attic needs properly sized vents to control moisture and heat build up. Without adequate ventilation, heat and moisture will cause mold, mildew, and deterioration of insulation, structure framing, and roofing. Air should enter the attic from the outside through vents installed in the soffits and exit the attic through vents at the ridge top or through gable-end louvers or ridge vents (Figure 15-6). If adequate ridge vents are installed, gable-end louvers can be the inlets. A combination of attic ridge vents, soffit vents, ceiling vapor retarder, and proper insulation is adequate for most attics. Attic vents will typically have screens, deflectors, and louvers on them to prevent birds, blowing snow, and dust from entering.

Your contractor can advise you about attic ventilation, but a good ventilation system should meet some simple basic requirements:

- If a vapor retarder is used in the ceiling, the attic ventilation should be 0.5 square foot of free air inlet and 0.5 square foot of outlet per 300 square feet of floor area.

• If a vapor retarder is not in the ceiling or if the vent exhaust openings are not more than 3 feet above the eave vents, the attic ventilation should be 0.5 square foot of free air inlet and 0.5 square foot of outlet per 150 square feet.

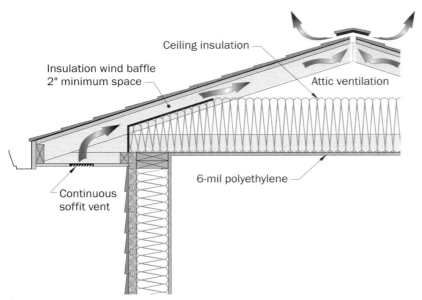

FIGURE 15-6.
Air entering through soffit into attic space and exiting through the ridge vent.

Adapted from *Moisture Control Handbook: Principles and Practices for Residential and Small Commercial Buildings.* 1993. Lstibureck and Carmody.

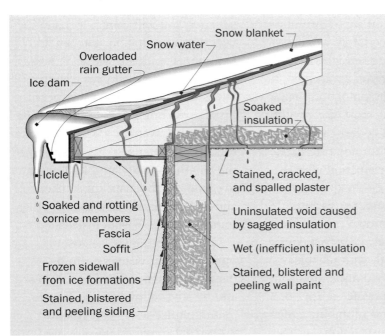

Ice Dams
Ice dams occur when escaping heat melts snow on the room, and the water freezes when it reaches the cooler surface near the eave. Water from ice dams can enter wall cavities, causing insulation to be ineffective, leading to rotting of structural wood, staining wall and ceiling coverings, and creating conditions conducive for mold growth. The potential for ice dams can be minimized by sealing air leaks from the living space to the attic and providing adequate attic insulation and ventilation to keep the roof cold.

Adapted from *Keep Your Home Healthy.* 2001. K. Hellevang.

- Where adequate natural ventilation cannot be provided, a powered, roof-attic ventilator with thermostat or humidistat control can be installed on the roof or gable ends.
- If a powered, roof-attic ventilator is installed, it must be properly sized because operation of powered, roof-attic ventilators without adequate intake area can create suction in the house and interfere with proper operation of vents and chimneys.

Water and Sewer Systems

If your home is in an urban or suburban area, the municipality in which you live will install and manage the water and sewer systems that serve your property. As a homeowner, you will be responsible for the connections to the public systems and for the systems within your house. If you live in a rural area, you may be connected to a rural water system, or you may have a private water system. If you are in a rural area, you almost certainly will have an on-site domestic sewage disposal system. Wherever you are located, the design and installation of your water and sewer systems most likely will be governed by local codes. Usually you must get a permit for any proposed water or sewer system, and a local inspector will check the quality of work on these systems at various stages of construction.

As a homeowner, your best course of action is to work with reliable contractors and subcontractors. You should check your state, county, or city regulations and plumbing codes before starting construction, and be sure that the installation of these systems follows the prescribed code.

For additional information on water systems, refer to *Private Water Systems Handbook* (MWPS-14). For additional information on sewage systems, refer to *On-site Domestic Sewage Disposal Handbook*, (MWPS-24).

Water

A properly designed water system should supply the quantity of water needed every day all year. It should deliver water at a rate that meets the temporary large demands that occur each day, and in certain rural or suburban locations, it should be able to provide enough water to fight small fires.

As a homeowner, your main concern will be with having a system that meets your needs now and is expandable to meet any future needs you might anticipate. If you have a private water supply, you will need space inside the house (probably in the basement) for a water pump, pressure tank, and perhaps a water softener. You will want adequate water pressure in your kitchen and bathrooms, and you will want at least two exterior hose bibs for watering lawns or washing cars. Many people install hose bibs on all four sides of a house for convenience. Good contractors install water systems to minimize the length of water runs, and often try to economize by installing kitchens and bathrooms adjacent to each other to minimize the cost of installation.

You can cut down the cost of operating your water system by installing water-conserving fixtures and by advocating lifestyle choices that minimize water use. About 70 percent of the total water used in a home is for toilet flushing, laundry, and baths. Choose water-conserving toilets that use 1.6 gallons or less per flush. To reduce water use and energy consumption to heat the water, install clothes washers with adjustable fill levels for small loads and dishwashers with water-conserving cycles. Select water-saving faucets and showerheads. Recent advances in technology have provided a variety of choices for homeowners. For example, new, water-conserving showerheads provide satisfactory results while using one third of the water used with older fixtures.

Sewer

The sewer system should be able to handle all household sewage, including washer water, bath water, and garbage disposal scraps. The home sewer system must connect to an approved sewer connection usually either a central sewer system or a permitted on-site wastewater (septic) system. Do not try to cut corners with the sewer system because the health and safety of the home's occupants are at stake.

The sewage system for a house includes sewer pipes, vent pipes, and water traps. The sewer pipes carry the household sewage from all sources and all appliances including sinks, laundry, stools, tubs, and showers to the sewer outlet for the home. The vent pipes allow airflow to prevent interference with proper drainage and carry away sewer gases from all parts of the system. The water traps prevent gases from escaping into the house through the fixtures.

As with a water system, the homeowner's main concerns will be with having a system that meets current needs now and is expandable to meet any future needs without requiring major reconstruction efforts. During building or remodeling, consider having an outlet for a bathroom stool installed in the basement or in unused space on the second floor or in the attic. Ask your contractor about installing sufficient and well-located vent pipes in case you want to add an additional bathroom or laundry sink. Thinking about future needs will save time, money, and frustration later.

Electrical System

The electrical system in a typical house consists of many components: conductors (wiring), breakers, a service entrance panel (SEP), outlets, and lights. An electrical circuit consists of all wiring controlled by one circuit breaker. The breakers are located in the SEP, which distributes power to various parts of the house. The breakers act as protective devices for the circuits, automatically cutting off power from the main breaker during an overload or short.

Develop a plan

A good electrical plan is essential in making sure enough outlets or sufficient lighting is available in a room. To ensure that everything is wired properly, all electrical wiring must be completed according to the National Electrical Code, and should be installed by a licensed electrician and approved by an electrical inspector.

Consider electrical needs for office equipment, lighting, entertainment systems, and communication systems. Plan for long-range

One way to minimize the danger of people being injured due to an electrical problem is to have ground fault circuit interrupters (GFCIs) installed (Figure 15-7). These devices protect people from dangerous shock by cutting the circuit almost immediately upon detecting a ground fault (current is escaping to ground somewhere in the circuit). The GFCI monitors the current going out and the current returning. If these current levels are not equal, then a ground fault is detected, and the hot wire is disconnected in about 0.125 seconds. This protection is required on bathroom outlets, kitchen outlets near the sink, and outdoor and garage outlets, or any location where floors may be wet. A GFCI breaks the circuit much more quickly and at lower currents than a circuit breaker does.

Receptacle GFCIs can be used to replace 120-volt receptacles that have no equipment ground. In these applications, the circuit can be operated without an equipment ground.

For 120-volt circuits, both the circuit neutral and hot wire connect to the GFCI. The GFCI has a white lead to connect to the neutral bar.

FIGURE 15-7.
GFCI circuit breaker.

wiring needs; it is less expensive to provide extra capacity than to add it later. Providing access from the basement or attic simplifies adding or changing wiring. Consider using "Smart House," an electrical wiring system that standardizes the wiring in a house. By hiring a contractor who can install Smart House wiring, you will have conduits for low voltage and specialized wiring so wiring can be added or changed later by pulling additional wires through the conduit.

You should plan to install convenience outlets on every wall, and to locate them no more than 12 feet apart. Numerous outlets minimize the use of extension cords, allow equipment and lighting to be moved easily, and make it easier to arrange furniture. To reduce noise transmission between rooms, avoid placing outlets back to back in the same wall. Protect outlets with ground fault interrupters, arc-fault interrupters, and surge protectors.

The kitchen and home office need more outlets than other rooms. In the kitchen, you will need to provide separate outlets for the refrigerator, microwave, dishwasher, and garbage disposal. A good design limits each kitchen circuit to less than the 10-outlet maximum. Another good strategy is to install outlets above the counter backsplash, alternating adjacent outlets between two circuits. In a kitchen, outlets should be close enough to appliances to allow the use of 24-inch appliance cords. For more information about kitchens and lighting, see **Chapter 6. Kitchens.**

Consider an emergency system

In an emergency, a properly sized electric generator can supply the electrical power for lights, gas-fired heating appliances, sump pumps, refrigeration equipment, and other critical needs. A small generator used conservatively can help you cope with an emergency (for example, operate the furnace for two hours and then run the refrigerator and freezer for two hours). A larger generator will allow several appliances to operate simultaneously. Also consider a generator that can burn natural gas or LPG; these units can be connected to the supply for a gas-fired furnace and will operate for long periods without refueling. However, electric heating units require larger amounts of power than is generally available from residential generators.

If you are going to install an emergency system, you will need to provide an outdoor electrical connection and double-throw disconnect switch. Failure to properly disconnect the generator from the electric service can feed high-voltage power back through supply transformers and injure or kill workers repairing the electric service. Have a qualified electrician install the system, and inform the electric utility that you have a generator.

Lighting

Proper lighting enhances your living areas and provides convenience, security, comfort, and dramatic effects. Factors to consider in selecting and installing lighting include the size of the room, the mood that you wish to create, and most important, the types of activities that will occur in each area. Plan your lighting needs as you design your living areas to save money on future installations and to have the most effective lighting possible. To ensure that your home has adequate, well-placed lighting, you might consider working with a lighting designer.

Make a lighting plan

A good lighting plan combines general, task, and accent lighting to meet the interior and exterior lighting needs of a home (Table 15-2). General lighting provides overall illumination with chandeliers, ceiling or wall-mounted fixtures, recessed lighting, or track lights. Task lighting provides illumination for specific activities, such as reading, cooking, studying, or hobby work. Track and recessed lighting, pendant lighting, and portable lamps can provide glare-free, shadowless lighting for performing these tasks. Accent lighting, usually provided by track, recessed, or wall-mounted fixtures, adds drama to rooms by spotlighting prized possessions like paintings or by

Table 15-3. Estimated illumination levels.

Use this table to help provide a baseline when estimating a room's illumination level.

Comparison item	Level of illumination (foot-candles)
Moonlight	0.01
Dimly lit restaurant	1.0
Bright room	100
Bright sunlight	10,000

highlighting curtains, outdoor landscaping, or the texture of a wall.

A variety of lighting options in a room or space provides the flexibility to meet different needs. You can also take advantage of natural light by installing skylights and other privacy windows. Nightlights are a safety feature for persons who often get up during the night. For people whose sleep is disturbed by light, motion- or sound-activated nightlights are available that can be plugged into an outlet near the bed.

Understand the characteristics of light

Five characteristics of light that can be used to compare light performance are power use, total light emitted, efficiency, color rendering index (CRI), and lifespan, Table 15-4. Power use is the amount of electricity a bulb uses, which is measured in watts. Total light emitted is the amount of light a bulb produces; it is measured in lumens. The efficiency of a light bulb is measured in lumens of light produced divided by the watts of electricity used. The CRI measures the effect a light source has on perceived color of an object. A high CRI value means a bulb makes all colors look natural; low

Table 15-2. Recommended lighting levels for various tasks.

See Table 15-3 to get a perspective on illumination levels.

Task	Illumination level (foot-candle)*
General lighting	2-10
Dining	10-20
Kitchen general	20-50
Detailed work	50-100
Laundry	20-50
Normal reading	20-50
Prolonged reading or studying	50-100

* 1 foot-candle = 1 lumen per square foot

CRI values mean a light will cause some colors to wash out or appear to be a completely different hue. The lifespan of a bulb is an estimated number of hours a light bulb will last.

Energy efficiency

Save on future energy bills by using energy-efficient options whenever possible. When choosing lighting, consider initial cost, light quality, appearance of bulbs and fixtures, and their heat production. The most common choices are incandescent and fluorescent.

Incandescent lights

Consider incandescent fixtures (Figure 15-8) when light is needed for short periods and when lights are turned on and off frequently. They reach full output almost immediately. Their initial cost is relatively low, and they operate well in most conditions

**FIGURE 15-8.
Incandescent bulb.**

**FIGURE 15-9.
Spiral compact fluorescent.**

Table 15-4. Characteristics of lights.

Total amount of light emitted is equal to the average lumens. Efficiency (lumens per watt) is based on converting electricity into light.

Lamp	Rated size (watts)	Power use (watt)*	Total light emitted(lumens)	Efficiency (lumens/watt)*	CRI	Lifespan (hours)
Incandescent						
Standard	40	40	410	10	100	1,500
	60	60	780	13	100	1,000
	100	100	1,580	16	100	750
	150	150	2,500	17	100	750
	300	300	5,860	20	100	750
Fluorescent						
Compact						
Spiral, T3	26	26	1,700	65	82	8,000
Spiral, T4	42	42	2,650	63	82	10,000
Biax, T4	20	20	1,200	60	82	12,000
	28	28	1,750	63	82	12,000
Tube (T8) (cool white or warm white)						
24-inch	17	19	1,325	70	75	20,000
48-inch	32	35	2,800	80	82	20,000
	44	50	4,000	80	86	18,000
60-inch	55	61	5,050	83	86	18,000
96-inch	51	56	4,000	71	75	7,500
	86	95	8,200	86	86	24,000

*Including the ballast for fluorescents.

including low temperatures. Incandescent light efficiency is relatively low, so they are the most expensive light to operate. Note that their efficiency increases with wattage, (Table 15-2). Incandescent lights are short lived—only 750 hours for 100- to 150-watt bulbs. Light output decreases to 80% to 90% of its initial value as the bulb approaches its rated life. A 100-watt incandescent bulb radiates 10% of the input energy as visible light and 72% in the infrared spectrum, accounting for the low efficiency. The high infrared output can also be detrimental in some applications. Incandescent lights produce a warm flattering light similar to daylight. They have the highest CRI value so should be used in areas where determining natural colors is important.

Fluorescent lights

Fluorescent fixtures cost more than incandescent fixtures but produce 3 to 4 times more light per watt (Table 15-4). Turning these lights on and off frequently or leaving them on for only 2 to 3 hours at a time reduces lamp life. Near the end of its life, a typical fluorescent lamp emits only 60 to 80 percent of its initial light output. Standard white fluorescents give the highest light output, but are not desirable for color matching tasks. Deluxe white fluorescents are about 25 percent less efficient than the standard bulb. Fluorescents have high CRI characteristics; however, some of them may produce light more in the blue light spectrum, which enhances the colors in the green, blue, violet, and magenta range. The deluxe cool white produces light nearest to daylight.

The deluxe warm white produces light that is closest in color to the incandescent. Fluorescents produce little infrared light.

Compact fluorescents are available to screw into incandescent light fixtures (Figure 15-9). They are available in several wattages. They are energy efficient, saving up to 70 percent versus incandescent bulbs. Compact fluorescents are more expensive than incandescent bulbs, but can last up to 16 times longer because of their lower power usage. They may not hold up to power surges well, so they should be used in areas where power surges are not a concern. Today's compact fluorescents have very high CRI values and start almost immediately, so they are closer in performance to incandescent lights.

Safety and Convenience Systems

Incorporating a safety system in a house can save property and possibly lives. Smoke, fire, and carbon monoxide alarms are common. Security systems are becoming standard in many homes, and more and more homeowners are installing fire suppression systems.

Smoke and carbon monoxide alarms

Alarms are available to warn of dangerous conditions such as smoke (Figure 15-10), carbon monoxide, gas, and security breaches or equipment failures such as sump pump or freezer outage. Single-station, stand-alone alarms, which sound a warning at the alarm location, are relatively inexpensive and easy to install. Centrally installed alarms that sound a

FIGURE 15-10.
Smoke alarm.

Purchase carbon monoxide alarms listed with recognized testing laboratories, such as Underwriters Laboratory or International Approval Services. These alarms make a loud noise that will awaken most people. Carbon monoxide alarms are available both with and without displays; consider purchasing at least one carbon monoxide alarm with a digital readout showing current concentrations of carbon monoxide and a memory that stores the peak reading. Carbon monoxide alarms do not indicate low carbon monoxide levels and do not sound at low levels. However, low concentrations can cause health problems if you are exposed for long periods or are at high risk. To avoid carbon monoxide exposure, eliminate smoking in the house, use only vented gas appliances, do not leave a vehicle running in a garage attached to the house, and hire a qualified heating contractor to inspect all fuel-burning appliances yearly.

warning throughout the house when an alarm at any location detects a problem are a different matter. They are more expensive and usually require professional installation. If you think you might install a central alarm system in the future, plan for the wiring installation when building a new home or remodeling an existing home.

Smoke and carbon monoxide alarms can save lives. All houses should have smoke and fire alarms, and all houses that burn fossil fuels should have carbon monoxide alarms. Install the alarms on each level of the house and outside each sleeping area. Placing a detector in the hallway outside bedrooms with an additional one in the bedroom is recommended. The alarms on these devices should be able to wake sleeping occupants. Smoke detectors can be purchased that operate a strobe light to wake hearing-impaired occupants; they should be installed inside the bedroom. Smoke detectors should be installed on or near the ceiling, while carbon monoxide detectors can be installed at any height. Both battery and line-powered alarms with battery-powered backup are available. Check with building code officials and insurance representatives to determine the proper number and type of smoke and carbon monoxide alarms for your home.

Two types of smoke alarms are available: ionization and photoelectric. Ionization alarms are best at detecting quick-burning fires while photoelectric are best at detecting slow-burning smoldering fires. Consider installing at least one of each type or an alarm with a combination response. Experts recommend

installing smoke alarms with exit lighting in hallways, above stairwells, and in exit routes.

Security alarms

Security alarms (Figure 15-11) with sensors on doors and windows sound an alarm when an intruder enters the house. Interior motion detectors can be set to warn when unexpected motion occurs. Alarms can be set to sound within the house, outside the house, or at a remote location. Because alarm systems require wiring that is best concealed, it is wise to install the wiring when building a new home or when doing extensive remodeling. It is a good idea to install the wiring even if there is no plan to install the alarm right away.

Fire suppression

To protect life and property, residential sprinkler systems use plastic pipes and sprinkler heads designed for houses. These professionally installed systems are a cost-effective means of protecting residential properties, especially in areas where high-value items area located. You will need controls and larger water supply lines for the house, and the system must be checked periodically. Individual benefits include reduced homeowner's insurance rates and the security of knowing your house is protected against fire. The damage caused by a sprinkler is much less than the damage caused by smoke and fire.

Indoor air quality systems

Many people have health problems when poor indoor air quality exists. Filtering systems to control dust and fine air particles can help people with allergies. Controlling the humidity

FIGURE 15-11.
Security alarm control panel.

level in a house also can help create a healthier environment for people and can preserve furniture and structural components of the house.

Air filtering

High-efficiency filtering systems reduce dust and fine particulates, which can cause respiratory problems. Electronic air filters and HEPA (high efficiency particulate air) filters are commonly used in houses. Both are effective at removing fine particulates. The effectiveness of a filtering system depends on the quantity of air that is filtered and the efficiency of the system. A product of these two factors (for a given pollutant) is expressed as the unit's clean air delivery rate (CADR).

Air filtering systems can be installed in the central air handling system or can be individual room units. Consider installing a central filter first. Central systems are installed in the air return ductwork, and filtering occurs when air is passing through the filter. To increase

its effectiveness, consider operating the unit continuously. A high-efficiency electric motor and variable speed control reduce energy costs and noise level.

As is the case with most house-wide systems, you should plan to install a central air filtering system during construction or remodeling. Contact a heating contractor for advice, products, and installation of central units.

Humidification and dehumidification

Acceptable relative humidity is a compromise among humidity levels that enhance human health, levels that do not harm the house structure or promote mold growth, and the costs of achieving the desired level.

In winter, loose houses are dried by air leaks and become too dry, while tight houses trap moisture and pollutants and are too wet. In houses without controlled ventilation systems, relative humidity is difficult to control. Humidifiers can be added to loose, dry houses, but because the water in humidifiers can harbor bacteria and spread it throughout the house, they can be a source of air contamination. In a loose house, moisture released into the house passes out of the house through cracks and holes and can collect in the house structure and damage insulation and framing.

To forestall these kinds of problems, many homeowners add an interior ventilation system while building or remodeling. In cold climates, indoor humidity can be lowered by ventilating with cold, dry outdoor air. To reduce operating costs, consider using a heat recovery ventilation system. Control the ventilation system with a dehumidistat.

If needed, individual air filtering consoles can be used to clean the air in a single, closed room.
Individual room units are available with either electronic air filters or HEPA filters. Most air filters are labeled with a Minimum Efficiency Reporting Value (MERV) rating number, which measures a filter's ability to trap particles ranging in size from 0.3 microns to 10.0 microns as specified by ANSI/ASHRAE Standard 52.2. Residential filters commonly have MERV ratings of 1-12. The higher the MERV rating, the more efficient the filter is, and the more particles it can filter. A MERV 5-8 rated filter is adequate for most residential applications, and a MERV 9-12 rated filter provides residential filtration for special needs. HEPA filters are the most efficient mechanical filters for removing small particles, which can be breathed deep into the lungs. HEPA filters remove 0.3 micron sized particles at a minimum of 99.97% efficiency. Some manufacturers also have their own rating systems. For portable air cleaning systems, ANSI/AHAM AC-1 (Association of Home Appliance Manufacturers) may be useful in estimating the effectiveness of the units.

Avoid extremely low and extremely high relative humidities. Winter relative humidities lower than 30 percent can cause chapped skin and lips, breathing problems, scratchy nose and throat, and static electricity that can lead to shocks when touching metal objects. Winter relative humidities higher than 50 to 60 percent can lead to mold growth and excessive moisture condensation on windows and walls. As a rule-of-thumb during cold weather, when the outdoor temperature is 15°F or lower, the indoor relative humidity should be 30 percent. The relative humidity can be higher during cold weather as the outdoor temperature increases. In summer, relative humidities lower than 40 percent are difficult to achieve without excessive dehumidification, and relative humidities higher than 70 percent promote condensation and mold growth.

In summer, naturally ventilated houses depend on outside airflow through openings to cool the house. Inside temperatures and humidities depend on those outside conditions, and if temperatures and humidities are not acceptable, mechanical cooling and dehumidification are required.

Hot, humid climates require the use of mechanical air conditioning, which lowers both the temperature and the relative humidity. Contact a qualified contractor to assist with sizing the air conditioning unit. Smaller units, with longer run times, provide better temperature and humidity control at lower operating cost. Multi-capacity units easily handle extremely hot days or provide additional cooling when guests are visiting. Operate dehumidifiers as needed for additional moisture control.

Convenience systems

The best time to install conveniences in a house is during construction or major remodeling. If finances do not allow these items to be installed immediately, provide space for these items so they can be easily installed in the future.

Sound, communication, and entertainment

Sound, communication, and entertainment systems including home theaters, surround sound speakers, computers, video and music systems, and elaborate television systems are rapidly evolving. For example, a whole-house audio package enables homeowners to control the music in any room with the touch of a button. While the most complex systems are typically

installed in high-end houses, homes that are more modest are being built or remodeled to incorporate these systems. Even if you do not plan to install such a system when you are building, consider reserving space and installing wiring and outlets during construction. That will enable you to add systems when you want without the need for major modification to your house. You will save money, time, and effort by having the wiring in place.

Vacuum

Vacuuming picks up dust and dirt. Individual vacuum sweepers, with low-efficiency collection bags, blow the fine particulates back into the house, and fine particulates can cause respiratory problems. Installing a central vacuum system (Figure 15-12) can help minimize air quality problems. A central vacuum system allows the fine particulates to be exhausted immediately to the

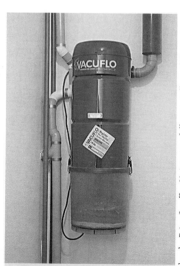

FIGURE 15-12.
Central-vacuuming power unit.

Photo taken by Brian Stauffer, University of Illinois, College of ACES.

outside of the house, reducing health problems caused by house dust. Central vacuum systems also are convenient and provide ample cleaning power. Installing a central vacuum system requires space for the central vacuum unit along with special piping and electrical wiring, so if you are going to install a central vacuum system, do it during original construction or during a major remodeling project. Specialty contractors are available to help you select and install products.

Resources

ASHRAE Standard 62.2-2003, Ventilation and Acceptable Indoor Air Quality in Low-Rise Residential Buildings.

Energy Star: http://www.energystar.gov

Greiner, T. 1984. *Heating Fuel Cost Comparison*. Extension Publication: Iowa State University. Publication no. PM-1068.

Hellevang, K. 2001. *Keep Your Home Healthy*. 2001. North Dakota State University Extension Service. Publication no. AE-1204. (http://www.ext.nodak.edu/extpubs/ageng/structu/ae1204.pdf)

Lstibureck, J., and John Carmody. 1993. *Moisture Control Handbook: Principles and Practices for Residential and Small Commercial Buildings*. Van Nostrand Reinhold, 115 Fifth Avenue, New York, New York 10003.

Mancl, Karen, Marty Sailus, and Linda Wagenet, 1991. *Private Drinking Water Systems Supplies* (NRAES-47), Ithaca, NY: Northeast Regional Agricultural Engineering Service, nraes@cornell.edu.

Manual D from the Air Conditioning Contractors of America.

Manual J from the Air Conditioning Contractors of America.

MidWest Plan Service (MWPS), 1982. *Onsite Domestic Sewage Disposal Handbook* (MWPS-24). Ames, IA: MWPS, Iowa State University, http://www.mwpshq.org, 1-800-562-3618.

MidWest Plan Service (MWPS), 1979. *Private Water Systems Handbook* (MWPS-14). Ames, IA: MWPS, Iowa State University, http://www.mwpshq.org, 1-800-562-3618.

Rose, William B., Henry R. Spies, and Rose Geier-Wilson. 1994. *Heating the Home* (BRC Notes G3.1) Urbana-Champaign, IL: Building Research Council (BRC), University of Illinois, 1-800-336-0616.

Section R806 Roof Ventilation, 2000 International Residential Code for One and Two-Family Dwellings. International Code Council.

Sneed, Bruce. *Building a Radon-Resistant New Home*, Kansas Radon Program, Engineering Extension Kansas State University, 800-693-5343, http://radon.oznet.ksu.edu

CHAPTER 16

Building Materials

PROSPECTIVE HOMEOWNERS MUST CHOOSE among a variety of alternative building materials used to construct a house. Materials including wood, concrete, steel, masonry block, fiberglass, and even straw have been used in the construction of a house. Wood is still the most popular material used throughout a home. For longevity and other reasons, concrete and steel are commonly used, in appropriate places, even for wood frame construction. For aesthetics or other personal reasons, some homeowners may prefer a specialty wood material system, such as timber or log frame construction, or straw. House construction typically uses several different materials and systems in combination during the construction process. This chapter will focus on the light wood frame system and the accompanying use of other materials such as steel and concrete where appropriate.

Today's technology-driven home marketplace offers a bewildering array of choices in the materials that can be used to construct a house. By considering the principles in this chapter, you can reach decisions about incorporating technology into a home, making it more attractive, affordable, convenient, efficient, and healthy. The effort you expend in making these choices can pay huge dividends over the life of your home.

Guidelines for Selecting the Right Materials

In today's building market, many more kinds of building materials are available today than 20 years ago. Synthetics can replace metal; plastic roofing gives the same appearance as wood shakes; composite engineered wood products for framing can replace dimension lumber. Some of the alternatives to conventional materials have track records that instill confidence in their performance as building components. You can, however, still benefit by following the advice of the proverb, "Be not the first by whom the new is tried nor yet the last to put the old aside." Before you buy, get references and view the new materials in use. If you want an affordable home, incorporate tried-and-true methods in your new house.

Consider the balance between quality and initial price. As another proverb warns, "The bitterness of poor quality remains long after the sweetness of low cost is gone." When you select materials, you decide a large part of the finished cost and future maintenance needs of your house. Ask yourself the following questions about components that receive frequent use or face maximum weather exposure, thus requiring special attention:

The process of selecting materials for your house requires you to make judgments that reflect some of your personal preferences and needs, while taking into account financial limitations. Those values relate to your definition of quality. In many respects, the themes throughout this book (affordable, attractive, convenient, efficient, and healthy) provide a framework for the way people think about quality. All such definitions of quality are legitimate, but families balance the themes in different ways as they make decisions about building the home.

- Are the windows easy to open, close, and seal?
- Do the roofing, gutters, and downspouts require minimum maintenance?
- Will the flooring clean easily, wear well with foot traffic, and not discolor with sunlight exposure?
- Are the strategically placed carpets of good quality?

As you choose your building materials, keep the following issues in mind:
- Codes and standards.
- Quality and appearance.
- Resource efficiency.
- Environmental safety.
- Cost.

Codes and standards

Many states, counties, or other municipalities have codes that restrict the types of construction materials that can be used. Often the material details of the building codes are based on fire safety or another judgment of human risk. If you are exploring the use of a type of building material that you do not see used elsewhere in the neighborhood, it may be wise to investigate through a local code authority whether use of the material is permitted. This approach can save considerable time and trouble later in planning and especially in construction. In addition, codes may dictate the type of structural system that is used and how it is used.

Standards usually establish certain minimum performance criteria and broadly regulate materials, design, and manufacturing. Standards ensure that materials are properly made or applied. The American Society for Testing and Materials (ASTM), for example, has written standards for the structural performance of caulks and sealants. By checking the fine print on the material label, you can more confidently match the material to the job. Standards can also give you information about the safe use of a material, such as the volatile organic compounds (VOCs) in paint formulated for indoor use. For standards to be of value, you must spend time becoming acquainted with them or else find a trustworthy contractor who knows the standards.

Many trade associations and other industry groups provide assurance that their products have met established standards. They use various methods, such as grade marks, labels, or seals, to state that a product meets or exceeds the appropriate industry standards. Some certifications of quality are of little value, while others are excellent. A certification issued by an independent testing laboratory is usually the most reliable.

Quality and appearance

To many homeowners, living within their means is a fundamental principle. This aspect of quality in the home may be legitimately reflected in the choice of building materials that are visible to the residents, visitors, and neighbors. For some people, quality in building materials is defined as "user friendly" or "no fuss." People who place a high value on convenience may consider the home to be important but prioritize other demands on their time and resources. For almost any application, alternative materials are available that will function well but are not extravagant.

Select materials that fit the purpose intended. For example, the functions of interior and exterior finishes include how well they resist weather, wear, and impact, and how easy they are to clean and repair. Functions of structural materials are strength, security, energy efficiency, and cost. Function takes into account your ability to provide periodic maintenance and repair.

Another aspect of the quality issue is the selection of the materials that are invisible once the house is constructed. Only the homeowner will likely remember the construction details, but he or she may continue to obtain lasting satisfaction with the quality decision that he or she made in selecting materials for the house.

The construction or installation of materials also affects quality. Find out if local builders have enough experience with a material to use it on your home in a competent manner. You probably do not want your home to be a training site for contractors to learn construction practices with unfamiliar materials. It may be wise to limit your list of materials to those that show time-tested success in the community.

Resource efficiency

More than at any time in our country's history, people seem to be aware of the need to use resources wisely. For the individual homeowner, quality in building materials may mean a strong emphasis on components that are recycled, recyclable, renewable, or especially plentiful. For such a person, the selection of building materials becomes an exercise in good stewardship.

For example, while old-growth western cedar and redwood make very durable siding, it is environmentally questionable to harvest timber from old-growth stands. Yet young wood is not as high quality. A resource-efficient decision on siding materials might be to substitute a composite wood siding material for timber siding.

A trend in some areas is deconstruction of older houses to make room for new houses. Deconstruction, unlike demolition, means carefully unbuilding the house so that materials or features can be used again in another house. Light fixtures, wood trim, interior paneling, staircases, and other components often can be recovered for a new building, thus saving resources. A forward-thinking homeowner might wish to consider deconstruction planning in the selection of materials for a house, so that someone else might enjoy the use of long-lasting materials in another structure.

Environmental safety

A historic function of the home is to provide a safe place to live. For some people, the safe and healthy aspect of building materials is paramount, and they go to great lengths to select materials that they believe provide the safest, healthiest environment. An example is the finish material for interior wood. Some finish materials give off more volatile organic chemicals (VOC) than others do. While the long-term health benefit of low-VOC interior finishes is not known, a homeowner might choose to select such materials for more peace of mind.

Although the aesthetic features of building materials can be hard to define, personal taste plays an important and perfectly valid role. If you view attractiveness as an important aspect of quality, you probably already know which finishing materials you like: the textures, patterns, colors, and the worth of traditional materials versus the manufactured replica look.

For the visible exterior materials, be very aware of harmony. To protect home resale value and project the desired statement, maintain the uniformity of the house with the neighborhood. Seek advice from a professional architect if you are not comfortable with the aesthetics of selecting exterior building materials.

Cost

You can address initial cost constraints by narrowing and refining your materials choices. An example of initial cost difference is the substitution of steel framing for wood. Steel, unlike wood, has dimensional stability, no shrinkage, and steel members are made to closer tolerances. In some construction details, steel can be fabricated to handle heavier load-bearing jobs than wood built up to the same cross-sectional dimension. Overall, a house built with steel framing will probably cost more to build. For unconventional house-framing jobs, the homeowner should get detailed bids with both materials for comparison.

A house will have additional cost during its life cycle. A time-tested rule of thumb is that homeowners should set aside about 1 percent of the initial cost of the house per year for maintenance and repair of the house structure. Whether that amount is insufficient or excessive depends to some degree on the materials. "Pay me now or pay me later" applies especially to the building shell exterior and the floor coverings in the home.

House Exterior

The house exterior includes the house frame or structure, the components that make up the wall such as insulation, and the windows, siding, and roof. You should select materials that are durable and that help to keep the house structurally sound and energy efficient.

Framing systems

The array of choices available to prospective homeowners includes the type of construction. The main type of construction remains light wood framing, but other types of construction are available. Homeowners must also consider and select between dimension lumber and engineered wood products as well as steel and wood. Other types of construction used are prefabricated, pre-cut, manufactured, modular, and panelized houses.

On-site construction

The majority of houses built today are constructed on-site, using wood framing, although light steel framing is coming into the market as a replacement for wood. Light-framed wood construction is also commonly referred to as stick-built or stick construction. The stick-built framing system is constructed from either dimension lumber or steel channel (Figure 16-1). Figure 16-2 shows two types of light-framed construction and common names for different components. Platform construction is built one level at a time. Balloon construction has continuous framing from the bottom to the top of the house.

The declining quality of framing lumber, widely fluctuating prices of wood, and environmental concerns have caused a renewed interest in steel framing. Steel channel has several advantages over wood in building walls. Steel has superior fire ratings, good earthquake resistance, good dimensional stability, and resistance to rot. Wood studs perform better as heat insulators than do steel studs. Both frames can be designed for equivalent insulation levels. Unfortunately, few builders have developed the skills or bought the specialized tools to use steel framing. To construct an energy-efficient,

FIGURE 16-1.
Light-framed, wood constructed house.

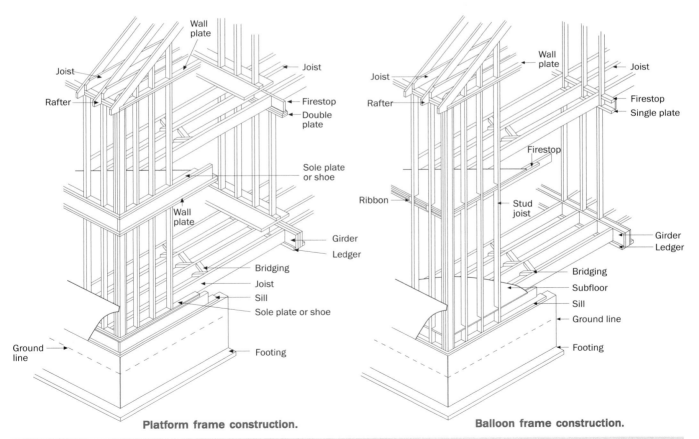

Platform frame construction.

Balloon frame construction.

FIGURE 16-2.
Two wall, floor, and roof systems.

**FIGURE 16-3.
Caulking gaps in wood to
reduce infiltration.**

steel-framed house, the amount of steel framing must be minimized in the exterior walls and ceiling. Builders must include thermal breaks in heat conduction paths and use caulks and sealants to tighten the shell of the home (Figure 16-3).

The invention of engineered wood products such as glulam (glue-laminated) beams, engineered studs, and I-joists makes it economical to use renewable wood material for wide floor span supports and tall walls. Using engineered wood products in a house requires careful design and clear communication between the on-site builder and the supplier of the product. However, this is one area where new types of materials may be able to (1) reduce the cost of a conventional house compared to the use of only dimension lumber, or (2) facilitate certain types of construction that could not be reasonably built using only dimension lumber.

Factory built

To simplify and speed up the construction process, homebuilders may use prefabricated or pre-cut pieces. Prefabricated or pre-assembled construction involves building the house in smaller pieces such as wall or roof panels or even room-sized modules. For example, wood or steel studs, engineered beams, and joists may be pre-cut for wall and floor construction, and trusses may be fabricated in a plant and transported to the site. The crew constructs the house piece by piece at the site with the pieces ready to install, eliminating some of the custom cutting. The framing members are spaced at between 12, 16, 19.2, or 24 inches on center for floor, wall, and roof sections.

Because the pieces are constructed under very controlled conditions, a prefabricated or pre-assembled house provides better quality control, reduces weather-related delays, and takes advantage of factory efficiencies. More builders than ever before are choosing to construct parts of houses in a factory. Prefabrication techniques ensure better quality at a lower price, and the units can be constructed quickly as well.

There are several variations of prefabricated house construction. The pre-assembled components can range from small wall panels to complete structures. Parts used in pre-assembled components include plywood, dimension lumber, and engineered wood products (composite cores with wood veneer such as plywood and hardboard). Such units as stress skin panels, sandwich panels, pre-framed panels (walls, floors, ceilings, or roofs), rigid frames, box beams, and curved or tapered units can be more easily assembled in a factory.

Factory workers can also apply finishes much more efficiently and with better quality control than workers can on-site. The assemblies are then transported to the job site for quick final setup. If your contractor is familiar with panelized construction and/or has a supplier for panelized components, you may be able to get a very competitively priced building shell, compared with light wood framing construction. (See the section titled **Light wood framing**.) In addition, you may be able to obtain components through pre-assembled construction that you could not get through on-site fabrication. Only imagination limits the range of building components and states of finish that can be incorporated into pre-assembled construction.

One disadvantage to pre-assembled walls and floors is that the incorporation of heating, air conditioning, electrical, and plumbing equipment requires very careful design. Some manufacturers design stress skin and sandwich panels to incorporate mechanical and electrical equipment into the panels. Some local building codes do not accept pre-assembled panels because the stud spacing in the panels is not the conventional 16- or 24-inch spacing. Check with all code authorities before using pre-assembled wall or floor panels.

A **pre-cut house** is another type of factory-built housing. Materials for this type of house are factory-cut (pre-cut) to design specifications, transported to the site, and then assembled. Pre-cut houses include timber frame, kit, log, and dome homes. These houses are built to meet either local or state building requirement codes.

A **manufactured house** is built entirely in the factory. Manufactured houses may be constructed as either a single section or as multiple sections. The section(s) is (are) then transported to the site and installed on a foundation.

A **modular house** is factory built and constructed to meet the state, local, or regional codes where the home will be located. Modular house construction involves building panels, units, or modules transported to the site and installed on a foundation.

A **panelized house** uses wall or roof panels complete with shingles, doors, windows, interior and exterior finishes, and wiring constructed in the factory; transported to the site;

and then assembled on a foundation. Panelized houses must meet the state or local building codes in effect where they are sited.

Insulation

Insulation is any material that reduces heat transfer from one area to another. During cold weather, insulation conserves heat, reduces heating, maintains warmer inside surface temperatures, and reduces condensation. During warm weather, insulation reduces heat gain, improves comfort, and reduces cooling costs.

The resistance of a material to heat flow is indicated by its R-value. When insulating a home, it is important to get the R-value specified by the builder or the local building code. Good insulators have a high R-value. While some manufacturers promote R-value per inch, the overall installed R-value is what counts. The recommended insulation levels depend on where you live in the United States. Your local building department, or gas or electric utility can inform you about the recommended R-value for your home. Table 16-1 shows a range of R-values based on location in the house, heating system, and climate.

Insulating materials are available in four main forms:

- **Batt** or **blanket.** This insulation form is one of the most common forms available. It comes in thicknesses of 1 to 8-inches and fits in widths of stud spaces. Batts are 4 or 8-feet long, and blankets are up to 100-feet long. The batt or blanket may have a paper or aluminum foil face to serve as a partial vapor retarder. An additional vapor retarder may be required.

Table 16-1. Cost-effective insulation R-values.

Table adapted from the U.S. Department of Energy 1997 Insulation Fact Sheet and on the *Recommended Levels of Insulation* found at: http://www.energystar.gov/index.cfm?c=home_sealing.hm_improvement_insulation_table

Climate	Heating system [d]	Recommended insulation level			
		Ceiling	Sidewalls (wood-framed)	Floor slabs	Basement or crawl space walls [f]
Warm (cooling and minimal heating) [a]	gas/oil or heat pump	R-22 to R-38	R-11 to R-13	R-11 to R-13	R-11 to R-19
	electric	R-38 to R-49	R-13 to R-25	R-13 to R-19	R-11 to R-19
Mixed (moderate heating and cooling) [b]	gas/oil or heat pump	R-38	R-11 to R-22 [e]	R-13 to R-25	R-11 to R-19
	electric	R-49	R-11 to R-28 [e]	R-25	R-11 to R-19
Cold [c]	gas/oil	R-38 to R-49	R-11 to R-22 [e]	R-25	R-11 to R-19
	heat pump or electric	R-49	R-11 to R-28 [e]	R-25	R-13 to R-19

[a] FL & HI; coastal CA; southeast TX; southern LA, AR, MS, AL & GA.
[b] VA, WV, KY, MO, NE, OK, OR, WA & ID; southern IN, KS, NM & AZ; northern LA, AR, MS, AL & GA; inland CA & western NV.
[c] PA, NY, New England, northern Midwest, Great Lakes area, mountainous area (e.g., CO, WV, UT, etc.).
[d] Insulation is also effective at reducing cooling bills. These levels assume your house has electric air-conditioning.
[e] R-values are for insulation only (not whole wall) and may be achieved through a combination of cavity and rigid board insulation.
[f] Do not insulate crawl space walls if crawl space is wet or ventilated with outdoor air.

- **Loose-fill.** This insulation is packaged as a loose material in bags. It is easy to pour or blow above ceilings, in walls, and in concrete block cores. Poor quality insulation can settle in walls, leaving the top inadequately insulated.

- **Rigid.** Typically, this insulation is available in 1/2- to 2-inch thick by 4-foot wide panels. Some types have aluminum foil or other vapor retarders attached to one or both faces. Rigid insulation can be used for roofs and walls or as a ceiling liner. It can also be used along foundations (perimeter insulation) or buried under concrete floors (if it is waterproof and protected from physical and rodent damage). Because insulation made is this form can be flammable, check with your insurance company to determine if there are requirements for protecting the insulation.

- **Spray-type foam.** This insulation is made by foaming organic materials with air or inert gases. Spray-type foam insulations usually are applied between stud spaces. The foam starts as a liquid that is pumped through a pressurized nozzle. Once the liquid lands on the surface, it expands to two or four times its original size, filling in cracks and forming a continuous insulating barrier. Application of these products usually requires a trained professional, and they are about 20 percent more expensive than the other material forms. Spray-type foam products are flammable and release toxic gases when burned. Check with your insurance company before using this type of insulation.

When calculating the total R-value of a wall, ceiling or floor, take into account the materials that form it, not just the material being used as insulation. When selecting insulation, it is important to know the insulating properties for the type of insulation used. Good insulation must be accompanied by a proper and well designed air infiltration and moisture control system.

Types of insulating materials

Insulating materials are bulky, porous, lightweight materials with many tiny air spaces. Generally, the more air pockets in a material, the better it insulates. Before choosing an insulation material, you should think about where it will be located. Many of the insulating materials are flammable and need to be protected from heat or fire. Insulating materials should not lie against recessed light fixtures, ceiling or ventilation fans, or chimney and gas flues.

You can choose from a variety of insulations. The two most common types of wall and ceiling insulation for residential applications are fiberglass and cellulose. Polyurethane is starting to become a more popular product for walls and ceilings. Polystyrene is used commonly for basement walls and underneath floor slabs.

Fiberglass or **glass wool** is a material that consists of long, thin glass fibers or filaments intertwined and fluffy in appearance. It can be pink, yellow, or white. This insulation typically has an R-value of 3.0 to 3.8 per inch of thickness. It is available in batts or blankets, but also can be purchased in loose bags for blown-in or pour installations. Fiberglass loose-fill insulations may settle approximately

1 percent, resulting in little impact on the thermal performance of the insulation. Fiberglass insulation is not absorbent, and if exposed to moisture, will not wick up or hold water. It will dry out and retain its original R-value. Fiberglass insulation requires no additional fire-retardant chemical treatments, but most facings attached to fiberglass insulation are combustible and should never be left exposed. Other special flame-resistant facings may be left exposed where desired, such as on a basement or crawl space wall.

Rock wool is similar to fiberglass, but instead of being made out of glass, it is made out of molten rock. It has similar properties as fiberglass. It is gray or brown and is available as a batt or blanket and as shredded loose-fill forms.

Cellulose or **wood fiber** is a fill-type insulation that is made primarily of ground-up or shredded newspaper. It has an R-value of 2.9 to 3.7 per inch thickness. It is the most common of the loose-fill blow-in type of insulating materials. It is commonly blown into walls of existing buildings and is also widely used for ceiling insulation. The process of blowing the material fluffs the insulation and directs it through a hose to place it in wall cavities or over ceilings. This material can be partly fluffed with a garden rake or pitchfork after placing, but blowing is usually best. Because cellulose is made from shredded newspaper, it will absorb and hold moisture, reducing energy savings. If soaked, cellulose will mat down, and the thermal performance can be permanently reduced. Cellulose insulation is naturally combustible. To protect against fire, cellulose insulation is heavily treated with fire-retardant chemicals. Though cellulose is treated with fire retardants, it is not fire proof, meaning that the insulation could still burn if exposed to a heat source.

Polystyrene is usually in rigid boards, but it is also available as a granular or pour-type insulation. It has an R-value of 3.5 to 6.0 per inch of thickness. Extruded polystyrenes (styrofoam) have a higher insulating value and are more resistant to moisture absorption. They often have a higher R-value when new because of the gases trapped during forming. The R-value decreases in time as the gases escape. Molded polystyrenes (bead board) have lower R-values and are not as moisture resistant. To tell the types apart, look at the particles making up the insulation. Bead board breaks up into many small ball bearing-type beads or pellets; extruded polystyrene is finer grained. Polystyrenes are flammable and should be covered with a fire-resistant material or used in locations where flammability is of little concern, such as perimeter foundation insulation. Check with your insurance company before using this type of insulation.

Synthetic insulating materials are usually **polyurethane foam**. This product is sprayed onto walls, ceilings, or other structural components. Polyurethane has an R-value of 3.5 to 6.0 per inch thickness. New urethane has a higher insulating value because of the gas used for foaming; but as the gas escapes during aging, the R-value decreases. Cover urethane with a fire-resistant material, such as plywood or drywall, to prevent rapid flame spread and to reduce the release of fumes in case of fire. Before using, check with your fire insurance company for special requirements.

Air Infiltration

The U.S. Department of Energy estimates that up to 40 percent of a house's heat loss can be from air infiltration. A properly constructed wall cavity using drywall, sheathing, and caulking will allow very little air to infiltrate a house regardless of the type of insulation. Most air infiltration occurs through sidewall cavities from around electrical outlets. This problem is best solved through careful construction, special boxes, and caulking of boxes and all exterior walls.

Air infiltration generally occurs in the areas of a home that are not insulated, such as around windows; doors; fireplaces; heating, ventilation, and air conditioning ductwork; and perimeter joints. It can and should be controlled with the use of housewrap; proper caulking and sealing of band joists, sill plates, header plates; and insulation around doors, windows, electrical outlets, and other openings (Figure 16-4).

Vapor retarders

Typically, the more insulated and airtight a house is the better the chance that moisture can collect in the walls or ceilings. Moisture collecting in sidewalls and ceilings can wet the insulation, which reduces the effective R-value of the insulation. In addition, wet walls and ceilings promote mold growth and wood rot, and cause paint failure.

Prevent moisture problems in building sections by installing a vapor retarder that keeps water vapor from entering areas where it is likely to condense into water. A vapor retarder is a material that does not easily allow water vapor to pass through it. The ability of a material to allow water vapor to pass through it is called permeability and is measured in units called perms.

Most building materials are highly permeable and **are not** good vapor retarders. A good vapor retarder will have a permeability of less than 1.0 perms, preferably less than 0.5 perms. A material that is a good vapor retarder is polyethylene. A 4- to 6-mil thick polyethylene will have a permeability of 0.4 to 0.6 perms.

A vapor retarder should be installed on the warm side of all insulated walls, ceilings, and roofs. Typically, the vapor retarder is located directly under the gypsum wallboard and near the heated side of the wall. Vapor retarders can be used underneath concrete floors and foundations to control soil moisture. Proper use of vapor retarders depends on the climatic region.

All electrical boxes, windows, and door frames in exterior walls should be sealed. For cold climates, the inside wall should be as air and moisture tight as possible. The outside wall should be able to breathe so any interior moisture that is trapped can escape. Using exterior flashing, building paper, and exterior house wrap is essential to help keep water from entering into a wall. In warm, humid climates, these recommendations are reversed.

Windows

Windows greatly improve the living spaces in your home. Consider using roof windows or skylights to bring light into a room or part of a room that is farther from an exterior wall. However, too many roof windows or skylights may aggravate summer overheating in a home and

FIGURE 16-4.
House wrap and taping around windows to reduce infiltration.

Photo courtesy Steve Theis, Rottlund Homes of Iowa, Inc.

heat loss in winter. It is best to use them sparingly. While good-quality windows are expensive, they can have a positive impact on the occupants' health, the cost of mild-weather space conditioning, and the market value of the home.

In a typical home, windows lose more heat in the winter and gain more in the summer than any other part of the structure. For several years following the 1970's energy crisis, homeowners were advised to minimize the number and sizes of windows in a new home. The vast improvement in energy-saving windows over the last couple of decades has made it possible to temper such advice.

Heat gain or loss through windows can be controlled by insulation, reflection, absorption, and shading. Specialized glass products such as insulating double- or triple-glazed assemblies, reflective-coated glass, tinted glass, and heat-absorbing glass can substantially reduce heat transmission. Shading of glass using awnings, draperies, and blinds also can reduce heat gain. Windows should be tightly sealed in all climates, regardless of whether the home is in a predominately hot or cold zone of the country.

Window frames can be constructed from aluminum, wood, vinyl, and composites of these materials. They also can be manufactured in various quality and/or performance grades. A performance grade system for wood windows allows side-by-side comparison of minimum performance in terms of structural test pressure, air infiltration, and water penetration. If you are building a house in a high-wind zone, you might select a window with a higher performance grade

that would normally be used for light commercial construction.

In general, windows that are double glazed insulate twice as much as single glazed windows. Additional glazing increases their insulating value. With double glazed windows, an air space is present between the panes of glass. Usually the wider the air space the better the insulating value. Air spaces filled with a gas such as carbon dioxide, krypton, or argon-krypton mixture will significantly reduce heat loss. Tinted windows will reduce heat gain through windows but also reduce sunlight. New types of window glazings are available that will reduce heat gain without a significant reduction in visible light.

When buying windows, compare three energy conservation performance measures:

- **U-Factor:** This measure is very similar to R-value. It is a measure of the amount of heat moving through the window. When comparing U-Factors, the lower the value the better.
- **Solar heat gain coefficient (SHGC):** This measure is the amount of solar energy passing through a window. Values usually range from 0.4 to 0.9. Colder climates want a high value, which will allow the solar energy to heat the house. Warmer climates want a low value, less than 0.4, so the cooling system will not have to work as hard.
- **Air infiltration:** This measure is the amount of uncontrolled leakage of air into the house through the windows. The best windows will have an air leakage

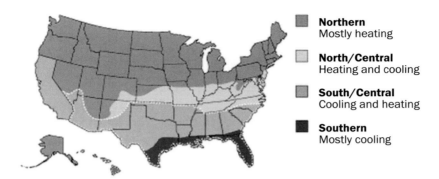

Northern
Mostly heating

North/Central
Heating and cooling

South/Central
Cooling and heating

Southern
Mostly cooling

FIGURE 16-5.
EnergyStar® climate zone map for windows, doors, and skylights.

Adapted from *Climate Zones for EnergyStar® Qualification Criteria* (http://www.energystar.gov/
index.cfm?c=windows_doors.pr_crit_windows)

**Table 16-2. Recommended EnergyStar®
U-Factor and Solar Heat Gain Coefficient
(SHGC) based on climate zone.**

Use with Figure 16-6. Residential Windows,
Doors, and Skylights Key Product Criteria

Climate Zone	U-Factor	SHGC
Northern	≤ 0.35	Any
North/Central	≤ 0.40	≤ 0.55
South/Central	≤ 0.40	≤ 0.40
	≤ 0.41	≤ 0.36
	≤ 0.42	≤ 0.31
	≤ 0.43	≤ 0.24
Southern	≤ 0.65	≤ 0.40
	≤ 0.66	≤ 0.39
	≤ 0.67	
	≤ 0.68	≤ 0.38
	≤ 0.69	≤ 0.37
	≤ 0.70	
	≤ 0.71	≤ 0.36
	≤ 0.72	≤ 0.35
	≤ 0.73	
	≤ 0.74	≤ 0.34
	≤ 0.75	≤ 0.33

Specific county information can be found at:
http://www.energystar.gov/ia/partners/manuf_res
ESTARClimateZonesbyCounty_City6_25_04FINAL.xls

between 0.01 to 0.06 cfm/ft.
Many window manufacturers
will not list this value on their
windows because the leakage is
higher than 0.06 cfm/ft.

Figure 16-5 and Table 16-2 show
the EnergyStar® recommendations for
window U-Factors and Solar Heat
Gain Coefficients based on region.
Figure 16-6 shows an example of a
window sticker that provides basic

FIGURE 16-6.
**Example of a window sticker detailing
window performance measures.**

comparison information. Visible light transmittance is another measure that is often listed on window stickers. This measure shows the optical property of the window. Most values fall between 0.3 and 0.8. A high visible light transmittance value is desirable to maximize daylight.

Siding

Homeowners can select from a wide array of exterior sidings for houses, including:

- Brick.
- Finished wood and wood composites.
- Cedar and other durable woods.
- Metal.
- Vinyl.
- Fiber cement.
- Stucco (synthetic one layer).
- External insulation and finish systems (EIFS).

Brick veneer remains a popular siding choice for many styles of houses. While its initial cost is high compared to other types of siding, its durability, appearance, and heat capacity put it high on the list of options for many houses. Brick veneer can be used for the entire siding job, for the street side(s) of the house only, or for accenting parts of the exterior in combination with other types of siding. One disadvantage of brick is the difficulty of finding matching brick if you have to perform repairs or if you decide to remodel or add on to the house in the future.

Wood clapboard and **lap siding** continue to be popular in many areas. The natural beauty of wood, its long life, and its ease of installation offset its relatively high cost and

need for periodic maintenance. In some regions, it may be possible to find and use wood siding from another building that is being deconstructed.

Wood composite siding, in contrast, costs much less than solid wood but may lack durability. The relative scarcity of high-quality wood siding has driven the development of many alternatively engineered wood products such as plywood, composites, and hardboard. A wide variety of textures and styles is available. When considering engineered wood for exterior use, check references for installations that have been in place for some time, and compare the manufacturers' warranties.

Durable wood siding is usually selected based on a certain "weathered look" that is difficult to duplicate with other materials. Durable woods are usually left unpainted although a sealer or transparent stain may be applied in some cases. A disadvantage to durable wood siding is that the weathering can be somewhat unpredictable and can sometimes cause an uneven appearance, especially where roof overhangs cause differences in sunlight and rain exposure. If you are considering durable wood siding, carefully consider how it will harmonize with other homes in the neighborhood.

Metal siding materials such as aluminum and steel have been used for many years. Advantages are low initial cost, long life, and durability. Fire resistance is very good, and resistance to hail damage is moderately good. However, metal siding must be periodically repainted. Houses located on coasts may undergo premature saltwater corrosion of steel siding. Be sure to check manufacturers' warranties for your application and geographic location.

Vinyl siding is used on many new homes in the United States. It has the advantages of easy installation, relatively low cost, and a wide variety of extruded shapes, textures, and colors. Because the plastic siding is colored throughout, it never needs painting. Its disadvantages include lower durability and greater thermal expansion than many other materials, so its proper installation requires careful attention to detail. As with many other materials, you should investigate the various grades of vinyl siding, and select a product based on availability, function, durability, and comparative cost.

Fiber-cement siding is rapidly becoming the most popular man-made siding material in the housing market (Figure 16-7). Manufactured in a variety of textures to simulate wood grain and other finishes, fiber-cement siding has advantages of lower cost, durability, and paintability over some traditional siding products such as wood and brick. The material is fairly new, so be sure your builder is familiar with the tools and skills needed to

**FIGURE 16-7.
Fiber-cement siding.**

apply fiber cement according to the manufacturer's specifications.

Stucco and **synthetic one-layer sidings** involve the on-site mixing and application of a material. The final appearance highly depends on the worker's skill. You should consider stucco only in close cooperation with your builder, considering the possibility of repairs and maintenance at a later date. Make sure the local home building and maintenance market will be able to support stucco siding.

Exterior insulation and finish systems (EIFS) are often called synthetic stucco. The finish is a reinforced plastered or painted-on coating over a layer of rigid insulation, which is in turn attached to a layer of sheathing applied to furring or framing. EIFS can be field applied or can be built up in pre-assembled panels and transported to the site. The advantages of EIFS include the ability to incorporate a variety of finished textures, colors, and so on. High R-values of wall insulation can be attained with the EIFS system. Some failures of EIFS have been traced to rain and condensation being trapped between the sheathing and the exterior foam board insulation. Unfortunately, EIFS failures are usually very expensive to correct. No nationally recognized standards-setting body publishes a standard for EIFS. Given the record of moisture-related failures, the very expensive repairs required to mitigate such failures, and the relatively brief history of EIFS in this country, use caution in choosing EIFS. Only experienced contractors who have good cooperation with their material and component suppliers should install EIFS.

Roofing materials should be selected to impart a certain amount of architectural beauty to the house or at least not detract from the appearance. Materials can be chosen that add texture or color to the roof, so that the roof becomes an architectural element. At the same time, it may not be advisable to select roof material that is markedly different from nearby roofs. Some parts of the country or a specific location are more fire prone than other types. Wood shakes and shingles are notoriously flammable, and as a result, the building codes adopted by some states and localities prohibit wood roofing materials. Likewise, in areas prone to earthquake activity, clay tile roofing may be dangerous because pieces of tile may break and fall off the roof during an earthquake.

Roofing

Roofs can be conveniently classified as steep or low sloped. Steep and low-sloped roofs generally require different roofing methods. Steep roofs have a slope greater than 1-1/2 inches per foot. Steep roofs are the most popular roofs for residential applications in the humid regions of the United States and will be the roofs discussed in this section.

Roofing choices vary considerably depending on your geographical location. Certain choices are aesthetically and functionally different in the Northwest than in the Southeast. Local codes may restrict choices depending on safety and function.

The durability of roofing directly relates to several considerations. Resistance to hail, high winds, earthquakes, and fire are all concerns for insurance companies and the housing industry. In some parts of the country, mold, moss, and fungal growths are serious threats to roofing durability. Exposure to freeze-thaw cycles can severely damage some types of roofing materials. In some climates, roofs need to be resistant to extremely high daytime temperatures. Some roofs can be damaged if a person walks on the surfaces without using special protection. Most types of roofing materials are covered by industry standards. In many cases, multiple grades govern application, appearance, and service.

Table 16-3 lists and compares several different roofing materials. Asphalt shingles, clay and concrete tiles, and slate are the most common roof covering materials.

One newer roof covering alternative is fiber-cement or cementitious roofing shingles. These shingles are made from Portland cement reinforced with cellulose fibers. They can be molded to mimic a wide variety of more conventional roofing materials and are resistant to weathering, insects, fungus, and fire. Because the fibers are made of renewable or recycled materials and Portland cement, fiber-cement shingles may be more environmentally friendly than asphalt-based, slate-coated shingles.

Another roof covering alternative is coated metal panels. This type of covering is made from metal panels that are stamped to look like "traditional" shakes or shingles. The advantages of metal include speed of installation, variety of colors and textures, weather resistance, fire protection, low shipping weight, and the use of recycled steel.

Decks

While they are not usually one of the structural components of a house, outdoor structures such as decks add considerable value to a home and provide many advantages to homeowners. In choosing materials for a deck, you may want to consider alternatives to the traditional preservative-treated wood. You can substitute redwood and other durable woods, or use recycled plastic planks and engineered wood products. Plastic composite railings can reduce maintenance and provide an attractive, though untraditional, appearance. For pressure-treated wood construction, hidden-fastener systems are available that improve deck appearance and long-term performance. Because of the continuous weather exposure and high wear on a deck, expect the life of

Table 16-3. Relative durability of roofing materials for steep roofs.

Durability issue	Roofing Material						
	Asphalt Shingles	Clay Tiles	Concrete Tiles	Slate	Wood Shakes/ Shingles	Fiber-Cement Shingles	Coated Metal
Expected life	Short/medium	Long	Long	Long	Medium	Long	Long
Freeze-thaw resistance	Good	Good	Varies with treatment	Good	Good	Varies with treatment	Good
Hail resistance	Fair	Good	Good	Fair/good	Good	Fair/good	Fair/good
Resistance to moss, mold, fungus growth	Fair/good	Good	Fair	Fair	Fair	Fair	Good
Wind resistance	Fair/poor	High	High	High	Fair/good	Good	Moderate/ high
Weight	Low/moderate	High	High	High	Low	High	Low
Heat reflection*	Poor	Fair/good	Fair/good	Fair	Fair/poor	Fair/poor	Good
Fire resistance	Moderate	Good	Good	Good	Poor/Fair	Good	Good
Disposal and/or recycling	Poor	Reusable	Reusable	Reusable	Poor but renewable	Poor	Fair/good
Cost	Low	High	Moderate	Varies by Region	Moderate/ high	Moderate	Moderate

*See U.S. EPA Energy Star® program for reflection minimum standards.

a deck to be short compared to that of the house structure, and plan maintenance and replacement accordingly.

House Interior

Inside the house, you have many opportunities to choose materials that can make life easier for you and reflect your quality values. Market forces have worked to the advantage of the homebuilder in making available a wide array of functional, attractive materials options. As with other materials selection assignments, you should make sure that your builder is familiar with the materials and installation techniques, so that your house does not become an expensive experiment.

When selecting finishing materials for walls and other surfaces in the house, consider ease of maintenance, appearance, cost, and expected wear life. Whenever possible, choose interior finishes that foster good health. For example, low-emitting volatile organic compounds (VOCs) options are available in wall coverings and other finishing materials. Such products as low-vapor paints and wood finishes benefit family members who have allergies or asthma or are sensitive to the chemicals used in these products.

In areas receiving heavy use like entryways, consider durability and

For basic painting, apply a primer before painting. A primer will fill in small holes and allow the paint to grip better and last longer. Applying a primer may seem like it will take extra time and cost money, but in the end it will save you money.

ease of maintenance in addition to appearance and cost. In figuring cost, include the product itself, the installation, and the cost of maintaining it over its expected lifetime. Refer to the manufacturer's specifications, recommended use, and safety factors for additional information about these products. This information can be obtained from the retailer or directly from the manufacturer, often by toll-free phone numbers or from their website.

Wall finishing

Drywall or *sheetrock* is the interior finish most commonly used in residential construction. Painting is usually the easiest and least expensive way to finish a wall. People can get imaginative with their painting by using different decorative techniques such as sponging, rag rolling, stenciling, combing, wood graining, and texturing.

There are two basic types of paints, flat and glossy. Flat paints will absorb light, so they will make a room seem darker. They also will have more problems with staining. A glossy paint will reflect more light so it will make a room seem brighter. Glossier paints will remain sticky even after they are dried. Top-rated paints usually are worth their extra cost. Work with your contractor and subcontractor to select a paint that is durable, attractive, and affordable.

Wall coverings are another option to finish a wall. The basic types of wall coverings are wallpaper, tiles, and paneling. Wallpaper comes in various patterns, colors, and finishes. It is usually the most popular type of wall finishing after painting. Vinyl coated is the most common type of

wallpaper. It has a vinyl coating that makes it ideal for scrubbing. Solid vinyl is a type of wallpaper that is durable and waterproof, making it ideal for humid climates. Other types of wallpaper include corked-faced, paper-backed fabric, flocked, grass cloth/burlap, and foil. Wallpaper can be an expensive option, and changing it is not nearly as easy as repainting a room, so, if you choose wallpaper, evaluate your alternatives carefully and choose wisely.

Glazed and porcelain wall tile are another wall covering option. These tiles are commonly used in bathrooms and kitchens, but now are starting to be found in other areas of the house as decorative borders. Today's type of wall paneling is much different than the old panel walls from the 1970s. Wainscoting is used in many homes. It is typically used on the lower halves of walls of kitchens and dining areas to give an old-fashioned appearance.

Flooring

Flooring materials are a good example of choices that must be made based on function, life-cycle cost, and appearance. While a general discussion of flooring materials is beyond the scope of this chapter, keep in mind the balance between wanting to use traditional flooring materials such as hardwood, carpet, and vinyl and the newer alternative materials and systems. Laminates, concrete, and ceramic tile are just a few of the materials to consider. Pay special attention to floor surfaces, because they tend to become wet. For this reason, choose non-slip floor surfaces. Matte-finished textured tile or vinyl is an excellent choice.

Resist the urge to install a lifetime flooring system that you may tire of and yet cannot justify removing and replacing. For example, many older homes have expensive hardwood floors beneath a layer of carpet. The hardwood seemed like the best investment at the time the home was built (very long life and low maintenance, and thus lower life-cycle cost), but that choice missed the mark—the comfort provided by carpet. Rather than take out the hardwood and make doors and moldings fit correctly, the carpet was added on top. On the other hand, hard or smooth surfaces rather than textured surfaces (for example, wood, vinyl, or tile floors rather than carpeting) are recommended for family members with allergies or asthma to help control dust and potential air pollutants. You may want to consider flooring as an expendable item and plan to make several changes of flooring and flooring styles over the life of the home. **Chapter 6, Kitchens,** has a comparison chart on basic types of flooring material for kitchens.

Resources

Windows. 1991. Raleigh, North Carolina: The Center for Universal Design, North Carolina State University. Publication number TP #7.00.

Doors and Doorways. 1991. Raleigh, North Carolina: The Center for Universal Design, North Carolina State University. Publication number TP #3.00

General Websites
American Council for an Energy-Efficient Economy (ACE[3]): http://www.aceee.org/consumerguide/

Ask the Builder: http://www.askthebuilder.com

BobVila: http://www.bobvila.com

Energy Star®: http://www.energystar.gov

National Fenestration Rating Council: http://www.nfrc.org

Hometime: http://www.hometime.com

Housing Education and Research Association (HERA): http://www.housingeducators.org

This Old House: http://www.thisoldhouse.com

Don Vandervort's Home Tips: http://www.hometips.com

The Journal of Light Construction (JLC): http://www.jlconline.com

North American Deck and Railing Association (NADRA): http://www.nadra.org/

National Association of Home Builders: http://www.nahb.org/

Flooring

Consumer Report—Wall-to-wall carpeting: http://www.consumerreports.org/cro/home-garden/home-furnishings/walltowall-carpeting-buying-advice-604.htm

Ask The Builder—Flooring: http://www.askthebuilder.com/Flooring.shtml

Framing

Timber Framers Guild: http://www.tfguild.org

Manufactured Housing Institute: http://www.manufacturedhousing.org

Insulation

Insulation Fact Sheet, U.S. Department of Energy: http://www.ornl.gov/sci/roofs+walls/insulation/ins_01.html

North American Insulation Manufacturers Association (NAIMA): http://www.naima.org

Cellulose Insulation Manufacturers Association: http://www.cellulose.org

Polyisocyanurate Insulation Manufacturers Association: http://www.pima.org

Spray Polyurethane Foam Alliance (SPFA): http://www.sprayfoam.org

Siding

Ask The Builder—Siding: http://www.askthebuilder.com/Siding.shtml

Wall Coverings

Consumer Report—Interior and Exterior Paints: http://www.consumerreports.org/cro/home-garden/paint/interior-and-exterior-paints.htm

HGTV—What's new for wall coverings: http://hgtv.com/hgtv/dc_design_kitchen/article/0,1793,HGTV_3375_3502807,00.html

Windows and Doors

Window & Door Manufacturers Association (WDMA): http://www.wdma.com

Selecting Windows for Energy Efficiency (U.S. Department of Energy): http://windows.lbl.gov/pub/selectingwindows/window.pdf

Consumer Guide to Home Energy Savings—New Windows: http://www.aceee.org/consumerguide/windo.htm

Choosing to Remodel

TODAY, MANY FAMILIES ARE CHOOSING TO REMODEL their current home rather than start over with a new one. Two of the reasons people choose to remodel are expectations of saving money and emotional attachment to the current home. This chapter is designed to help you decide if remodeling is right for you and your home. It also provides suggestions to make the project more successful.

Is Remodeling Right for You?

Before you decide whether to move or undertake a major remodeling project, you should ask yourself the following questions:

- Is the location right?
- Is your home worth remodeling?
- How much will remodeling cost?
- Do zoning laws allow the changes you plan?
- Would moving be cheaper than remodeling?

Is the location right?

Is the neighborhood changing or likely to change? If so, will you like the changes? Is there a great deal of traffic and noise? Are neighboring houses being converted to rental properties? Are homes turning over rapidly and people at a different point in the life cycle moving in? If you have children, will there be other children for them to play with as these changes occur? Would you rather live closer to work, schools, or shopping? Would you rather have more privacy or a more rural setting? If the answer is *yes* to some of these questions, maybe you should consider moving rather than remodeling.

Is your home worth remodeling?

When most people think about remodeling, they are considering updating a kitchen or adding space. However, before investing in such improvements, it is wise to critically evaluate the structural soundness of the house. Is the house structurally sound? Are floors level? Are rooflines straight? Is the plumbing system up to date or will you need to replace fixtures, pipes, or even a well or sewer system in the near future? Does the heating system keep the house warm, and is it efficient? If the house does not already have an air conditioning system, could one be easily added? Is the electrical wiring up to current code? Are outlets located on every wall? Are the outlets grounded? Is there at least a

As you begin investigating whether you should remodel your home, consider these major issues:

- Like designing a new house, you need to decide what you want before you make decisions about what you will do to achieve it.
- You need to understand that remodeling often takes longer than you think and costs more than you anticipate.
- You need to determine if the benefits of remodeling outweigh the costs.
- You should try to make the planned changes fit with the character and scale of the existing house.

An experienced housing inspector or contractor can help you determine what it would cost just to update and preserve your house without adding to it or upgrading it.

150-amp service panel? Is the foundation sound without major cracks or water damage? Are the roof and chimneys in good shape?

How much will remodeling cost?

List the specific improvements you want to make and then ask contractors for bids. Be sure to include the items necessary to update and preserve the house. Obtaining these initial estimates will help you understand the costs and scope of what you want to do and may raise issues you had not considered. Even if you plan to do part of the work yourself, you should get these preliminary estimates.

Do zoning laws allow the changes you plan?

Check with the local zoning and building inspection office to see if the type of work you plan is allowed and if additional work and expense will be involved to satisfy regulations. Zoning laws may limit how close you can build to your lot lines or how much of your lot you can cover with structures. In some states, for example, new houses cannot be built within 75 feet of a shoreline or other body of water.

Would moving be cheaper?

When all costs are included, remodeling is often cheaper than moving, but this is not always the case. Using your preliminary cost estimates, visit houses on the market in areas where you would like to live, and determine if you could get the features you want in another house for less money. Be sure to consider any updating or preservation work the potential house would require.

Are You Starting with Realistic Expectations?

While remodeling involves less change and uncertainty than starting over, it still involves some of both. Here are some factors to consider: cost, impact on house value, impact on real estate taxes, and doing the work yourself.

Cost

For several reasons, remodeling costs are likely to be proportionally higher than building an equivalent new house. First, demolition will be required. Second, after the demolition has occurred, it is common to discover unexpected problems, such as decay or structural weaknesses. Third, matching or at least blending old and new materials and mechanical systems can be costly both in terms of labor and materials. Fourth, you may need to deal with hazardous materials such as lead paint, asbestos, or mold, which may require hiring specialty contractors and add to your costs.

Impact on house value

Dollars and time spent remodeling will not necessarily increase the value of the house. The market value of home improvements is based on a comparison with other similar houses, not on the cost of the improvements. For example, fireplaces may add only $500 to the market value of houses in your area even though the cost of installing the fireplace may be as much as $3,000.

The market value of the improvements you plan will be determined by how your improved house will compare with neighboring houses. If you make the house larger or add features not common in your area, you may not recover the cost of improvements when you sell the house in the future. On the other hand, if the improvements make your house more like other houses in the neighborhood, your chances of recovering the costs of the improvements are greater.

Doing the work yourself

You may be able to substantially reduce the costs of remodeling by doing some of the work yourself, particularly if the job is labor intensive. Before you do the work yourself, however, you should consider the many hidden costs, including:

- **Tools and equipment**. To perform a job properly and efficiently, you need the right tools, but they can be expensive and may require special skills to use effectively.
- **Materials.** You will be buying materials at retail prices and then have to worry about getting them home. You may have to buy more than you need. It is also possible that you will waste some of the materials and will have to purchase even more.
- **Time**. If you are doing a project for the first time, you will be learning as you go and spending considerable time deciding what to do next or how to fix a mistake. You will probably also need to make repeated trips to suppliers to purchase things you forgot to order. If you are working evenings and weekends, you may spend nearly as much time setting up and cleaning up as you do on the task.
- **Skill and knowledge**. If you do not have the skills to do the job

right, the job may need to be redone sooner or may create unanticipated problems. You may even need to call in a contractor to rescue you when you realize you do not have the skill to complete the job. Finally, if the finished product is not "workmanlike," you may actually decrease the value of your house rather than increasing it, for example, if there are gaps between trim and drywall. Prospective buyers may feel they need to have the work redone and reflect these expected costs in their purchase offers.

- **Household concerns**. The time you spend on remodeling projects is time you could be spending with your family or friends. Household members may resent your lack of time for them. They may also resent having the kitchen or living room torn up for weeks or months. Do not underestimate this stress. You may also create safety or health risks. Power tools, exposed nails, or lead and asbestos dust can create serious safety issues.

Developing the Remodeling Plan

After considering the pros and cons, you may decide that remodeling is your best housing alternative. If so, begin by developing a remodeling plan. For any construction project, the time spent in planning is seldom wasted. Seek out multiple sources of information, and crosscheck your sources if you are not entirely comfortable with the answers you get.

Keep in mind that if you increase the market value of your home, you will probably also increase your real estate taxes.

It is usually much cheaper to make changes within the existing shell of the house so that you do not have to worry about foundation or roof changes.

Develop a list of goals for the project

Begin by listing what you want to accomplish with the remodeling project. Do you want more room for entertaining? Do you need more sleeping spaces? Do you need a play space or an office? Is your bathroom outdated? Does the kitchen lack work space or storage? It is a good idea for all household members to separately develop a list of what they would like to have in a remodeled house. Then the family should meet to set priorities. Be sure to plan for the future. Now is the time to widen doors and hallways and to incorporate a no-step entrance.

Look within for space

Some places to look for additional space are an attached garage, a porch, an attic, and a basement. You can also consider making changes that improve the functioning of existing space.

Attached garage

One source of cheap space is to convert an existing attached garage to additional living space. You can either do without the garage or add another garage beyond the existing one. When assessing whether this is the space you need, it is important to consider the function of the remodeled space within the existing floor plan, exterior views of the house, and location of the driveway. For example, a converted garage may not provide the privacy you want in a bedroom, but it might make a good family room. The height of a garage may allow the floor to be raised to match existing floor levels. This possibility has the added advantage of providing space for floor insulation.

The concrete floor of most garages is not insulated and can be very cold much of the year.

Porch

Many houses have open or screened porches that can be enclosed and insulated to provide additional living space. It is important to be sure that the support for the porch is sound. The footings or foundation of the porch may not be of the same quality as the main structure, causing it to settle or shift with the seasons. If the porch does not have a full foundation, it is a good idea to at least provide a solid skirt for the area between the ground and the floor. Before you do this, add insulation to the floor and cover the ground under the porch with a vapor barrier. (For more information on foundations, see **Chapter 14, Foundations**). When enclosing a porch, consider its effect on the appearance of the house. If the design is not carefully thought through, the resulting appearance can decrease the value of the house.

Attic

Some houses have space in the attic that can be converted to living space. Be aware, however, that not all attics are structurally designed to take the weight of regular foot traffic and furniture. If there is a stairway to the attic and windows, you can be pretty sure the attic was intended for expansion space. If not, you should consult an architect, builder, or engineer to be certain if the attic is usable. If there is no stairway, you will either have to sacrifice some existing living space for one or add a stair tower on the outside of the structure at a point where a door from the interior can be added.

This door should be accessed from a hall or living room rather than from a bedroom.

In addition to structural design, take a realistic look at head clearance. Most people feel comfortable in a room with 8 feet of head clearance. People can start to feel confined in a room with less than 7 feet of head clearance. Ask yourself if there is enough room once the space is finished for a person to walk upright in a majority of the room without hitting his or her head. If the answer is *no*, the attic may be better used as a storage space.

When finishing an attic area, make sure you handle the insulation properly. The design should provide enough space for the recommended amount of insulation and an air space between the insulation and the roof deck. This space should be connected to soffit vents at the lower edge of the roof and ridge or roof vents near or at the peak of the roof (Figure 17-1).

Basement

Basements are a frequent source of additional living space. However, there are several things to think about before you proceed. If you will be using basement space for bedrooms, you should include a second emergency exit in case of fire. Often, this exit is a window large enough for a person to crawl through. For details on bedroom exiting requirements, see **Chapter 8, Bedrooms**. If the basement is partially exposed on one side, the window can be installed there. If this cannot be done, a large window well can be created to accommodate such a window. This second exit should be accessible from all basement bedrooms.

These exit windows help solve another problem with basement living space—lack of natural light. You can compensate for this lack by creatively using artificial light and decorating with light-colored paint or wallpaper and flooring.

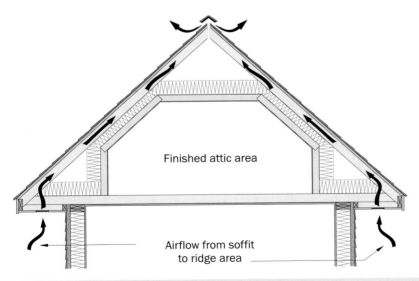

Finished attic area

Airflow from soffit to ridge area

FIGURE 17-1.
Ventilation and insulation for attic expansion.

If you need an additional half bathroom, consider space under a stairway, possibly combined with a closet. Perhaps doors can be moved and part of a hallway can be converted into the bath.

A third challenge faced when converting a basement to living space is the ceiling height and duct work and pipes that may make the ceiling height even lower. Developing a design that works around dropped ducts and pipes so that they are near or within walls can help. Recessing lights within open joist runs can also help.

Before you begin converting a basement to living space, make sure that the basement is leak free. If you are not sure if the basement has water problems, look for staining on the lower edge of the walls. There may be dark fungal stains or light stains left when water evaporated, leaving deposits of dissolved minerals on the surface.

Many basements have substantial condensation in the summer when warm air enters the cool basement. The temperature of basement walls and floors is often cool enough to cause moisture to condense out of the air. Insulating basement walls is a good way to deal with potential

condensation on walls. Because of the coolness of the floor, permanently installed carpeting in basements can easily become damp and a source of mold and mildew. Therefore use carpeting with extreme caution. For more information about basements, see **Chapter 14, Foundations**.

Rearrange existing walls and doors

Sometimes you can meet your remodeling goals without increasing the living space by changing existing walls and doors to improve the way the house functions for your family. Figure 17-2a shows the floor plan for the second story of a one and one half story home with four small bedrooms. The rooms are even smaller because the slope of the roof leaves some of the space with a ceiling height of less than four feet, making it unusable. The rooms are so small that they do not accommodate the owner's furniture. Except for possible under-eave storage, there is only one closet. Figure 17-2b offers one option for improving the situation.

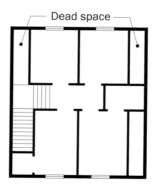

a. Before.
Story and a half house with small bedrooms.

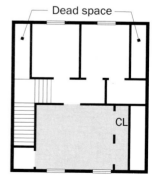

b. After.
Two bedrooms combined and closet opened to other bedroom.

FIGURE 17-2.
Remodeled house.

Taking out or adding walls or moving doors are often effective ways to improve the traffic flow and the functioning of spaces in houses. Before changing any walls or doors, however, you will need to determine the impact of the proposed changes on the structure and whether planned changes in the plumbing system are practical. Experienced remodeling contractors can often give you the information you need for simple changes. For more complicated changes, you will need to consult an architect or structural engineer.

Create an as-built drawing

Whether you will be working within the shell of the existing house or adding additional space, you should start with a drawing of your lot and the existing structure. You may have received a lot or plot plan when you bought your house, or you may be able to get one from local inspection or zoning officials. If not, you should draw one using the corner stakes on your property or the description in your deed. This step will be particularly important if you are planning to add on to the structure. You will need to keep the addition within setbacks established by local zoning and building officials. Measure the house on the outside and locate it on the plot plan. Then indicate approximately where water, sewer, gas, electric, and phone lines enter the house.

For the sections of the house that will be affected by the remodeling, develop detailed scaled drawings. These drawings should include the thickness of the walls, the widths of doors and windows, and the locations of heat registers or radiators. Graph paper with four or eight lines per inch and an architectural scale will make this job much easier.

Develop your plans

With your list of remodeling goals and your as-built drawings in hand, you are set to begin developing your plan. Tracing paper is a valuable aid at this point. Lay the tracing paper over your as-built drawings, and tape it in a couple of corners with removable tape. As you develop your plans, keep these issues in mind.

- Determining where your addition will go.
- Blending the addition with the house.
- Fitting furniture to the new or changed room.
- Incorporating accessibility features.
- Encountering hazards.
- Finding design ideas.

Determining where your addition will go

One of the first steps is to determine where your addition will go. Your lot is likely to limit where you can add on. If you have more than one option, look at your floor plan to see which one works best. Avoid options that require you to enter the addition through a bedroom. Determine if the addition will cover up existing windows and leave important rooms dark or bedrooms without exit windows.

One option that people on small lots find attractive is to raise the roof, either adding a full second story or changing the roof slope and adding dormers to make a story and a half house. If you do this, you will have to plan for a stairway to get to the

Before you begin any excavation, contact the utilities provider to locate underground lines.

second floor. You can add a stair
tower addition or sacrifice space on
the first floor to create the stairway.
Figure 17-3 shows an example of a
stair tower added to the rear of a
home.

Blending the addition with the house
Ideally, the addition will blend so

well with the original house that it is
indistinguishable from the original or
even improves its appearance. Of
course, this means matching siding
and window sizes and styles, and it
requires attention to roof design. Roof
slopes should blend. Figure 17-4
gives examples of rooflines that blend
and do not blend.

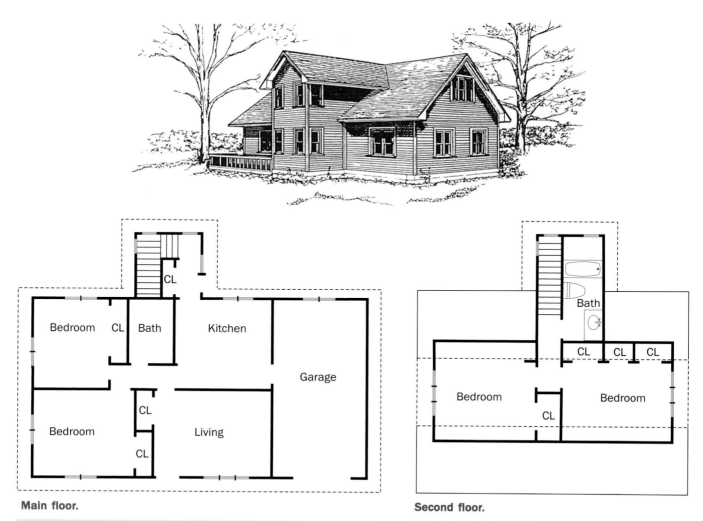

Main floor.   **Second floor.**

FIGURE 17-3.
Stair tower addition.

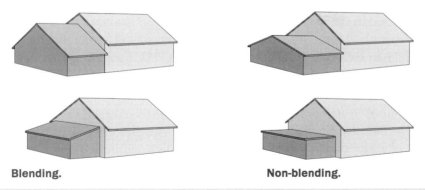

Blending.   Non-blending.

FIGURE 17-4.
Blending and non-blending rooflines.

*Fitting furniture to the new
or changed room*

Determine how furniture will fit in
the new and changed rooms. You can
make cardboard cutouts the size of
various pieces of furniture you plan
to use in the room. Make the cutouts
the same scale as your drawing and
place them on the drawing. Do they
fit? Will there be enough space left to
move around the room? The minimum width for a circulation route is
30 inches. A more comfortable width
is to allow 36 to 42 inches.

Incorporating accessibility features

Are you taking advantage of the
opportunity to incorporate accessibility improvements into the changes you
are making? If you are adding a new
exterior door, can you include a no-
step approach? If you are remodeling a
bath, can you provide the turn-around
room for a wheelchair and blocking in
the walls to support grab bars? Most of
the chapters in this book contain ideas
for incorporating universal design into
a house, and numerous other sources

of information about how to make
homes more accessible to people with
disabilities are available.

Encountering hazards

Have you thought about hazards
that you may encounter in the
remodeling process? When removing
materials, you many encounter dead
pests or an accumulation of dead
insects. The remodeling products
used may emit nauseous gases. In
older homes, remodelers can encounter two specific hazards: asbestos and
lead-based paint. Asbestos was used
in a variety of building products
including floor tile, pipe wrap, ceiling
tile, and "slate siding." If these
materials are sawed, sanded, or
otherwise turned into dust, that dust
is likely to contain asbestos particles,
which are linked to lung cancer. Left
undisturbed, most materials containing asbestos do not pose a threat.

Lead-based paint is a more common
concern in homes built before 1978.
When lead-based paint is sanded or
otherwise turned into dust, it poses a

serious health threat, particularly to young children. In fact, lead-based paint and other lead sources cause 2 million children each year to suffer mental retardation. If you are concerned that either of these hazards may be involved in your remodeling plans, check with your local public health or extension office for more information.

Finding design ideas

Numerous magazines and books are available with ideas for remodeling and decorating. They are a valuable resource as you try to resolve problems or decide on how space should look. However, remember that you will have to adapt these ideas so that they fit your situation. In addition to being attractive, they have to function for you. **Chapter 3, Designing a Home,** suggests additional ideas to think about as you develop your remodeling plan.

Remodeling Case Study

Figure 17-5 shows the stages of one representative remodeling project. The homeowner's concerns were twofold: not enough space for entertaining and only one bathroom in the house. A small existing breezeway room with a sliding glass door faced the neighbor's home about 15 feet away. Because it was inconvenient to the rest of the house, the breezeway was primarily used for access to the attached garage. The example includes a lot plan (Figure 17-5a), an as-built drawing of the portion of the home affected by the remodeling (Figure 17-5b), a detailed plan for the addition (Figure 17-5c), and a drawing that shows the new roofline (Figure 17-5d). The final design met the owner's design goals, and in addition, provided a new, no-step entry and a bath sized so that it could easily be made accessible.

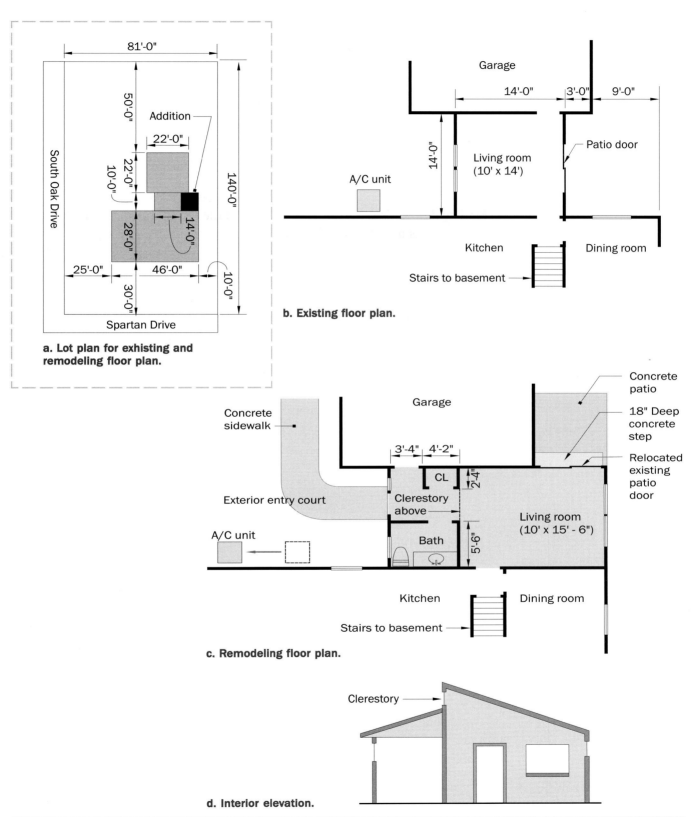

a. Lot plan for exhisting and remodeling floor plan.

b. Existing floor plan.

c. Remodeling floor plan.

d. Interior elevation.

FIGURE 17-5.
Remodeled house planning.

Resources

National Association of Home Builders, Remodeler Council: http://www.nahb.com/consumers/remodeling/remodelmain.htm

Planning for More Space, Building Research Council, School of Architecture, University of Illinois at Urbana-Champaign, Merrill, John. 1984.

Remodeling: Where to Begin. Madison, WI: University of Wisconsin-Extension. Publication NCR313.

Small Homes Council, University of Illinois. 1987. *Planning for Remodeling*. Council Notes C8.0.

Small Homes Council, University of Illinois. 1988. *Planning for More Space*. Council Notes C8.1.

U.S. Environmental Protection Service, Indoor Air Quality Publications: http://www.epa.gov/iaq/pubs/

INDEX